Pocket Guide to
Family Assessment
and Intervention

Pocket Guide to
Family Assessment
and Intervention

Karen Mischke Berkey, RN, PhD, CFLE

Associate Professor of Nursing
University of Hawaii School of Nursing (Manoa)
and Pacific Basin Geriatric Education Center;
Director of Continuing Education
Wainanae Coast Comprehensive Health Center
Honolulu, Hawaii

Shirley May Harmon Hanson, RN, PhD, FAAN, PMHNP, CFLE

Professor of Nursing
Department of Family Nursing
Oregon Health Sciences University
School of Nursing
Portland, Oregon

Illustrated

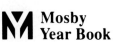

Mosby
Year Book

St. Louis   Baltimore   Boston   Chicago   London   Philadelphia   Sydney   Toronto

Mosby Year Book

Dedicated to Publishing Excellence

Editor: Linda L. Duncan
Project Manager: Peggy Fagen
Design: Laura Steube
Copyeditor: Mary Johnson

The FS³I is available to all family health-oriented caregivers. The authors request, in the interest of research and possible tool refinement, that users of it provide feedback, both positive and negative, to the authors. Such response will be greatly appreciated.

Mosby–Year Book, Inc.
11830 Westline Industrial Drive, St. Louis, Missouri 63146

CL/D/D   9   8   7   6   5   4   3   2   1

To my parents, **Carrol** and **Helen,**
and my brother, **Richard,**
for being an inspiring cheering section during their lifetimes;
to **Betty,**
my supportive and wise sister;
to **Jay,**
my husband and companion in the quest for genuineness,
openness, and sharing;
to **Tamara, Mark, Todd, Bebe,** and **Trenda,**
the most caring, appreciative, and thoughtful children
a mother could have;
to **Liette,**
my valuable friend and confidant through challenging times.

K.M.B.

To some of my friends and colleagues who have supported me
through difficult times:
**Doris, Karen, Jean, Vivian G., Vivian W., Marsha,
Fred, Perri, Susan, Ellen.**

S.M.H.H.

Foreword

In considering all that influences the family with its continuous energy exchange with environmental factors, changes are inherent within the total unit as a system. This living, dynamic, open family system moves along the health continuum with the many variables interacting to sustain the movement. This "mobile" of elements is alive and marvelous! No wonder Berkey and Hanson chose to work with families.

Throughout this book, the reader becomes fully aware of the respect and appreciation due the family as a unit and each member within it. The assessment tool designed by Karen Mischke Berkey and Shirley Hanson for assessing the health of the family system focuses heavily on strengths found therein. Their own service in family community health confirmed their conviction that every family has strengths that enable its members to respond to various stressors resulting in a positive and healthy outcome. This belief promotes their own sense of hope for families and for family-oriented professionals whose goal is optimum health for the entire family unit.

In assessment of a family's level of stability, one is challenged toward professionalism in considering all elements that make the family unique. The Neuman Systems Model provides the necessary structure for organization of these complex factors, thus preventing decisions based on one system variable to the exclusion of any or all others. The model forms the base for the practical Berkey-Hanson assessment tool for holistic family focused nursing. Inspiration for creating such a tool is related to their own experiences in family nursing and student family health teaching. Users of the tool will certainly be fascinated by and appreciative of the wide array of both family strengths and weaknesses, thus becoming more easily skilled in the understanding and support required for the family's movement toward optimal health and maintenance levels.

Theoretical contributions of other scientific disciplines are acknowledged as they relate to consideration and development of family health theories for the discipline of nursing. The book makes a unique contribution to the nursing profession as it considers the wide spectrum of system variables interacting with the environment, profiling the concept of wholism within the original context of the Neuman Systems Model.

Needless to say, I am delighted that the authors have chosen Neuman on which to base their work, and I sincerely hope it will enhance professional care of the family.

Betty Neuman

Preface

What society frequently considers a typical family is one in which the father is a rising young executive and the mother, choosing to stay home with the two children, actively participates in community activities. Their home is located in a middle class suburban community with easy access to schools and grocery stores. The media, via advertising and programming, portrays this family as being involved in a variety of problems ranging in severity from leaky faucets to hurricanes. However, most of their family problems can be easily "fixed" by hiring a handyman or obtaining the appropriate insurance policy. This so-called typical family is usually able to function well no matter what happens because they are perceived as having control over their world (Clements and Roberts, 1983).

It is quite apparent from our experience with families that this "typical" family is a figment of media imagination. We begin with it here, however, for the purpose of inviting you to examine your ideas about real families and how they function. Most of us have unexamined conceptions about families. However, we may not be aware of how these conceptions influence the judgments and evaluations we make about families—our own, those of our friends, the ones down the street, and most of all, the familes we serve.

In this handbook we have defined family in its broadest sense. The definition, synthesized from general systems theory, addresses the membership of the system, the relationship of the members to each other, and the factors of commitment and caring that make relationships meaningful.

The family is a group of individuals closely related by blood, marriage, or friendship ties (nuclear family, cohabiting couple, single parent, blended families, etc.) characterized by a continuum of stability, commitment, mutual decision making, and shared goals. Each family member is a composite of interacting variables (physiological, psychological, sociocultural, developmental, and spiritual) that affect individual and family health. The family as an open system interfaces with the environment.

The purpose of this handbook is to provide a framework by which nurses can assess families—the family system as a whole and its members as parts of that whole. As caring health professionals, nurses are becoming more and more concerned about family-focused health care. However, nurses need assessment and intervention instruments that elicit information about how families are functioning. Problems within a family are seldom the result of a single cause. Similarly, a family problem seldom has a single effect. The assessment instruments nurses require must provide them with direction as they plan intervention strategies that facilitate and restore optimal family functioning and health.

Currently, no one theoretical approach fully explains the relationships and dynamics of family life. Also, no single approach appears inclusive enough to provide a theoretical umbrella for the phenomena with which family nursing deal. Because of this, family nurses are forced to draw upon multiple theoretical frameworks in order to obtain the mechanisms by which they can organize observations, focus inquiries, and communicate findings.

In the early 1970s Betty Neuman designed a systems model for nursing that incorporates the concepts of problem-finding and prevention. This model has been used in a variety of nursing situations and is general enough to be useful in most health care settings. The goals of the Neuman Systems Model is to set forth a structure that depicts how a total system and the parts comprising the system function together. In applying this model to the family system, nurses are able to assess the level of family functioning and health. This includes the family as a whole and the individual members as parts of that whole.

The family assessment and intervention instrument described in this handbook is called the *Family Systems Stressor-Strength Inventory (FS³I)*. It is built on Betty Neuman's Systems Model and incorporates the concepts of family stressors, family strengths, and prevention as intervention. The *FS³I* assists nurses with the creation of therapeutic bridges between the theoretical base defining the family's current health status and the identified health goals established by both family and nurse.

The intended readers of this handbook are undergraduate health care professionals working with families; graduate students in family health, mental health, and community health nursing; and practicing nurses who assist families in any setting where the goal is to improve the family's optimal functioning. However, the theoretical and experiential foci are broad enough to warrant its use by health professionals outside the discipline of nursing, such as other clinicians, social workers, counselors, therapists, psychiatrists, and physicians.

This handbook has seven chapters. The first chapter presents a broad overview of selected theoretical orientations used to assess families. Three theory and three therapy approaches incorporating general systems theory concepts are described: structural-functional theory, symbolic interaction theory, developmental theory, structural therapy, interactional therapy, and family systems therapy. Chapter 2 focuses on nursing assessment as described in the Neuman Systems Model, with accompanying family member variables (physiological, psychological, sociocultural, developmental, spiritual) and family system categories (psychosocial relationship characteristics, physical status, developmental characteristics, and spiritual influence). Chapter 3 identifies and defines family systems stressors and family systems strengths as synthesized by the well-known family researcher, Delores Curran. Chapter 4 shows how the nursing process and the Neuman Systems Model are applied to families as units of care and describes the stages of the nursing process, nursing diagnosis, nursing goals, and nursing outcomes in relation to family assessment. The prevention as intervention modes using the lines of defense and resistance are delineated at the primary, secondary, and tertiary levels. *Family Systems Stressor-Strength Inventory (FS³I)*, a family systems assessment instrument for nurses, is described in Chapter 5. Intrafamily, interfamily, and extrafamily system stressors and family unit strengths are delineated. The two inventory forms with accompanying scoring formats are outlined, and explanations relative to the use of the quantitative and qualitative summaries are presented. The summaries serve as the basis for the family systems care plan, which is a negotiated effort between the nurse and family. Chapter 6 demonstrates how the Family Systems Stressor-Strength Inventory (FS³I) can be applied to actual family systems. Three case studies document its effectiveness for assessing optimal family function and family health. The seventh chapter presents an overview of family nursing assessment/measurement instrumentation. Components incorporated in this chapter include assessment/measurement definitions, assessment/measurement instrumentation, use of family assessment/measurement in family nursing curriculum, psychometric evaluations of nursing instruments, measurement strategies, and a listing of selected family instruments. The handbook also contains a foreword by Betty Neuman, the well-known nurse academician who is responsible for the development of the Neuman Systems Model.

The book progresses from the general overview of theoretical approaches applied to family systems to a specific way of therapeutically viewing the family. It culminates with the description of the Family Systems Stressor-Strength Inventory and a listing of family assessment/measurement instruments used by family-focused practitioners. We recommend a complete reading of the handbook prior to implementing the assessment and intervention inventory.

We believe this handbook builds a bridge from the theoretical world of beliefs, concepts, and propositions to the experiental world with which nurses deal daily. The theory base, which is described in detail, plays out the Neuman Systems Model. As such, it enables nurses to (1) organize their ideas or mental images about families and relate the ideas and images to each other, (2) incorporate a unique perspective from which they can view families, (3) predict family behavior and health in the face of stressor penetration at the lines of defense and resistance, and (4) use a nursing model to guide their family nursing practice from assessment through to intervention and outcome. The Neuman Systems theory base, which stresses prevention as intervention, culminates in the world of nursing action and family care. We believe this handbook will help nurses apply nursing theory to their practice by providing them with a foundation for incorporating the family system as a unit of care and by presenting an instrument for assessing family health and stability, which is the real impetus for implementing family-focused care plans.

Karen Mischke Berkey
Shirley May Harmon Hanson

Acknowledgments

Many people helped and encouraged us in the development of this handbook. We especially wish to mention the following people:

Linda Duncan, from Mosby–Year Book, Inc., whose warm interest, trust, and well-paced encouragement stimulated our productivity

Peter Warner, colleague, friend, and a family systems counseling expert, who helped us with an earlier version of the Family Systems Stressor-Strength Inventory (FS³I)

Colleagues and students who have shared our ideas and challenged us to refine our thinking; particularly we thank **Mary Post** who helped with the FS³I content validity analysis

Virginia Nufer, whose nimble fingers and eye for detail helped ensure that the manuscript met high editorial standards

Contents

1   Theoretical Orientations Used to Understand Family Systems, 1

2   Nursing Assessment Applied to Family Systems, 20

3   Family Systems Stressors and Family Systems Strengths, 38

4   Families, the Nursing Process, and the Neuman Systems Model, 51

5   Family Systems Stressor-Strength Inventory (FS^{3}I), 72

6   Family Systems Stressor-Strength Inventory (FS^{3}I) Applied to Family Case Studies, 84

7   Family Nursing Assessment/Measurement Instrumentation, 226

References and Suggested Readings, 263

Appendix, 279

Theoretical Orientations Used to Understand Family Systems

The purpose of this chapter is to present an overview of selected theoretical approaches that have been used to assess families. Conceptual and semantic links must be established between family-focused disciplines to enable professionals to share a common language unrestricted by subject matter boundaries (Sills and Weaver, 1985). A basic understanding of theoretical perspectives enhances the likelihood that meaningful dialogue between professionals will occur in the midst of increasing specialization and knowledge fragmentation (Sills and Hall, 1985).

When a client/patient enters a hospital, clinic, or physician's office, an evaluation process begins. It continues until the client's problems are resolved or therapeutic interventions are no longer needed. Included in this evaluation process are judgments as to the nature of the client's problem, the client's potential for resolving the problem, and the expected outcomes. Professionals make these judgments with minimal awareness as to the client's strengths, limitations, or family context (Filsinger, 1983). Whether conducted formally or informally, this evaluation process can be considered the beginning of assessment.

The position taken here is that clients coming to hospitals, clinics, or physicians' offices can benefit from attention being given to their family as a unit of care (Friedman, 1986; Jones and Dimond, 1982). This focus includes factors, such as who the family members are, how they relate to one another, how they interact and communicate with each other and how they spend their time together.

A central assumption of this handbook is that clinical nursing practice should be guided by theory. The definitions of theory that appear to be most useful for family nursing are those developed by Chinn and Jacobs (1983) and Fawcett (1989a). Chinn and Jacobs (1983, p. 70) define nursing theory as "a set of concepts, definitions, and propositions that projects a systematic view of phenomena by designating specific inter-relationships among concepts for the purpose of describing, explaining, predicting, and/or controlling phenomena". Fawcett (1989a, p. 23), in supporting this definition, states that nursing theory is a "relatively specific and concrete set of concepts and propositions that purports to account for or characterize phenomena of interest to the discipline of nursing." The nurse needs to use a theoretical framework in assisting families to obtain optimal health (Fawcett, 1989a).

Nurses should base decisions regarding the selection of a theoretical perspective for use in clinical nursing practice (assessment, diagnosis, planning, and intervention) on practical, pragmatic grounds. Those working with families need to choose theory that best explains family situations and suggests meaningful and effective nursing goals and actions (Chinn and Jacobs, 1983; Fawcett, 1989; Friedman, 1986; Grotevant, 1989).

Family Systems as Units of Care

Over the last 10 years, nurses have become keenly aware of the importance of the family environment and its effect on the family's perceptions of health and illness (Barnard and Neal, 1977; Fawcett, 1989a; Fitzpatrick and Whall, 1983; Gilliss, Roberts, Highley, and Martinson, 1989; Murphy, 1986). The nursing profession now recognizes the family as the primary social structure for its members. This primary social structure provides the context in which family members learn and practice health promoting and illness preventing behaviors (Pender, 1987). Families are responsible for undertaking certain tasks that affect the health and well-being of each member. Encouraging optimal health should be an integral part of the family life-style (Houldin, Saltstein, and Ganley, 1987; Pender, 1987). Included in these basic responsibilities are activities related to:

1. Developing competencies in the individual members that enable them to care for themselves (Pender, 1987)
2. Providing family members with sufficient social and phys-

ical resources so that they are able to function (Duvall, 1977; Duvall and Miller, 1985; Pender, 1987)

3. Defining when a family member is sick or well (Jones and Dimond, 1982; Litman, 1974; Pratt, 1973)
4. Facilitating autonomy and individuality for each member (Friedman, 1986; Pender, 1987)
5. Promoting family behaviors that contribute to and enhance the family's well-being and quality of life (Litman, 1974; Wright and Leahey, 1984)

Recognizing families' responsibility for promoting and preserving the health of its members, nurses need to be alert to the importance of assessing family units. The assessment process subsequently described focuses on family dynamics, strengths, and relative state of health and well-being. It includes an evaluation of selected health variables germane to family members as individuals and to the family as a unit and gives direction to the assessment of the complex interactions and relationships incumbent in family systems. Variables involved in individual family member assessment are physiological, sociocultural, psychological, developmental, and spiritual. Grouping of these variables into categories facilitates overall assessment of the family. These categories encompass the family's general physical status, psychosocial relationship characteristics, developmental characteristics, and spiritual influence. Used synergistically, variables and categories create a framework for assessing an interacting holistic family system in intimate relationship (Neuman, 1983). Since nurses are concerned with promoting, maintaining, and restoring family health, an assessment of the family unit is vital.

Theoretical Approaches Used to Study Families

Historically, there have been two broad conceptual approaches used by family-focused professionals to understand the structure, function, and dynamics of family units. These two approaches, *family theory models* and *family therapy models* (Broderick, 1971; Grotevant, 1989; Jones and Dimond, 1982), group selected ideas, beliefs, and values pertaining to families and how they should function. They also designate how these ideas, beliefs, and values relate to one another. Terms used for the various theory and therapy models are similar in name but are defined differently for each assessment process approach.

The family theory and family therapy models originated in

the behavioral, natural, and physical sciences and therefore differ in their implications for family assessment and intervention. Theory models, developed by sociologists and anthropologists, assist health professionals in analyzing family structure and processes. They approach assessment from the standpoint of family normality and health and center on describing essential family functions, marital interactions, and family needs and tasks over time (Jones and Dimond, 1982). Therapy models, on the other hand, were developed by clinicians in psychology, psychiatry, social work, and marriage and family (Jones and Dimond, 1982). Their practice focus is on explaining how family structures and processes break down. These health professionals are concerned with determining how ambiguity of family rules and role relationships occurs and how anxiety is transmitted from parents to children. The starting point of therapy models is pathology and family dysfunction (Jones and Dimond, 1982).

Integration of General Systems Theory with Theoretical Approaches

The majority of professionals using family theory and family therapy modalities subscribe to general systems theory, which views the family as a system. Their explanations of how families function differ, however, as does the point at which entry into the family system occurs. For example, some begin assessment of the family at the emotional system level, some at the communication system level, and still others at the structural system level. Since systems theory permeates the practice of family-focused professionals, a brief description of the theory follows.

General systems theory, introduced in 1936 by von Bertalanffy, came to the forefront after World War II as an outgrowth of developments in cybernetics and computers. Individuals attempting to understand large systems such as cities created the notion that the whole is greater than the sum of its parts. This notion became the unifying concept in the diverse fields whose professionals sought to understand systems, whether mechanical, biological, or human (Miller and Winstead-Fry, 1982). The type of general systems theory developed by von Bertalanffy (1968) began to filter into nursing thought and literature by way of Roger's A Science of Unitary Human Beings (1970, 1989), Roy's Adaptation Model (1980, 1989), Neuman's Systems Model (1982, 1983, 1989), and King's General Systems Framework and Theory (1981, 1989).

A number of trends become apparent as one reviews the systems literature: (1) there is no clear agreement as to the primary concepts of systems theory, (2) many of the concepts described in systems theory are seldom applied to clinical practice with families (Wright and Leahey, 1984), and (3) "explanatory concepts of general systems theory have not been fully organized into predictive relationship" (Scoresby, 1979, p. 24). Allmond, Buckman, and Gofman (1979, p. 16) use a mobile analogy to highlight systems concepts and how these concepts may be applied to family systems:

Visualize a mobile with four or five pieces suspended from the ceiling and gently moving in the air. The whole is in balance, steady yet moving. Some pieces are moving rapidly; others are almost stationary. Some are heavier and appear to carry more weight in the ultimate direction of the mobile's movement; others seem to go along for the ride. A breeze catching only one segment of the mobile immediately influences movement of every piece, some more than others, and the pace picks up with some pieces unbalancing themselves and moving chaotically about for a time. Gradually the whole exerts its influence in the errant part(s) and balance is re-established but not before a decided change in direction of the whole may have taken place. You will also notice the changeability regarding closeness and distance among pieces, the impact of actual contact one with another, and the importance of vertical hierarchy. Coalitions of movement may be observed between two pieces. Or one piece may persistently appear isolated from the others; yet its position of isolation is essential to the balancing of the entire system.

Applying the definition of a system to families enhances nurses' understanding of how families function. Nurses then view the family as a set of complex elements in mutual interaction, a whole system in relationship, as opposed to examining each member separately. In attempting to analyze how systems function, nurses look for behavioral linkages that often occur between events. These events form sequences, and sequences form patterns (Wright and Leahey, 1984).

The rule structure operating in the family often governs family behavioral patterns. These rules contribute to family health and well-being when they are appropriately used. When inappropriately used rules jeopardize the family's health. Keeping the mobile analogy in mind, consider the following systems concepts put forth by Wright and Leahey (1984, pp. 10-14):

1. A family system, composed of subsystems, is part of a larger suprasystem
2. The family as a whole is greater than the sum of its parts

3. A change in one family member affects all family members

4. The family is able to create a balance between change and stability

5. Family members' behaviors are best understood using a circular point of view rather than one of linear causality

The key ideas of general systems theory are divided into two broad areas: elements addressing system structure and elements addressing system control. System structure refers to family organization and the pattern of relationships among family members, as exhibited by wholeness, boundaries, and hierarchies. System control is the process by which a family operates and the effectiveness with which a family meets its goals. Concepts incorporated into system control include resources, homeostasis, feedback, and energy (Clements and Roberts, 1983; Friedman, 1986; Miller and Janosik, 1980).

According to Chin (1980, p. 24), "the analytic model of system demands that we treat the phenomena and the concepts for organizing the phenomena as if there existed organization, interaction, interdependency, integration of parts and elements." The boundary determines which elements belong inside a designated system and which go outside, with varying degrees of boundary permeability found in different types of systems. Auger (1976 p. 24) defines a boundary "as a more or less open line forming a circle around the system where there is greater interchange of energy within the circle than on the outside. It is helpful to visualize a boundary as a 'filter' which permits the constant exchange of elements, information, or energy between the system and its environment . . . The more porous the filter, the greater the degree of interaction possible between the system and its environment."

All living systems have semipermeable boundaries that allow for the exchange of matter, energy, and information across their environmental boundaries (Sills and Hall, 1985). The differences in permeability result in varying degrees of matter, energy, and information exchange (Auger, 1976).

Family systems may undergo stress caused by internal interactions of family members or by external factors in the environment. Family systems interacting with the outside environment receive information or feedback that can be used for system operations. All systems, including family systems, attempt to achieve a state of equilibrium, or balance, between forces within the system and those impinging on it from the outside. Systems resist disturbances and attempt to restore balance, resulting in a new equilibrium based either on the status quo or on change (Bertrand, 1972).

Miller (1978, p. 234) describes system balance and feedback as follows:

There is a range of stability for each of numerous variables in all living systems. An input or output of either matter, energy or information, which by lack or excess of some characteristics forces the variables beyond the range of stability, constitutes a stress and produces a strain within the system. Information that a stress is imminent constitutes a threat to the system: stress may be anticipated. The totality of the strains within a system constitute a value; while the relative urgency of reducing these specific strains represents a system's hierarchy of values.

Therefore, decisions in family systems are based on information entering the system. This input, in the form of feedback, regulates the adjustments and adaptations required to maintain system equilibrium. As the information feedback increases, so does the probability of effective decision making and system stability (Sills and Hall, 1985). The goal and purpose of the open system are to determine the desired degree of stability. The family system works to produce decisions that will maintain a continuum of stability and purposeful direction in the internal and external environments. All open family systems seek some range of stability, as determined by their values, goals, and purposes (Sills and Hall, 1985). Each family system decides what adaptations it can make in regard to stability, for there is always a cost-efficiency factor linked to such decisions in terms of matter, energy, and information (Sills and Hall, 1985). As Miller (1965, p. 234) purports:

How efficiently a system adjusts to its environment is determined by what strategies it employs in selecting adjustment processes and whether they satisfactorily reduce strains without being too costly. Relevant information available to the decider can improve decisions . . . consequently, it is valuable.

A general systems perspective presents a humanistic view of families as holistic, goal-directed, self-maintaining, self-creating individuals of intrinsic worth. Family members are capable of reflecting upon their uniqueness as family members (Sills and Hall, 1985). This approach "allows for consideration of individuals at their subsystems levels, as human beings and as social creatures who network themselves with others in hierarchically arranged human systems of increasing complexity. Thus, the person, from the level of the individual to the level of society, can be conceptualized as client and become the target system for using intervention" (Sills and Hall, 1985, p. 28).

Nursing proponents using the systems model endeavor to understand (1) how family members interact, (2) family norms and expectations, (3) how family decisions are made, (4) how effectively family members communicate, and (5) how the family deals with individual needs and family expectations (Clements and Roberts, 1983; Friedman, 1986; Wright and Leahey, 1984).

Family Theory Approach

Since the early 1950s family theorists have attempted to gather information about families and organize it so that selected aspects of family behavior and patterns could be described and explained (Christenson, 1964; Hill, Katz, and Simpson, 1957; Jones and Dimond, 1982; Nye and Berardo, 1981). Three theory approaches are considered useful and viable by nurses and other health care professionals: structural-functional, symbolic interaction, and developmental (Adams, 1980; Broderick, 1971; Burr, Hill, Nye, and Reiss, 1979; Hill, Katz, and Simpson, 1957; Holman and Burr, 1980;). Each of these theories will be discussed briefly, along with the major nursing proponents supportive of the overall approach. Concepts embodied in each approach will be explained. Nurses must be cognizant of the theoretical and conceptual bases they use in evaluating families.

Structural-functional theory approach.   The structural-functional theory approach is a major theoretical frame of reference in sociology, particularly in the areas of family and medical sociology (Eshleman, 1974). Its scope is broad when applied to the family. The structural-functional theory views the family as an open social system. The family members are parts of that social system or function as subsystems (Bronfenbrenner, 1979; Friedman, 1986; Parsons and Bales, 1955). Families as social systems interact with other social systems comprising the world around them, such as the systems of education, employment, religion, and health care (Leslie, 1976). Because the family system can be examined holistically (as a unit), in parts (as subsystems), and interactionally (as a system interacting with other institutions), it is a useful framework for assessing family life. The theory emphasizes examining the functions that the family performs for society, as well as the functions that society performs for the family, and views the family and its members as reactive and passive instead of active elements capable of producing change.

Ultimately, the family structure is evaluated by determining how well the family fulfills its functions (Duvall, 1977; Eshleman, 1974; Minuchin, 1974). Family assessment using the structural-functional approach focuses on two areas: (1) defining the basic functions that families perform, such as reproduction, socialization of children, and provision for physical needs and economic functions, and (2) understanding family processes, including all of the internal and external forces affecting the family (Clemen-Stone, Eigsti, and McGuire, 1987; Friedman, 1986; Hymovich, 1983; Knafl, 1986; Neuman, 1982, 1989; Wright and Leahey, 1984). Health professionals direct therapeutic interventions toward changing family organization or structure to change its function. Altering the positions of family members transforms their experiences and leads to changes in family functioning (Minuchin, 1974).

Several family assessment instruments use concepts from this theory approach. Two of these are the Calgary Family Assessment Model (Leahey and Wright, 1984) and Guidelines for Family Assessment (Friedman, 1986). Systems concepts are also basic to the Behavioral Systems Model for Nursing (Johnson, 1980).

Symbolic interaction theory approach.   A basic assumption of the symbolic interaction theory approach is that humans live in a symbolic as well as a physical environment (Mead, 1933). Human behavior reflects the meanings that people give to their own actions and to those of others (Mead, 1933). When applied to assessing families, this approach is used to examine family dynamics by analyzing the behaviors of the individual members (Burgess, 1926; Clark, 1978; Hanson, 1987; Jones, 1986; Mead, 1933; Mischke-Berkey, Warner, and Hanson, 1989). These internal family dynamics consist of role playing, communication patterns, status relations, coping patterns, decision making, and socialization (Friedman, 1986). Family members are a set of interacting personalities, each occupying a position within the family group and having a number of assigned roles (Hill and Hansen, 1960). Individual members define their role in each external or internal situation that the family confronts. These role expectations take into account the reference group, the event, and the member's self-concept (Schraneveldt, 1973). Each family member then acts out the role in interactions with other family members (Jones and Dimond, 1982; Schraneveldt, 1973). The theory emphasizes the internal aspects of family dynamics, almost to the exclusion of collateral associations or the family's relationship to society (Hill and Hansen, 1960). Symbolic interaction theory is useful not only in providing a practical way of assessing the family but also in isolating and specifying potential sources of difficulty as family members relate to one another and to their community (Friedman, 1986).

Concepts from interaction theory are widely used by nurse theoreticians in developing models for nursing practice. Among these are the Riehl Interaction Model (Riehl-Sisca, 1989), Barnard's Parent-Interaction Model (Barnard and Neal, 1977); King's Theory of Goal Attainment Model (King, 1981), and Travelbee's Human-to-Human Relationship Model (Travelbee and Doona, 1979).

Developmental theory approach. The developmental approach, fashioned from major themes from sociology, child psychology, and human development, focuses on the family unit that progresses and changes as it moves through a life cycle (Duvall, 1977; Duvall and Miller, 1985, Hill and Rodgers, 1964; Jones and Dimond, 1982; Rodgers, 1964). This approach combines the large social system orientation of the structural-functional approach with the smaller family social system approach of symbolic interaction.

Developmental theory supports the belief that families have life cycles that are divided into a series of discrete and well-defined stages (Duvall, 1977; Duvall and Miller, 1985). The notion of life cycle rests on the assumption that there is a great degree of interdependence in families. For example, families are forced to change each time the number of members changes or each time the oldest child moves to a new developmental stage (Friedman, 1986). Each stage in the life cycle is thought of as a period of relative stability that is qualitatively and quantitatively distinct (Mederer and Hill, 1983). For example, roles, the marital relationship, child-rearing, and discipline change from one stage to another, which requires the family to adjust if growth is to continue (Friedman, 1986; Mederer and Hill, 1983; Murray and Zentner, 1985).

Each stage contains a number of developmental tasks that contribute to healthy family functioning and stability. Duvall and

Miller (1985, p. 45) defines family developmental tasks as "growth responsibilities that arise at a certain stage in the life of a family, successful achievement of which leads to satisfaction and success with later tasks, while failure leads to unhappiness in the family, disapproval by society, and difficulty with later family developmental tasks". Duvall and Miller (1985) lists nine ever-changing developmental tasks that span the family life cycle. These tasks are to establish and maintain the following:

1. An independent home
2. Satisfactory ways of getting and spending money
3. Mutually acceptable patterns in the division of labor
4. Continuity of mutually satisfying sex relationships
5. Open system of intellectual and emotional communication
6. Workable relationships with relatives
7. Ways of interacting with associates and community organizations
8. Competency in bearing and rearing children
9. A workable philosophy of life

In studying this family development concept, nurses should realize that family members face individual developmental tasks while simultaneously at different stages of human development. Moreover, adults who are parents have additional developmental tasks relating specifically to parent-child relationships that are not present in families without children.

The developmental approach focuses on three dimensions of family behavior (Jones and Dimond, 1982). These dimensions are (1) the changing developmental tasks and role expectations of the parents, (2) the changing developmental tasks and role expectations of the children, and (3) the developmental tasks of the family as a unit, which flow from cultural dictates at various stages in the family life cycle (Duvall and Miller, 1985; Jones and Dimond, 1982).

Nurses applying this approach in practice view the family as a series of interacting personalities woven together into paired positions or paired roles, such as wife-mother, husband-father, and daughter-sister (Duvall and Miller, 1985; Jones and Dimond, 1982). Each position or role has designated behaviors that dictate how to maintain reciprocal relations. These role behaviors are examined over time as ages of family members and their positions change (Kandzari and Howard, 1981; Knafl and Grace, 1978; Knafl, 1986).

Concepts from developmental theory that are of particular interest to nurses are family life cycle and family developmental tasks (Reed, 1986). Nurses have developed family assessment instruments incorporating these concepts. Examples of these instruments include Guidelines for Family Assessment (Friedman, 1986), Calgary Family Assessment Model (Wright and Leahey, 1984), and An Assessment/Intervention Tool based upon the Neuman Systems Model (Neuman, 1982, 1989). Developmental models for nursing practice include: Nursing: A science of unitary human beings (Rogers, 1989), Watson's philosophy and theory of human care in nursing (Watson, 1989), Man-Living-Health: A Theory of Nursing (Parse, 1989), and The Systems-Developmental-Stress Model (Chrisman and Riehl-Sisca, 1989).

Family Therapy Approaches

Family therapists, like family theorists, attempt to organize information about families so that they can understand family activities and behaviors. However, the starting point at which therapists engage families and their purposes for doing so differ (Duvall and Miller, 1985; Jones and Dimond, 1982).

The family therapy approach began in the late 1940s and early 1950s when several therapists, unknown to each other, began to see families for treatment. This usually occurred in relation to the symptoms expressed by one family member (Jones and Dimond, 1982), and therapists considered the identified family member as the unit of care. Over the years the focus shifted. Therapists came to consider the whole family as the unit of care (Clements and Buchanan, 1982). They viewed individual symptoms as by-products of relationship and communication struggles. They geared their interventions toward understanding individual behavior patterns that arose from and fed back into the complex matrix of the overall family system (Belew and Buchanan, 1982; Jones, 1980). Family therapy approaches considered the locus of pathology to be in the family per se, so interventions focused on the whole family. Alterations in overall family behavior would result in positive outcomes for individual members as well as for the family as a whole (Foley, 1974).

Family therapists agree that the primary purpose of family therapy is to improve overall family functioning, although they disagree on how to accomplish this (Beels and Ferber, 1973). They also disagree on where to enter into the family system.

Family therapists group themselves into two categories: those following *role relationship models*, like Ackerman (1972), and those following *systems models*, such as Bowen (1978), Jackson (1973), Haley (1976), Watzlawick (1977), and Satir (1967). Clinicians using a systems approach divide themselves into those who enter the family system at the emotional level, such as Bowen (1978), and those who enter at the communication level, including Jackson (1973), Haley (1976), Watzlawick (1977), and Satir (1967).

The family therapy approach is called a "practice" model approach, because it provides the practitioner with a selection of the most effective means for reaching the desired therapeutic ends (Woolridge, Skipper, and Leonard, 1968).

Structural therapy approach. The structural therapy approach views the family in distress as an open system in the process of transformation (Minuchin, 1974). Families are composed of individual members whose relationships and actions are governed by an invisible set of functional demands (Minuchin, 1974). These demands or rules regulate family behavior (Minuchin, 1974). The family, as a behavioral system, is made up of interlocking behaviors that occur through transactional patterns (Jones and Dimond, 1980). Although invisible in the context, the transactional patterns govern how family members interact over time. The patterns control how, when, where, and to whom the family members relate (Jones and Dimond, 1982).

The structural therapy approach views the family system as being structured in a hierarchical fashion. The family members as subsystems, or parts of the larger family system, associate according to the affinity existing among them. For example, grouping can occur by generation, gender, interest, or function (Jones and Dimond, 1982). Boundaries separate all subsystems, including parental and sibling. The structural transactions developed by the family over time control the boundaries (Jones and Dimond, 1982; Minuchin, 1974). For example, when a father tells a teenage daughter to be home at 10:30 PM and she complies, this interaction defines the teenager's role in relation to the father and the father's relationship to the daughter in that context.

The goal of structural intervention is to help the dysfunctional family change its organization so that new patterns of behavior may evolve. According to Minuchin (1974), the interventions are based on three assumptions: (1) the context in which a family member lives influences that member's psychic life, (2) psychic processes are changed through changes in family structure, and (3) professionals working with families become part of the family system (Popkin, 1980).

Therapists supporting this approach join the family, experience its interaction cognitively and affectively, and function as a participants-observers-facilitators (Popkin, 1980). They use the unstable situation to change and restructure the family (Minuchin, 1974). Strategies include advocating family guidance, modeling, and teaching to improve family problem-solving skills.

Selected structural therapy concepts are integrated into nursing family assessment instruments. Concepts most commonly seen are subsystems, boundaries, roles, coalitions and alliances, family solidarity, power, and status (Friedman, 1986; Popkin, 1980; Wright and Leahey, 1984).

Interactional therapy approach. The interactional therapy approach has its roots in symbolic interactionism as it focuses on the internal functioning of the family. It rejects the concept of role behavior found in symbolic interaction theory and focuses instead on the family as a fairly closed communication system (Jones, 1980). Central to this approach is the idea that interactions involve more than one person. Therefore, the family is a system in which each member influences the actions of all of the other members. In addition, families interact with social suprasystems (Auger, 1976; Bertrand, 1972; Hall and Weaver, 1985). Schraneveldt (1973) noted that interaction is a process rather than a state.

When family systems become dysfunctional, the focus for intervention is on the dynamics of interchange between and among individual members. The interactional therapy approach uses the systems concept of homeostasis to explain how change in one family member is related to change in another family member (Haley, 1976; Jackson, 1973; Satir, 1967; Watzlawick and Weakland, 1977). The family as a unit attempts to maintain system balance or a steady state by using internal, ongoing interactional, and communication processes. These processes and the subsequent balance achieved determine how the family functions.

Family rules and information exchanges between the family and the environment contribute to the maintenance of system stability (Jones and Dimond, 1980). The family system is corrected or calibrated in response to feedback from the surrounding environment (Satir, 1967). Therefore, the family attempts to reestablish system balance in any way possible when the family unit or a family member feels threatened in any way.

Hill and Hansen (1960) delineate three major assumptions of the interactional therapy approach. These are as follows:

1. Social conduct is most immediately a function of the social milieu
2. A human is an independent actor as well as a reactor to his or her situation
3. The basic autonomous unit is the acting individual in a social setting

The value of using the interactional approach for family assessment is enhanced when nurses use knowledge of the context in which interactions occur. This means that being aware of the family's developmental stage is basic to assessing the interactional processes (Bertrand, 1972; Hall and Weaver, 1985). The family members, when assessed with the developmental concept in the foreground, can be viewed as developing members of a changing family group. Nurses using this approach are able to isolate specific problems as family members interact with each other and with society.

Three conceptual frameworks for nursing employ concepts from the interactional approach. These are Levine's Theory of Nursing (Glass, 1989; Levine, 1971), Orem's Self-Care Nursing Theory (Feathers, 1989; Orem, 1979), and Riehl's Interaction Model (Riehl-Sisca, 1986, 1989).

Family systems therapy approach.   The family systems therapy approach, also referred to as Bowen's Multigenerational Approach, fits into the broad framework of general systems theory as developed by von Bertalanffy (1968). However, it is inaccurate to think of family systems theory, or the Bowen approach to family therapy, as synonymous with general systems theory (Bowen, 1976). Bowen's family systems approach (1976) views the family in distress as a combination of emotional and relationship systems (Bowen, 1976). The term *emotional* refers to the force that motivates the system and *relationship* refers to the ways that it is expressed (Bowen, 1978).

Family systems therapy approaches conceptualize the family as an automatic emotional system, which establishes, maintains, and balances member relationships (Phipps, 1980). Family member responses to emotional stimuli within the family system determine the degree to which members are able to function. Members can respond to emotional stimuli either objectively or subjectively. Their ability to distinguish between an objective thinking response and a subjective feeling response contributes to their sense of identity. It also provides them with the opportunity to develop greater problem-solving flexibility in coping with stressful situations (Phipps, 1980). If one family member learns to respond in an objective manner, then the significant other's response is more likely to be objective because of the nature of family interactions. Movement toward a cognitive, rational means of relating, in place of a reliance on emotionalism, provides opportunities for improved family relationships (Miller and Winstead-Fry, 1982).

Bowen (1976) views the family as a multigenerational system characterized by patterns of emotional interaction (Miller and Winstead-Fry, 1982). No individual family member is free from his or her family of origin; the family member and the family as a whole are intimately connected. Individual family members may seem unique, but they have more similarities than differences (Miller and Winstead-Fry, 1982).

There are eight basic concepts in the family systems therapy approach, all of which attempt to explain how the family functions. These concepts, which describe and predict the patterns of emotional interactions within a family, are (1) differentiation of self, (2) societal regression, (3) emotional cutoff, (4) sibling position, (5) nuclear family emotional system, (6) triangles, (7) family projections, and (8) multigenerational transmission process.

Each of the eight concepts is to some extent operational in all families (Miller and Winstead-Fry 1982). To understand a selected family using this approach the nurse must comprehend each of the concepts and their interrelationship within the family system or family member.

The goal of using this approach is twofold: (1) the differentiation of the self of each family member from other members and (2) the reduction of a family's emotional "stuck-togetherness." Family members must be able to make their own choices and take independent stands on issues instead of reacting in response to what other members say or do. This differentiation of self needs to occur on both the emotional and intellectual levels (Bowen, 1976, 1978). Frequently the intellectual level is overpowered by what is happening on the emotional level. When this occurs the intellect is not autonomous, and logical reasoning is impaired. The decisions that result from the emotional level are based on reactions to the behaviors of others rather than on intellectual reasoning. Reactions family members generally follow are those that "feel right" (Bowen, 1978; Dimond and Jones, 1982).

Practitioners using the family systems approach strive to remain objective and detached from the family's emotional system. They work primarily with the marital couple, supporting their leadership positions in the family and focusing on their emotional response patterns. Their premise is that, as each member of the marital couple grows in self-differentiation, the family system will change, enabling other family members to grow also. Bowen (1971) uses the terms *coach* or *teacher* to describe the practitioner's role in this process.

Miller and Winstead-Fry (1982), in their book *Family Systems Theory in Nursing Practice,* address how nurses can use this approach in their own family nursing practice. Other nurse academicians demonstrate its use via the case study approach (Clements and Buchanan, 1982; Jones, 1980; Miller and Janosik 1980).

Implications of Theoretical Orientations to Nursing Practice

The three theory approaches described (structure-function, symbolic interaction, developmental) and the three therapy approaches (structural, interactional, family systems) are closely aligned even though each views family health differently (Whall, 1986). Each approach represents an attempt to understand the family and how it functions. Although the theory and therapy models differ in their origins and purposes, each approach contributes useful conceptual knowledge. This knowledge is relevant to family assessment and to viewing the family as the unit of care. Family theory approaches focus on family behavior and normality. This includes how families function, the environment-family interchange, interactions within the family, how the family changes over time, and the family's reaction to internal and external events. Family therapy models focus on family pathology and dysfunction. They are designed to be used with families experiencing varying degrees of relational, emotional, and communication dysfunction. These families have often been labeled as having a member with severe emotional problems (Bowen, 1978).

Currently no one approach from family theory or family therapy fully explains the relationships and dynamics of family life (Fawcett, 1989a; Friedman, 1987; Grotevant, 1989; Pender, 1987; Whall, 1986). None of the approaches by itself appears inclusive enough to provide a theoretical umbrella for the phenomena with which family nursing deals (Fawcett, 1989a; Friedmann, 1989). Therefore, nurses are forced to draw upon multiple theoretical and therapeutic approaches to provide the means for organizing observations, focusing inquiries, and communicating findings.

Nurses must understand how the theory and therapy approaches contribute to nursing practice (Whall, 1986), to be certain that information gleaned from both approaches supports a nursing perspective. Nurses attempting to develop assessment and intervention instruments based on the orientations described must modify or reformulate them to fit the nursing perspective (Fitzpatrick, Whall, Johnston, and Floyd, 1982; Whall, 1986).

Family therapy approaches, which were "developed outside of nursing, are at a more specific or less abstract level than the nursing models" (Whall, 1986, p. 5). As currently used, the approaches are not consistent with the nursing perspective articulated in the American Nursing Association's (ANA) Social Policy Statement (1980), the ANA Standards of Nursing Practice (1976), or the majority of nursing models currently in use (Whall, 1986). Therefore, reformulations or modifications of family theory and therapy approaches need to be considered if nurses plan to use them for family assessment (Fitzpatrick and Whall, 1989). As Whall (1986, p. ix) states, "If nursing is to develop a cohesive body of knowledge upon which to base practice, it is counterproductive to our efforts to use without change theories from other disciplines that are not consistent with the perspective of nursing."

The application of nursing theory to the family as the unit of care appears to be superficial or, at best, incomplete (Clements and Roberts, 1983; Whall, 1986). The majority of recognized nursing theorists—Henderson, Johnson, King, Levine, Neuman, Orem, Peplau, Rogers, Roy, Travelbee, and Weidenback—tend to focus their assessments and interventions on individual patients as client, as opposed to the families as client (Clements and Roberts, 1983, Friedman, 1986; Gonot, 1986; Johnston, 1986; Neuman, 1989; Wright and Leahey, 1986). However, despite the current stage of theory development, nursing theories hold great promise for being able to describe and explain how families function in health and illness and spell out the nurse's role in the family assessment and intervention process (Friedman, 1986; Reed, 1986).

Chapter 2 describes how selected concepts from these theoretical orientations are interwoven into the family nursing assessment process.

Nursing Assessment Applied to Family Systems

2

Orientation to Nursing Assessment as Applied to Family Systems

The purpose of this chapter is to describe a nursing model that incorporates selected concepts from the theoretical approaches and applies them to a family systems nursing assessment.

The assessment process provides an opportunity for families and health professionals to acquire relevant information from which to develop individually tailored plans for promotive, preventive, and rehabilitative health care (Carlson, 1989; Filsinger, 1983). Assessment enables nurses to organize their thinking in ways that facilitate an understanding of complex family behavioral patterns. It also helps nurses identify underlying family member problems that are not readily observed.

The family has long been recognized as the most important contextual influence in human growth and development (Belsky, Lerner, and Spanier, 1984). As such it provides the environment in which family members learn and practice health promotion activities and health-generating behaviors. Family members frequently carry these health-focused activities and behaviors forward as they age, thereby creating a life-style pattern (Pender, 1987).

Nurses are taught to practice with the recognition that each individual is a unified whole—people exist as individuals and as members of a family within the larger context of the community. Most nurses also embrace the notion that their profession is family centered, even though the family as the unit of service for client assessment and intervention is a relatively new nursing concept (Fawcett, 1989a; Pender, 1987; Reed, 1982, 1989; Whall, 1986; Wright and Leahey, 1984). Little documentation exists relative to the family-centered nature of actual family nursing practice or what family nursing practice includes (Murphy, 1986; Speer and Sachs, 1985; Whall, 1990). There is also some confusion as to where the "family" fits into the nursing paradigm, due, in part, to how nursing practice is perceived by both those within the profession and those outside of it. For example, does nursing practice serve individuals within family environments, or do nurses provide care for families as units? If one's theoretical or therapeutic stance focuses primarily on the individual therapeutic nurse-client relationship, then "family" is either treated as context for the therapeutic interaction or is ignored (Murphy, 1986). In practice, Murphy (1986, p. 191) suggests that "nurses provide care to both individuals and family units—whether or not theoretical frameworks conceptualize these adequately."

Nurse theoreticians are attempting to build nursing models that are both pertinent to family-centered care and supportive of the nursing perspective (Fawcett, 1989). These beginning models take into account the concepts of family as client, health, illness, environment, wellness, prevention activities, family stability, and nursing. Other forward-thinking nurse academicians, recognizing the importance of viewing the family as client, are continuing to develop assessment instruments that can be used with families (Clemen-Stone, Eigsti, and McGuire, 1987; Feetham, 1983; Friedman, 1986; Hanson, 1985, 1986; Hymovich and Barnard, 1979; Pender, 1987; Stanhope and Lancaster, 1984; Wright and Leahey, 1984; Neuman, 1983, 1989). These assessment instruments, like those developed in the social and behavioral sciences, incorporate selected concepts from the theory and therapy modalities presented.

As the nursing profession progresses into the twenty-first century, it must continue to broaden its scope of practice and accept responsibility and accountability for including the family as client in the assessment and intervention process (Fawcett, 1989a; Fawcett and Downs, 1986). Nurses will need to make conscious, explicit efforts to assess families as units of care. The rationale for this explicitness is based on the numerous deterrents that have prohibited nurses from attempting to use family-centered health promotive and preventive approaches in the past. The lack of time, organizational support, economic incentives, traditional care settings, and knowledge about the family assessment process are but a few obstacles to implementing family approaches (Speer and Sachs, 1985; Fawcett, 1986; Gilliss, Roberts, Highley, and Martinson, 1989). As insurmountable as these obstacles appear, it is nonetheless vital to conduct family assessments since the information obtained greatly influences nursing practice.

The family assessment inventory described in this handbook is built on a nursing model, the Neuman systems model. It is designed as a tool for assessing family health and identifying the entry level at which prevention and intervention activities should begin. The foundation upon which the model rests will be discussed first, then the inventory itself.

Neuman Systems Model Applied to Family Systems

The Neuman systems model incorporates conceptual knowledge gained from both theory and therapy modalities, with general systems theory providing its central approach. The systems viewpoint is helpful in conceptualizing appropriate nursing assessment and intervention actions applicable to family health. Neuman (1980, 1982, 1983, 1989) and others (Gray, Rizzo, and Duhl, 1969; Putt, 1978; Reed, 1982, 1989) believe that general systems theory provides a framework that is useful in addressing the large number of variables, relationships, and developments that occur within families.

This open systems approach embraces a holistic concept of persons and their environmental interactions. Concepts germane to nursing have been drawn from several of the theory and therapy approaches described in Chapter 1. These concepts, modified and reformulated to fit the nursing perspective, include open system, environment, holism, stability or homeostasis, structure, interaction, roles, life cycle, communication, and relationship patterns.

Neuman (1989) also uses principles from Gestalt and field theories to describe the movement and organization that occur within and outside of the client system. Concepts from Gestalt theory imply that each family or family system is surrounded by a perceptual field that is in dynamic equilibrium. Field theory concepts endorse the holistic view that all parts of the family system are intimately interrelated and interdependent and contribute to the total organization of the system (Neuman, 1989).

Gestalt theory concepts, defined and operationalized to be consistent with a nursing perspective, are interaction of person and environment (Neuman, 1989). Additional concepts synthesized for this model are stress, adaptation, interaction with environment (Selye, 1976), levels of prevention (Caplan, 1964), and totality of life (de Chardin, 1955).

Neuman Systems Model Basic Assumptions

The basic assumptions inherent within the Neuman systems model relate to an individual client as a system or to a group of any size as client (Neuman, 1989, pp. 17, 21-22). The following assumptions, termed *propositions* by Fawcett (1989a), define, describe, and link the concepts of the model. For purposes of clarity and focus the authors have used the word *family* instead of *client*.

1. Though each family as a family system is unique, each system is a composite of common, known factors or innate characteristics within a normal, given range of response contained within a basic structure.

2. Many known, unknown, and universal environmental stressors exist. Each differs in its potential for disturbing a family's usual stability level, or normal line of defense. The particular interrelationships of family variables — physiological, psychological, sociocultural, developmental, and spiritual — at any time can affect the degree to which a family is protected by the flexible line of defense against possible reaction to one or more stressors.

3. Over time, each family/family system has evolved a normal range of response to the environment, referred to as a normal line of defense, or usual wellness/stability state.

4. When the cushioning, accordion-like effect of the flexible line of defense is no longer capable of protecting the family/family system against an environmental stressor, the stressor breaks through the normal line of defense. The interrelationships of variables — physiological, psychological, sociocultural, developmental, and spiritual — determine the nature and degree of the system reaction or possible reaction to the stressor.

5. The family, whether in a state of wellness or illness, is a dynamic composite of the interrelationships of variables — physiological, psychological, sociocultural, developmental, and spiritual. Wellness is on a continuum

of available energy to support the system in its optimal state.

6. Implicit within each family system is a set of internal resistance, factors known as lines of resistance, which function to stabilize and return the family to the usual wellness state (normal line of defense), or possibly to a higher level of stability, following an environmental stressor reaction.

7. *Primary prevention* relates to general knowledge that is applied in family assessment and intervention in identification and mitigation of risk factors associated with environmental stressors to prevent possible reaction.

8. *Secondary prevention* relates to symptomatology following reaction to stressors, appropriate ranking of intervention priorities, and treatment to reduce their noxious effects.

9. *Tertiary prevention* relates to the adjustive processes taking place as reconstitution begins and maintenance factors move the client back in a circular manner toward primary prevention.

10. The family is in dynamic, constant energy exchange with the environment.

Neuman Systems Model Definition of Terms

The Neuman systems model initially focused on the assessment of individuals, as the name Total-Person Approach (Neuman, 1980, 1982, 1989) implies, although it was not limited to individuals. The model's scope was and is broad enough to encompass the assessment of families, groups, and communities (Goldblum-Graff and Graff, 1982; Reed, 1982, 1989; Mischke-Berkey, Warner and Hanson, 1989; Mirenda, 1986).

The Neuman systems model can be explained in relation to a family as a system that is subject to the impact of environmental stressors (Neuman, 1989). Concepts from the model can be applied to the family, the health care provider, and the health care system.

These concepts assist nurses in identifying actual and potential family health problems as well as problems surrounding the delivery of needed family services. Family concepts include: open system, environment, holism, wellness/illness, health, stressors (intra-family, inter-family, extra-family) basic structure, normal line of defense, flexible line of defense, lines of resistance, degree of reaction, adaptation/reconstitution, variables, man/person/family. Concepts related to the nurse or health care providers and the health care system are primary, secondary, and tertiary prevention as intervention, nursing diagnosis, nursing goals, nursing outcomes, and the profession of nursing (see Table 2-1).

Table 2-1   Neuman systems model definitions

Terms	Definitions
Basic structure	The basic structure consists of common client survival factors, as well as unique individual characteristics.
Boundary lines	The flexible line of defense is the outer boundary of the client. All relevant variables must be taken into account, as the whole is greater than the sum of the parts; a change in one part affects all other parts.
Client/client system	A composite of variables (physiological, psychological, sociocultural, developmental, and spiritual), each of which is a subpart of all parts, forms the whole of the client. The client as a system is composed of a core or basic structure of survival factors and surrounding protective concentric rings. The concentric rings are composed of similar factors, yet serve varied and different purposes in either retention, attainment, or maintenance of system stability and integrity or a combination of these. The client is considered an open system in total interface with the environment.
Content	The variables of man in interaction with the internal and external environment comprise the whole client system.

From Neuman, B. (1989). *The Neuman systems model*. Norwalk, CN: Appleton-Lange, pp. 48-50. Copyright © 1985 by Betty Neuman; revised 1987 by Betty Neuman.

Continued.

Table 2-1   Neuman systems model definitions—cont'd

Terms	Definitions
Degree of reaction	The degree of reaction is the amount of system instability resulting from stressor invasion of the normal line of defense.
Entropy	A process of energy depletion and disorganization, moving the system toward illness or possible death.
Environment	The environment consists of both internal and external forces surrounding the client, influencing and being influenced by the client, at any point in time, as an open system.
Feedback	The process within which matter, energy, and information, as system output, provide feedback for corrective action to change, enhance, or stabilize the system.
Flexible line of defense	The flexible line of defense is a protective, accordionlike mechanism that surrounds and protects the normal line of defense from invasion by stressors. The greater the expansiveness of this line from the normal line of defense, the greater the degree of protectiveness. Examples are situational, such as recently altered sleep patterns or immune functions.
Goal	The system goal is stability for the purpose of client survival and optimal wellness.
Health	A continuum of wellness to illness, dynamic in nature, that is constantly subject to change. Optimal wellness or stability indicates total system needs are being met. A reduced state of wellness is the result of unmet systemic needs. The client is in a dynamic state either of wellness or illness, in varying degrees, at any given point in time.

Table 2-1 Neuman systems model definitions—cont'd

Terms	Definitions
Input/output	The matter, energy, and information exchanged between client and environment, which is entering or leaving the system at any point in time.
Internal lines of resistance	Internal protection factors activated when stressors have penetrated the normal line of defense, causing a reaction or symptomatology. The resistance lines ideally protect the basic structure and facilitate reconstitution toward wellness during the following treatment, as stressor reaction is decreased and client resistance is increased.
Negentropy	A process of energy conservation which increases organization and complexity, moving the system toward stability or wellness.
Normal line of defense	An adaptational level of health developed over time and considered normal for a particular individual client or system; it becomes a standard for wellness-deviance determination.
Nursing	A unique profession concerned with all variables affecting clients in their environment.
Open system	A system in which there is a continuous flow of input and process, output and feedback. It is a system of organized complexity, where all elements are in interaction. Stress and reaction to stress are basic components.
Prevention as intervention	Intervention typology or modes for nursing action and determinants for entry of both client and nurse into the health care system. Primary prevention: before a reaction to stressors occur. Secondary prevention: treatment of symptoms following a reaction to stressors. Tertiary prevention: maintenance of optimal wellness following treatment.

Continued.

Table 2-1   Neuman systems model definitions—cont'd

Terms	Definitions
Process/function	The function or process of the system is the exchange of matter, energy, and information with the environment and the interaction of the parts and subparts of the client system. A living system tends to move toward wholeness, stability, wellness, and negentropy.
Reconstitution	Represents the return and maintenance of system stability, following treatment of stressor reaction, which may result in a higher or lower level of wellness than previously.
Stability	A state of balance or harmony requiring energy exchanges as the client adequately copes with stressors to retain, attain, or maintain an optimal level of health, thus preserving system integrity.
Stressors	Environmental factors, intra-, inter-, and extrapersonal in nature, that have potential for disrupting the system stability. A stressor is any phenomenon that might penetrate both the flexible and normal lines of defense, resulting in either a positive or negative outcome.
Wellness/illness	Wellness is the condition in which all system parts and subparts are in harmony with the whole system of the client. Wholeness is based upon interrelationships of variables, which determine the amount of resistance an individual has to any stressor. Illness indicates disharmony among the parts and subparts of the client system.

Table 2-1   Neuman systems model definitions—cont'd

Terms	Definitions
Wholistic	A system is considered wholistic when any parts or subparts can be organized into an interrelating whole. Wholistic organization is one of keeping parts whole or stable in their intimate relationships; individuals are viewed as wholes whose component parts are in dynamic interdependent interaction.

Neuman Systems Model Operationalized

This model defines the family as "a group of two or more persons who create and maintain a common culture; its most central goal is one of continuance" (Neuman, 1983, p. 241). When placed in the context of a systems framework, this definition appears to develop a life of its own—one that is rich in meanings, values, movement, and identifiable relationship patterns. As Neuman states (1983), "the family as a system . . . is composed of individual family members harmonious in their relationships—a cluster of related meanings and values that govern the family and keep it viable in a constantly changing environment" (p. 241).

The Neuman Systems Model views the family as an open and dynamic system in interaction with its environment. As such the system is subject to the tensions produced when stressors, in the form of situations, problems, or concerns, impinge on or penetrate through the family's defense system. The reaction from the family system depends on how deeply the stressor penetrates the family unit and how capable the family is in adapting to maintain its stability. For example, did the stressor (situation, problem, event) impinge on the flexible line of defense or penetrate through the normal line of defense to the lines of resistance? The lines of resistance protect the family's basic structure, which includes variable characteristics, functions, and energy resources of the family unit. It also contains the patterns of family interactions and unit strengths. The basic structure must be protected at all costs; otherwise, the demise of the family system will occur.

Reconstitution or adaptation is the work a family undertakes to preserve or restore impaired family unit functions and family stability after the stressor penetrating the family lines of defense has in some way altered family unit functions.

Nursing interventions are actions instituted to assist, modify, and/or regulate the family system's ability to generate its own health-promoting care or to respond to stressful situations. Nurses intervene by implementing health-promoting and health preventive actions as primary, secondary, or tertiary interventions that focus on intrafamily, interfamily, and extrafamily forces. The purpose of implementing nursing preventions as interventions is to assist the family in stabilizing its system.

Keeping these ideas in mind, the goal of nursing becomes one of identifying and manipulating environmental factors that curtail the family's ability to retain, attain, or maintain itself in an optimal state of health. The family's wellness state is defined in terms of system stability, homeostasis, or balance. This wellness state depends on the family's functional ability to cope with the myriad of environmental factors that internally or externally impinge on the family system. As a system, the family attempts to perform the necessary functions that contribute to the personalized growth and development of its individual members. The individual family members are considered to be subcomponents of the total family system.

Nurses can assist families with the process of retaining, attaining, and maintaining stability by being knowledgeable about the components of family systems, how these systems function, and the environmental factors that affect system balance. With this understanding nurses can develop individually tailored nursing action plans that facilitate unit stability and contribute to optimal family health.

Family member assessment variables. It is difficult to assess the family as a system without first assessing the individual family members as subcomponents of that system. Each family as a whole, and each member, as part of that whole, has identifiable boundaries. Boundaries refer to "who participates and how" (Minuchin, 1974, p. 53) or "the point which differentiates what is inside from what is outside the system; the point at which the system has little control over, or impact on outcomes" (Grubb, 1974, p. 163). Nurses need to identify these boundaries, along with the elements or parts contained therein, to make accurate family assessments. In addition, the boundary permeability needs to be assessed. Nurses can begin to define the boundaries by identifying the five variable areas that are incumbent in any human system—individual or family. These variables are physiological, psychological, sociocultural, developmental, and spiritual (Neuman, 1989). All five variables contribute to the individual family member's profile as distinct from the identity of the family composite. Each variable is separate from the other, yet intimately related, and each functions synergistically as well (Eberst, 1984). Each has its own nature and for assessment purposes can be viewed separately or in combination with one or more of the others. In addition, assessment of these variables can be applied to the subcomponents of the family system, such as individual family members, or to the whole family as a unit (Eberst, 1984). When the variable areas of one family member interface with those of other family members, a host of interactive styles and relationship patterns develops. For example, processes occurring within individual members or externally to them can affect the relating patterns of the total family unit (Messer, 1970). What the nurse observes during the family assessment procedure is the playing out of these variables in the context of the family system.

The five variable areas and their subcomponents are defined here in general terms.

Physiological variable.   The physiological variable is probably the easiest to assess, since most nursing efforts have been directed toward improving individuals' physical functioning and integrity over the life span. This variable refers primarily to the bodily structure and physical functioning of individual family members (Neuman, 1989). It includes the members' ability to carry out daily tasks with sufficient energy left over to handle unforeseen circumstances that may occur (Greenberg, 1985). Other contributing elements, whether directed at individuals or at whole family units, encompass: level(s) of fitness; presences or absence of disease; general state of physical health; past and present level of physical functioning, including motor skills, etc. (Whall, 1981); genetic factors affecting level of functioning (Whall, 1981); presence or absence of predisposing risk factors; life-style patterns; level of exposure to abuse—alcohol, stress, nicotine, drugs; nutrition, metabolism, and flexibility (Greenberg, 1985).

Psychological variable.   The psychological variable, as used by Neuman (1989), is divided into two components, mental processes and relationships. It encompasses the overall level of functioning with regard to cognitive and affective elements oper- ating in the family. Academicians outside of nursing call these components mental and emotional health (Eberst, 1984; Green- berg, 1985; Russell, 1980). Mental health and/or mental pro- cesses refers to the ability to learn—"cognition" or "knowing." Selected subcomponents contributing to this variable include in- tellectual capacity; psychological growth, sexuality; perception of others, adaptability, decision-making ability; ability to cope, ability to relax, tolerance, and judgment.

Emotional health is the ability to control emotions so that one feels comfortable expressing them when appropriate and does so appropriately (Greenberg, 1985). It also includes the ability not to express emotions when it is not appropriate to do so. Emo- tional health relates more to "feelings" and how they are ex- pressed (Eberst, 1984; Greenberg, 1985). Elements subsumed under this subcomponent are the ability to relate to personal val- ues; self-knowledge; self-love and feelings of self-importance; self-perception; sexuality, empathy, honesty, and the ability to express feelings and emotions appropriately (Sorochan, 1976).

Sociocultural variable. The sociocultural variable is defined in terms of combined social and cultural functions (Neuman, 1989). The social subcomponent refers to the family's ability to interact satisfactorily with people and the environment and, as a consequence, experience satisfying interpersonal relationships (Greenberg, 1985; Neuman, 1989). The cultural subcomponent addresses situations, patterns, and characteristics of the social system (Neuman, 1989) and includes the level of social skills that an individual family member and/or family system pos- sesses. It also addresses family members' comfort in being in- volved with others (social functioning), interactional patterns, communication patterns, sibling relationships; role relationships; attachment patterns (Whall, 1981); the ability to see oneself as a member of a larger society; and the extent of concern for others (Eberst, 1984).

As can be expected, the social dimension depends to a much greater extent on the quality and quantity of interaction with oth- ers and is much less "independent" than the psychological di- mension (Eberst, 1984). Additional sociocultural components in- clude job satisfaction, gaining a new perspective on problem solving, impact of quality of life on others, financial "success," career advancement, sharing of life experience with others, ser- vice to others, fulfillment of goals related to the "greater good," meeting new nonrecreational challenges, and expanding personal and professional horizons (Neuman, 1989; Reed, 1989; Eberst, 1984; Paltrow, 1980).

Developmental variable. This variable refers to life developmental processes that begin with birth and end with death (Neuman, 1989). Families, as well as individuals, have life cycle continuums, and as such they are involved in carrying out certain developmental tasks at specific developmental stages (Duvall, 1985). Duvall and Miller (1985) identifies eight stages of family development: married couples (without children), childbearing families (oldest child birth to 30 months), families with preschool children (oldest child 30 months to 6 years), families with teenagers (oldest child 13 to 20 years), families launching young adults (first child gone to last child leaving home), middle-aged parents (empty nest to retirement), aging family members (retirement to death of both spouses). Each of these developmental stages has eight accompanying tasks, as identified in Chapter 1.

The tasks of the family system at each stage support and complement individual and family development. Families must successfully complete all tasks in their current stage to function optimally. Developmental processes contribute to balancing change and consistency over time (i.e., changes and consistency of family members as individuals and as a family unit and the impact of change and consistency on the individual and/or family's physiological, psychological, sociocultural, and spiritual health behaviors and practices) (Schuster and Ashburn, 1986).

Spiritual variable. The spiritual variable refers to the influence of spiritual belief for individuals, families, and communities (Neuman, 1989). Only relatively recently have nursing assessment instruments formally acknowledged this variable. Also, the term *spiritual health* seems to defy a concrete definition, and the elements or subcomponents contained therein are difficult to validate (Eberst, 1984). Russell (1980), Banks (1980), and Greenberg (1985) identify several elements that contribute to an understanding of spiritual health. These elements bring meaning and clarity to the variable and involve a belief in or commitment to a unifying life force or a higher process or being. For some family members or family units the life force or higher process will be nature, for others it will be scientific laws, and for others it will be a godlike force (Greenberg, 1985). Spiritual elements involve trust, integrity, principles and ethics, the ability to love

and be loved, the purpose or drive in life, basic survival in-
stincts, feelings of selflessness, creativity, degree of pleasure-
seeking qualities; grief, loss, and the ability to believe in concepts that are not subject to "state of the art" explanation
(Eberst, 1984).

These variable subcomponents are ones that would seem to
have a great impact on a family member's overall personal
health (Eberst, 1984). Elements like confidence, life force, en-
thusiasm, moral code, and ethics would seem to be pivotal to an
individual's physiological, psychological, sociocultural, and developmental health, as well as to the health of the family unit
(Eberst, 1984). If this is true, then it is possible to suggest that
the spiritual aspect of health is much more than just one of the
five health variables. It may also provide the supporting mechanism or basic structure around which the other four dimensions
articulate and interact with each other (Eberst, 1984).

Family systems categories.   The five variables present in each family member as a subsystem can also be isolated in the whole
family as a system. The family system has physiological, psychological, sociocultural, developmental, and spiritual variables
that grow and develop over time. These variables, encircled by
their identifiable boundaries and varying degrees of permeability, contribute to and maintain family health. Neuman (1989)
groups the five variables applicable to each family member into
a family assessment variable arrangement that connotes holism,
interaction, and relationship. This grouping of variables is sifted
into four categories: (1) psychosocial relationship characteristics,
(2) physical status, (3) developmental characteristics, and (4)
spiritual influence (Neuman, 1989). These categories, serving as
a format for family assessment, assist nurses in determining the
levels of family stability (relative state of wellness) and instability (illness state). Stability levels are viewed on the basis of a
continuum that ranges from stability at one end to instability at
the other. Optimal family stability can be equated with optimal
family health (Neuman, 1989).

Some specific family concerns, concepts, and interaction patterns included in the four categories are listed in the box (Neuman, 1983, p. 242).

The magnitude of the interactive and relationship factors become very apparent when nurses consider the rearrangement of
the five variable areas into the four major categories. Because
the human condition is not static, there is constant change of all

Possible Family Concerns, Concepts, and Interaction Patterns

Category 1: Psychosocial relationship characteristics

Family relationships are clear and flexible, and interaction patterns predominate

Individual needs: components contributing to the needs of individual family members are age, sex, developmental state, individual differences, and environmental influences

Individual and family composite of behavioral patterns: values and family interaction patterns determine the family structure and process; components germane to this category are decision making, coping style, role relationship, communication styles and interaction patterns, goals, boundaries, socialization process, individuation, and sharing

Family adjustment needs: the degree to which each family member's need is satisfied within the family composite of behavioral relationship pattern characteristics

Category 2: Physical status

Components of this category include (1) optimal energy to carry out system requirements and responsibilities and (2) homeostatic system balance, which enables family system to function at its optimal wellness level (Neuman, 1983). Factors germane to family system energy levels and system balance involve the overall physiological health status of the family unit, the immediate and culmulative effects of individual family member health variance on the family unit, and family system life-style patterns that facilitate wellness and/or contribute to illness.

Category 3: Developmental characteristics

Components include age/stage appropriate processes and a determination if they are within normal limits (Neuman, 1983). The family developmental age/stage processes include basic tasks confronting the family as a group in all social classes and subcultures, through changing times and throughout the family life cycle (Duvall and Miller, 1985). The tasks of all families are implemented by the roles family members play in interaction (Duvall and Miller, 1985). These tasks and their inherent characteristics are:

1. An independent home—providing shelter, food, clothing, health care, etc.
2. Satisfactory ways of getting and spending money—meeting family needs and costs; apportioning material goods, facilities, space, authority; giving respect, affection, etc.
3. Mutually acceptable patterns in the division of labor—deciding who does what, assigning responsibility for pro-

Continued.

Possible Family Concerns, Concepts, and Interaction Patterns—cont'd

   curing income, managing the household, caring for family members, and other specific tasks

4. Continuity of mutually satisfying sex relationships
5. Open system of intellectual and emotional communication—guiding the internalization of increasingly mature and acceptable patterns of controlling elimination, food intake, sexual drives, sleep, aggression, etc; maintenance of order—providing means of communication and establishing types and intensity of interaction, patterns of affection, and sexual expression—by administering sanctions ensuring conformity to group norms affection
6. Workable relationships with relatives—incorporating new members by marriage and establishing policies for inclusion of others: in-laws, relatives, stepparents, guests, family friends, etc.
7. Ways of interacting with associates and community organizations—fitting into the community; relating to church, school, organizational life, political and economic systems; and protecting family members from undesirable influences
8. Competency in bearing and rearing children—bearing or adopting children and rearing them for independent life
9. A workable philosophy of life—maintenance of motivation and morale, rewarding members of achievements, satisfying individual needs for acceptance, encouragement and affection, meeting personal and family crises

Category 4: Spiritual influence
Component of this category includes identifiable and definable support (belief influence) (Neuman, 1983). Family's spiritual beliefs in life force, higher process, or godlike force involves trust, integrity, ethical principles, feelings of selflessness among family members. Also included are ability to love and be loved, purpose or drive in life

The three categories of physical status, developmental characteristics, and spiritual influence are not as explicitly described by Neuman as is the psychosocial relationship characteristics category (Neuman, 1983). Therefore, additional interactive and relational effects of these categories have been expanded (Reed, 1989; Duvall and Miller, 1985; Johnson, Vaughn-Wrobel, Ziegler, et al, 1982; Hoffman, 1982; Mischke-Berkey, Warner, and Hanson, 1989).

variables in all people and consequently in all families. Whenever one element of a variable is rearranged or "worked on" separately, the activity affects almost every other element in every variable. This also holds true for its effect on all family system categories.

Awareness of this rippling effect is important because most family members seeking to improve their family's health, or nurses helping them with this process, focus on only one variable at a time. For example, consider the sociocultural element of employment. Many family members will "sacrifice" a degree of their physiological, psychological, developmental, and spiritual health in an effort to reach their maximum potential in the vocational area. They may work long hours, forego a balanced nutritional intake, expose themselves to excess stress without adapting to it, spend less "prime" time with significant others, defer relaxation, and end up being too busy to experience and express their feelings (Eberst, 1984). To assist families involved with this kind of experience, nurses need to focus on all family member variables or on all categories rather than just one variable or one category. This simultaneous, holistic focusing is a necessary and challenging responsibility.

The family member variables and the family systems categories are subject to the effects of a myriad of stressors and strengths. These are described in Chapter 3.

Family Systems Stressors and Family Systems Strengths

3

Family Systems Stressor Orientation
What is this Thing Called Stress?

The purpose of this chapter is to describe the effects of stressors on the family system and to identify strengths operating in family systems.

If you are alive, you experience stress. No family members, no family system, is immune. Like it or not, stress is going to be with all family members daily. Also, family members constantly react to people and events in their lives.

Listening to a funny story or touching a hot element on the stove both cause reactions. Each actually produces a type of stress. Stress occurs whenever the mind and body react to some real or imagined threatening event or situation (Haney and Boenisch, 1983). Events that cause stress reactions are called *stressors*. Some family system stress is beneficial and stimulating. Other types of stress, especially if prolonged, can fatigue or damage the basic structure of the family system to the point of excessive instability, dysfunction, and illness (Haney and Boenisch, 1983; Neuman, 1982, 1989).

Stress is inherent in the majority of day-to-day activities involving family members. However, the object is not to eliminate stress from the family system but to assist family members in adapting to it. Family members need moderate levels of stress to help them stay alert and perform well (Haney and Boenisch, 1983). The key is control. Stress can be beneficial as long as family members have some feelings of control (Phares, 1976).

When families are not in control of their life situations, ongoing stress may result in the demise of the system (Neuman, 1989).

Distinctions can be made between stress that is harmful and negative and that which is beneficial and positive (Selye, 1976). Harmful stress often contributes to family instability and culminates in feelings of helplessness, frustration, and disappointment. Positive stress can be beneficial and contribute to family stability, thus enabling families to live effective lives (Selye, 1974). Positive stress produces feelings of achievement and exhilaration. Therefore, it is not so much the stressor or its intensity that determines whether it is beneficial or harmful but the family's perception of the event (Bomar, 1989). The family system's perceptions trigger their reactions (Bomar, 1989; Haney and Boenisch, 1983; Phares, 1976).

Recalling the systems theory principles typified by the hanging mobile example cited in Chapter 1, family nurses are actively using systems principles to help them understand family stress (Wright and Leahey, 1984). Curran (1983), a well-respected family specialist, asks health professionals to think of a family unit as being suspended in midair by a thin nylon cord. When family life is proceeding smoothly all members are in balance. However, forces impinging on the system can quickly alter the system balance. These forces can arise from inside the family system as normal maturational and transitional stresses and/or as catastrophic events. For example, when a stepparent, a new baby, or an elderly parent enters a family unit, the additional member creates a temporary system imbalance. This culminates in a shaky family mobile.

It is normal for family members to experience some sleepless nights when a new baby enters the family. Reduced spousal time and role displacement for the youngest child occur as well. Everyone in the family system is forced to change, at least temporarily, as new behaviors and adaptations come into play. If a family member dies, a child goes off to college, or the parents divorce, then the family unit is more violently affected and for a longer period of time (Curran, 1985). Family resources and strengths eventually determine how long it takes for the family to regain system balance.

Forces arising from outside the family can also influence system balance and stability. These forces usually take the form of societal pressures, including family moves, teenage peer pressure, loss of employment, inflation, added taxes, natural disasters, and so on. These outside forces contribute to fluctuations in family system balance, as can be demonstrated by a rapidly flagellating family mobile.

Families are called upon to continuously and simultaneously negotiate changes caused by inner and outer stressors (Curran, 1985). Some families are able to mobilize their strengths and resources, thereby adapting effectively to multiple pressures, while others fall apart. Nurses must carefully assess family units to determine how families use their strengths and resources to retain, attain, and maintain system balance. They must also be able to recognize the family dynamics that enable some families to control their stress levels.

Families adapting effectively to stressful events share common reactive patterns. Curran (1985 p.12) identified the following family reactions:

1. A tendency to recognize that stress is temporary and that it may even be positive
2. A working together on solutions to minimize stressors, which, in turn, strengthens family skills
3. A development of new rules, which include prioritizing time and sharing responsibilities
4. An expectation that some stress is a normal part of family life and that the family is not a failure because it exists
5. A good feeling about themselves for having dealt effectively with the new stressor

Families dealing with stressful events ineffectually also share common characteristics (Curran, 1985, p. 12). These characteristics are expressed as follows:

1. Feelings of guilt for permitting a stress to exist
2. Looking for a place to lay blame rather than for a solution to the problem
3. Giving in to stress and giving up trying to master it
4. Focusing on family problems rather than on family strengths
5. Feeling weaker rather than stronger after the normal stress experience
6. Growing to dislike family life as a result of the buildup of stresses

Family scholars Olson, McCubbin, Barnes et al, (1983) describe research linking stress and family life. They state that satisfied families were not stressed families, but that families under stress were dissatisfied families. Also, couples under stress were equally dissatisfied with their marriages, with their family lives, and with the quality of their individual lives. Family members are not born with undesirable reactions to stressors; they learn how to react to tension-producing events and situations. They learn by watching others, responding to selected parental demands, incorporating the neighbors' hearsay, painful coincidences, etc. Over time the reactions of family members to different situations become self-perpetuating habit patterns (Haney and Boenisch, 1983).

All family systems experience somewhat similar stressors as they grow and develop over the life cycle. Some families are more successful in stressor management than others; consequently they transform stresses into positive forces. These families are able to maintain and retain system stability and health. Other families facing similar growth and developmental demands tend to lose control and react in ways that jeopardize family system function.

Family units living with distress and instability as a way of life exhibit symptoms that nurses can recognize while performing a family assessment (Curran, 1985, p. 13). These include the following:

- A constant sense of urgency and hurry; no time to release and relax
- Tension that underlies and causes sharp words, sibling fighting, and misunderstandings
- A mania to escape—to one's room, car, garage, away
- Feelings of frustration over not getting things done
- A feeling that time is passing too quickly; children are growing up too fast
- A nagging desire for a simpler life; constant talk about times that were or will be simpler
- Little "me" or couple time
- A pervasive sense of guilt for not being and doing everything to and for all of the people in one's life

Most families experience these symptoms at one time or another, but for some the symptoms become the family's modus operandi. The family members learn to live with negativity, distress, and instability.

Most families and health care professionals have notions about family stress and what constitutes a family stressor. Curran (1985) identified 45 stressful situations commonly found in family life. These included such things as communication with children, spousal relationship, health/illness, insufficient "me" time, retirement, housekeeping standards, and so on. Curran's initial research (1985) also showed a pattern of disagreement between husbands and wives as to what constituted a stressor. Stresses selected differed particularly among three basic groups: married men, married women, and single mothers. The box below shows the 10 situations most often selected by married men, married women, and single mothers as causing the most stress in their families (Curran, 1985, p. 20).

One of the dilemmas facing nurse academicians who are attempting to identify and define family stressors relates to how families and nurses conceptualize stressful situations. Do nurses focus on the family and its perception of stress, or do nurses assess the situational demands and coping resources of the family independent of the family's perceptions? The Neuman systems model attempts to take both orientations into account, to learn how families view their stressors and how they use their internal and external strengths and resources to handle stress effectively over the life cycle. The model gives consideration to the type of stressor and its intensity as well as the stability level (resistance level) operative in the family system. These variables determine whether a stressor becomes noxious.

Family Stressors and the Neuman Systems Model

Neuman (1989, p. 9) in defining stressors as "tension producing stimuli or forces occurring within both the internal and the exter-

---

Top Stressors in Order of Priority for Total Group

1. Economics/finances/budgets
2. Children's behavior/discipline/sibling fighting
3. Insufficient couple time
4. Lack of shared responsibility in the family
5. Communicating with children
6. Insufficient "me" time
7. Guilt for not accomplishing more
8. Spousal relationship (communication, friendship, sex)
9. Insufficient family play time
10. Overscheduled family calendar

From Curran, D. (1985). *Stress and the healthy family.* Minneapolis, MN: Winston Press, Inc., p. 20. Reprinted by permission of Harper & Row, Publishers, Inc., New York, NY.

nal environmental boundaries of the client/client system," provides a mechanism by which family stressors can be defined. These stressors include "all forces (problems, conditions, situations) that either are or could produce instability within the family system" (Neuman, 1983, p. 246).

Family stressors are categorized into three broad areas based on the the family system's internal and external environment. Stressors arise from intrafamily, interfamily, and extrafamily sources; that is, they are present within as well as from outside of the family system. All stressors in some way affect the physiological, psychological, sociocultural, developmental, and spiritual variables operating in family members as parts of a system and in the family as a whole system.

Nurses need to take into account several factors pertaining to intrafamily, interfamily, and extrafamily stressors when assessing families. These factors include cultural differences, stressor intensity, family coping ability and style, stressor reaction and adaptation, change in role function, and negative family adjustment (Neuman, 1983). These family system stressor factors are listed below.

Family System Stressor Factors

1. Cultural differences can become stressors, especially when change is imposed by family or societal needs. Cultural factors create differences in adaptation needs to stressors.
2. Measurement of a stressor is dependent on an individual's subjective perception of it.
3. When a stressor is severe, adaptive function is temporarily satisfied to control or cope with it; that will allow for invasion of the basic structure.
4. The mere fact of reactions to stressors indicates adaptive ability.
5. The degree of family flexibility for change and past coping styles are variables in relation to resolution of stressors.
6. Family stressors usually require some change in role function. The change process itself may become a stressor.
7. A negative adjustment to unresolved encounters with stressors can, in part, be defined by the rigidity of continued use of defensive behaviors.

From Neuman, B. (1983). Family intervention using the Betty Neuman Health-Care Systems Model. In I. Clements and F. Roberts (Eds.), *Family health: A theoretical approach to nursing care* (p. 247). New York: John Wiley and Sons.

Identifying sources of stress as well as the stressors themselves depends on both family and nurses' perceptions, which sometimes differ. For example, one family member may conclude that a particular stressor originates within a designated family member while another may think that the stressor arises out of the interaction between two family members. A nurse assessing the situation might infer that the stressor originates outside the family system, that it involves a community social policy, for example. Each person is viewing the source of stress from a different perspective. How a stressor is perceived is crucial since nursing interventions are based on how the problem is perceived.

Intrafamily Stressors

Intrafamily stressors are all things that occur within the boundary of the family/family system that have the potential for disrupting the stability of the family system (Neuman, 1983). This includes stressors that are routinely thought of as being intrapersonal in nature. Intrapersonal stressors experienced by one family member may affect the stability of the whole family. For example, what happens to one family member may affect the stability of the whole family. Nurses assessing families must consider the environmental source of stress and view each stressor in terms of the five variables inherent in every human system. Examples of intrafamily stressors are found in the box below.

Intrafamily System Stressors

1. Family member(s) feeling unappreciated
2. Guilt for not accomplishing more
3. Insufficient "me" time
4. Self-image/self-esteem/feelings of unattractiveness
5. Perfectionism
6. Dieting
7. Health/illness
8. Drugs/alcohol
9. Widowhood
10. Retirement
11. Homework/school/grades

From Curran, D. (1985). *Stress and the healthy family*. Minneapolis, MN: Winston Press, Inc. Reprinted by permission of Haper & Row, Publishers, Inc., New York, NY.

Interfamily Stressors

Interfamily stressors are all things occurring between the boundary of the family/family system and the immediate or direct external environment (Neuman, 1983). Examples of problems or concerns relevant to this category are found in the box below.

Each of these concerns must be filtered through the assessment lenses of the five family member variables (physiological, psychological, sociocultural, developmental, spiritual) and the four categories of a family system (psychosocial relationship characteristics, physical status, developmental characteristics, and spiritual influence).

Extrafamily Stressors

Extrafamily stressors are all things occurring between the boundary of the family/family system and the distal or indirect external

---

Interfamily System Stressors

1. Communication with children
2. Housekeeping standards
3. Insufficient couple time
4. Insufficient family playtime
5. Children's behavior/discipline/sibling fighting
6. Television
7. Overscheduled family calendar
8. Lack of shared responsibility in the family
9. Moving
10. Spousal relationship (communication, friendship, sex)
11. Holidays
12. In-laws
13. Teen behaviors
14. New baby
15. Houseguests
16. Family vacations
17. Remarriage
18. Relationship with former spouse
19. Summer
20. Weekends
21. Religious differences
22. Predinner hours
23. Older parents

From Curran, D. (1985). *Stress and the healthy family*. Minneapolis, MN: Winston Press, Inc. Reprinted by permission of Harper & Row, Publishers, Inc., New York, NY.

Extrafamily System Stressors

1. Economics/finances/budgets
2. Unhappiness with work situation
3. Overvolunteerism
4. Neighbors
5. Unemployment
6. Nuclear and environmental fears
7. Church/school activities
8. Unsatisfactory housing
9. Organized sports activities
10. Change in work patterns
11. Two-paycheck family

From Curran, D. (1985). *Stress and the healthy family*. Minneapolis, MN: Winston Press, Inc. Reprinted by permission of Harper & Row, Publishers, Inc., New York, NY.

environment (Neuman, 1983). Keeping in mind the family member variables and the family system categories, consider the examples found in the box above.

• • •

Families and society are interdependent. What enriches one enriches the other; what damages one damages the other (Curran, 1985). Nurses can assist families experiencing varying degrees of stressor penetration by designing appropriate adaptational strategies with them. These strategies begin with the identification of family strengths and resources.

Family Systems Strength Orientation

The purpose of family assessment is to determine the quality of family health and stability. This encompasses not only the identification of family system weaknesses but also the all-important challenge of identifying family system strengths. Family strengths are those caring, nurturing, and growth-facilitating qualities held by individual family members that are given meaning and substance when played out in the interactive and relationship patterns of a family system. In nursing there is a tendency to concentrate on family needs, problems, and weaknesses (Daniel, 1986; Spradley, 1981). One reason for this might rest with the point at which family members first interface with the health care system, which is usually when the family is experiencing symptoms of overwhelming instability. Nurses meet the distraught families at this juncture, when system viability is in question. Another reason nurses might focus more on weaknesses then strengths is that nursing tends to be problem-oriented or illness-oriented, rather than strength- and wellness-oriented. It seems to suit our role as helper to look for people and things that need our help (Spradley, 1981).

Family nurses recognize that most families are able to identify their problems but are unable to identify their inherent system strengths. It is imperative for nurses to help families identify their strengths, then to acknowledge and reinforce these strengths since they are the basis for therapeutic strategies. Emphasizing family strengths encourages family members to feel better about themselves (Stinnett and DeFrain, 1985; Stinnett, 1979) by fostering a positive self-image, promoting self-confidence, and decreasing the family's feeling of hopelessness. Focusing on family strengths also energizes the family's efforts and unleashes their potential for developing their system's capacities (Pratt, 1976; Spradley, 1981). This does not mean that nurses ignore family concerns. On the contrary, holistic family assessment takes into account all factors and forces that affect family stability and health, positive and negative. Emphasizing strengths says, in effect, "your family is important to me"; "I value you"; and "I see many growth-facilitating aspects inherent in your family system." All of these aspects can contribute to system health and stability.

Now is the time to shift gears from a problem orientation to a strength orientation and look closely at why some families are healthy and strong. The knowledge gained from incorporating strengths into a family care plan can contribute significantly to the family's ability to resolve problem issues (Stinnett, 1979).

A number of researchers have attempted to delineate characteristics and behaviors of healthy families. Otto (1973) was a pioneer in researching family strengths. His original work identified several strengths of families: communication patterns, support system, relationship, and ability to deal with crises or solve problems. These "family strength factors are not isolated variables but clusters or constellations that are dynamic, fluid, inter-related and variable at different stages in the family's life cycle" (Otto, 1973, p. 9). They contribute to family unity and solidarity and foster the development of inherent family potential.

Otto's family strengths have been incorporated into the Calgary Family Assessment Model (CFAM) developed by Wright and Leahey (1984). In using the CFAM nurses are encouraged to identify and list family strengths and problems in three assessment areas: structural, developmental, and functional. This listing gives purposes and direction to the development of therapeutic interventions.

One of the current leading investigatory teams in the area of family strengths is led by Nick Stinnett at the University of Nebraska (Stinnett, Chester, DeFrain, et al, 1979; Stinnett and De-Frain, 1985; Stinnett, DeFrain, King, et al, 1981; Stinnett, Sanders, and DeFrain, 1981; Stinnett, DeFrain, King, et al, 1982). This team of researchers defines strong two-parent families as those in which members express appreciation for each other, spend a good deal of quality time together, enjoy good communication, maintain a high degree of commitment to each other, share a religious orientation, and demonstrate the ability to handle crises positively.

Pratt (1976) conducted research to identify what she called the "energized family." By examining the dimensions of family structure, Pratt concluded that the energized family was one in which (1) all members were actively engaged in varied and regular interaction with each other; (2) the family had ties to the broader community through active participation of its members; (3) the family had a high degree of autonomy and a tendency to encourage individuality; and (4) the family engaged in reactive problem solving and active coping.

Additional family health parameters have been described by Lewis (1979), Glasser (1970), Satir (1972), and Peters (1981). Lewis (1979) identified nine dimensions of what he called "healthy" families. Glasser and Glasser (1970) delineated five general criteria for the "adequate" family, Satir (1972) discussed patterns of vital and nurturing families, and Peters (1981) compared strengths of black families to strengths of white families.

Curran's research (1983) on healthy families built on the contributions of the previously mentioned academicians. She focused on acquiring answers to the following questions: (1) what strengths or traits of health do professionals agree are found in healthy families?; (2) on what family traits do they disagree? and (3) do families get different messages about good family living from different institutions in their lives? Professional groups in five institutional areas of American culture were selected as participants. The sample included individuals in education (principals, counselors, teachers), churches (pastoral staffs, counselors, educators), health (pediatricians, nurses, family physicians, pediatric nurse practitioners), family counseling (counselors, therapists, mental health personnel, social workers), and voluntary organizations (directors, leaders, coaches).

Curran (1983, pp. 23-24) asked the professionals working with families to rank 15 traits, from a list of 56, that they believed facilitated family stability and health. The traits or strengths that they agreed upon are ranked in the box according to prevalence of selection. For example, "communicates and listens" was listed most often; "affirms and supports one another" received the next most votes.

Five additional traits that Curran (1983) identified were added to the listing of 15, to facilitate a broadening of the family strength and resource base. Additional strengths of healthy families include honoring its elders, accepting and encouraging individual values, valuing work satisfaction, financial security, and being able to "let go" of grown children. Each of the 20 strengths has identifiable hallmarks of success by which nurses and families are able to assess goal attainment. Hallmarks of success can be thought of as short-range goals and incorporated

---

Fifteen Strengths or Traits Found in Healthy Families

1. Communicates and listens
2. Affirms and supports one another
3. Teaches respect for others
4. Develops a sense of trust
5. Develops a sense of play and humor
6. Exhibits a sense of shared responsibility
7. Teaches a sense of right and wrong
8. Has a strong sense of family in which rituals and traditions abound
9. Has a balance of interaction among members
10. Has a shared religious core
11. Respects the privacy of one another
12. Values service to others
13. Fosters family table time and conversation
14. Shares leisure time
15. Admits to and seeks help with problems

From Curran, D. (1985). *Stress and the healthy family*. Minneapolis, MN: Winston Press, Inc. Reprinted by permission of Harper & Row, Publishers, Inc., New York, NY.

into the family care plan. For example, a family focusing on the long-range goal of communicating and listening to each other may design short-term goals that include sharing emotional feelings and power; tuning into family members' nonverbal messages, encouraging individual feelings and independent thinking, recognizing turn-off words and phrases that put family members down, and developing reconciliation patterns (Curran, 1983). Each of these short-range goals supports the family's long-range goal of communication and listening.

Nurses must be able to make thorough family assessments, given the effects of stressors on the family system and the need to identify family strengths that enhance system stability. Chapter 4 assists nurses with this task by presenting information relative to families, the nursing process, and the Neuman Systems Model.

Families, the Nursing Process and the Neuman Systems Model

4

The purpose of this chapter is to apply the nursing process to the care of families, using the Neuman Systems Model. The American Nurses Association, (1980, p. 9-10) stated in the Nursing Social Policy Statement that:

The phenomena of concern to nurses are human responses to actual or potential health problems. . . . The human responses of people toward which the actions of nurses are directed are of two kinds: (1) reactions of individuals and groups to actual health problems (health restoring responses), such as the impact of illness-effects upon the self and family, and related self-care needs; and (2) concerns of individuals and groups about potential health problems (health supporting responses), such as monitoring and teaching in populations or communities at risk in which educative needs for information, skill development, health-oriented attitudes and related behavioral changes arise.

Nursing Process

The nursing process is based on two assumptions: (1) professional nursing is interpersonal in nature and (2) professional nurses view human beings as holistic units (Stanton, Paul, and Reeves, 1985). The interpersonal nature of the nursing process is apparent when one considers the effects of the nurse's relationship with clients. In addition, a holistic view of clients gives credence to the notion that mind and body are not separate but function as a whole (Stanton, Paul, and Reeves, 1985). What happens in one part of the body or mind affects the whole body. People respond as whole beings.

The nursing process is a volitional, logical, and rational activity whereby the practice of nursing is performed in a systematic manner (Griffith-Kenney and Christensen, 1986). It is the underlying scheme that provides order and direction to nursing care and is the essence of nursing practice (Stanton, Paul, and Reeves, 1985). Nurses use the nursing process to acquire and analyze data concerning the health of family members and family systems. Analysis of this data culminates in specific statements that identify existing or potential health problems (Houl-

Table 4-1   Nursing process

Category	Description of Nursing Process
Assessment	1. Continuous process of collecting both subjective and objective data about client's health status, strengths, and concerns 2. Data systematically recorded serves as data base for all other components of nursing process
Diagnosis	1. Data base is analyzed and synthesized through selected theoretical approach 2. Nursing diagnostic statements written in clear, concise language
Planning	1. Nursing diagnoses prioritized 2. Goals mutually established by nurse and client 3. Objectives established 4. Implementation strategies developed 5. Nursing orders written in terms of client and nursing behaviors for each objective 6. Scientific rationale for planning clearly identified
Implementation	1. Activities performed by client, nurse, or other consistent with plan 2. Actions performed with skill and efficiency 3. Actions documented appropriately
Evaluation	1. Comparing client's status with objectives and goals to determine client's progress toward goal achievement 2. Summative evaluation performed that describes client's overall progress toward meeting the goal 3. Nursing care plan revised to reflect changes in client's condition or when goals or objectives have not been adequately met

From Griffith-Kenney, J.W., and Christensen, P.J. (1986). *Nursing process: Application of Theories, frameworks, and models.* (2nd ed). St. Louis: The C.V. Mosby Co.

din, Saltstein, and Ganley, 1987). These statements are referred to as nursing diagnoses. Each diagnostic statement provides the focus for the nurse's plan of care (Houldin, Saltstein, and Ganley, 1987). Griffith-Kenney and Christensen (1986) describe five interacting phases of the nursing process with accompanying steps (Table 4-1).

This five-phase process, which serves as the core of nursing practice by providing the needed structures for nursing care, is viewed somewhat differently by Neuman (1989). Neuman designed a specific format for the nursing process to facilitate the use of the systems model. This format contains three categories: nursing diagnosis, nursing goals, and nursing outcomes. The essential elements, explicitly defined in Table 4-2, incorporate the five-phase process described by Griffith-Kenney and Christensen (1986).

Table 4-2   Nursing process according to Neuman

Category	Description of Process
Nursing Diagnosis	1. Based on acquisition of appropriate data base, the diagnosis identifies, assesses, classifies, and evaluates the dynamic interaction of the biopsychosociocultural-developmental-spiritual variables
	2. Variances from wellness (needs/problems) are determined by correlations and constraints through synthesis of theory and data base.
	3. Broad hypothetical interventions are determined (i.e., maintain flexible line of defense)
Nursing Goals	1. Nurse/client system negotiates for prescriptive change
	2. Nurse intervention strategies postulated to retain, attain, and maintain client system stability
Nursing Outcomes	1. Nursing intervention using one or more prevention modes
	2. Confirmation of prescriptive change or reformulation of nursing goals
	3. Short-term goal outcomes influencing determinations of intermediate/long-term goals
	4. Client outcome validating nursing process

From Cross, J. (1985). Betty Neuman. In J. Georgh (Ed.). Nursing theories: The base for professional nursing practice (2nd ed.), Englewood Cliffs, NJ: Prentice-Hall, Inc.

Table 4-3, compares the traditional nursing process (Griffith-Kenney and Christensen, 1986) with the Neuman Systems Model nursing process.

Nurse academicians, clinicians, and educators have applied the nursing process primarily to their care of individual clients, but now its usefulness is broadening to include families as units of care. The nursing process, according to Neuman, has the capability of focusing on families as units of care with minimal alterations in the theoretical base (Reed, 1982; Mischke-Berkey, Warner, and Hanson, 1989). Inherent in the Neuman systems model are nine basic principles supporting a four-pronged client focus that includes the individual, the family, the group, and the community. Referencing the family as client, the principles inculcate the following beliefs: (1) good assessment requires

Table 4-3   Comparison of nursing processes

Griffith-Kenny and Christensen	Neuman Nursing Process
	1. Nursing diagnosis
1. Assessment	A. Accurate data base
	B. Synthesize theory: define problem and "variance from wellness;" prioritize needs
2. Diagnosis	C. Hypothetical intervention postulated
3. Planning	2. Nursing goals
	A. Mutual negotiation with client for prescriptive change to correct problem
	B. Appropriate intervention strategies planned (retain, attain, maintain client stability)
4. Implementation	3. Nursing outcomes
	A. Nursing intervention (using one or more modes of prevention)
	B. Confirmation of change (or reformulation of goals)
5. Evaluation	C. Short-term goals influencing long-term goals for subsequent nursing action
	D. Client outcome validating nursing process

From Cross, J. (1985). Betty Neuman. In J. George (Ed.). Nursing theories: The base for professional nursing practice (2nd ed.), Englewood Cliffs, NJ: Prentice-Hall, Inc.

knowledge of all factors that influence the family's perceptual field; (2) the meaning a stressor has to the family is validated by the family as well as the care-giver; (3) factors in the care-giver's perceptual field that influence the assessment of the family's situation should become apparent (Neuman, 1980). Additional principles and beliefs that assist nurses with the application of the nursing process to families have been articulated by other family-oriented academicians (Pender, 1987; Reed, 1989). These include (1) most nursing care delivered to families occurs during transition periods such as transitions to parenthood or developmental transitions of children, (2) the well family demonstrates a spectrum of abilities, insights, and strengths, and (3) family members of the dynamic unit are engaged in tasks aimed at personal development and continuation of the family system.

Nursing Diagnosis

The currently accepted nursing diagnosis categories are, for the most part, centered around the actual or potential harmful effects of illness on the health status of individuals (Houldin, Saltstein, and Ganley, 1987). However, nurses make client decisions and design intervention strategies that are not limited to the treatment of problems as articulated by the Ninth National Conference on Classification of Nursing Diagnoses (see the box).

Nurses focus their professional practice on assisting individuals, families, groups, and communities to attain, retain, and maintain their optimal health potential. Maintaining this potential increases the likelihood that the family system will be able to meet its health care needs (Houldin, Saltstein, and Ganley, 1987). Nurses and families must be committed to promoting health and preventing illness, along with recognizing and intervening with illness processes.

Formalized nursing diagnostic statements related to health promotion and disease prevention are not found in the literature, according to Houldin, Saltstein, and Ganley (1986 pp. 4, 9, 10). These nurse educators state:

As nurse educators, interested in teaching nursing students to promote health, prevent illness, and capitalize on clients' strengths, we have repeatedly lamented the fact that no identification or classification of wellness-related diagnoses is available in the literature. Our nursing students are forced to rely on a haphazard, nonspecific classification method to identify and incorporate client strengths into their nursing care planning. Whether the nursing goal is to maintain and promote health activ-

NANDA Approved Nursing Diagnostic Categories*

This list represents the NANDA approved nursing diagnostic categories for clinical use and testing (1988). Changes have been made in 15 labels for consistency.

1.1.2.1	Altered Nutrition: More than body requirements
1.1.2.2	Altered Nutrition: Less than body requirements
1.1.2.3	Altered Nutrition: Potential for more than body requirements
1.2.1.1	Potential for Infection
1.2.2.1	Potential Altered Body Temperature
**1.2.2.2	Hypothermia
1.2.2.3	Hyperthermia
1.2.2.4	Ineffective Thermoregulation
*1.2.3.1	Dysreflexia
1.3.1.1	Constipation
*1.3.1.1.1	Perceived Constipation
*1.3.1.1.2	Colonic Constipation
1.3.1.2	Diarrhea
1.3.1.3	Bowel Incontinence
1.3.2	Altered Urinary Elimination
1.3.2.1.1	Stress Incontinence
1.3.2.1.2	Reflex Incontinence
1.3.2.1.3	Urge Incontinence
1.3.2.1.4	Functional Incontinence
1.3.2.1.5	Total Incontinence
1.3.2.2	Urinary Retention
1.4.1.1	Altered (specify type) Tissue Perfusion (renal, cerebral, cardiopulmonary, gastrointestinal, peripheral)
1.4.1.2.1	Fluid Volume Excess
1.4.1.2.2.1	Fluid Volume Deficit
1.4.1.2.2.2	Potential Fluid Volume Deficit
1.4.2.1	Decreased Cardiac Output
1.5.1.1	Impaired Gas Exchange
1.5.1.2	Ineffective Airway Clearance
1.5.1.3	Ineffective Breathing Pattern
1.6.1	Potential for Injury
1.6.1.1	Potential for Suffocation
1.6.1.2	Potential for Poisoning
1.6.1.3	Potential for Trauma
*1.6.1.4	Potential for Aspiration
*1.6.1.5	Potential for Disuse Syndrome
1.6.2	Altered Protection
1.6.2.1	Impaired Tissue Integrity
1.6.2.1.1	Altered Oral Mucous Membrane
1.6.2.1.2.1	Impaired Skin Integrity

NANDA Approved Nursing Diagnostic Categories — cont'd

1.6.2.1.2.2	Potential Impaired Skin Integrity
2.1.1.1	Impaired Verbal Communication
3.1.1	Impaired Social Interaction
3.1.2	Social Isolation
3.2.1	Altered Role Performance
3.2.1.1.1	Altered Parenting
3.2.1.1.2	Potential Altered Parenting
3.2.1.2.1	Sexual Dysfunction
3.2.2	Altered Family Processes
*3.2.3.1	Parental Role Conflict
3.3	Altered Sexuality Patterns
4.1.1	Spiritual Distress (distress of the human spirit)
5.1.1.1	Ineffective Individual Coping
5.1.1.1.1	Impaired Adjustment
*5.1.1.1.2	Defensive Coping
*5.1.1.1.3	Ineffective Denial
5.1.2.1.1	Ineffective Family Coping: Disabling
5.1.2.1.2	Ineffective Family Coping: Compromised
5.1.2.2	Family Coping: Potential for Growth
5.2.1.1	Noncompliance (specify)
*5.3.1.1	Decisional Conflict (specify)
*5.4	Health-Seeking Behaviors (specify)
6.1.1.1	Impaired Physical Mobility
6.1.1.2	Activity Intolerance
*6.1.1.2.1	Fatigue
6.1.1.3	Potential Activity Intolerance
6.2.1	Sleep Pattern Disturbance
6.3.1.1	Diversional Activity Deficit
6.4.1.1	Impaired Home Maintenance Management
6.4.2	Altered Health Maintenance
6.5.1	Feeding Self-Care Deficit
6.5.1.1	Impaired Swallowing
*6.5.1.2	Ineffective Breastfeeding
6.5.1.3	Effective Breastfeeding
6.5.2	Bathing/Hygiene Self-Care Deficit
6.5.3	Dressing/Grooming Self-Care Deficit
6.5.4	Toileting Self-Care Deficit
6.6	Altered Growth and Development
7.1.1	Body Image Disturbance
**7.1.2	Self-Esteem Disturbance
*7.1.2.1	Chronic Low Self-Esteem
*7.1.2.2	Situational Low Self-Esteem
7.1.3	Personal Identity Disturbance
7.2	Sensory/Perceptual Alterations (specify) (visual, auditory, kinesthetic, gustatory, tactile, olfactory)
7.2.1.1	Unilateral Neglect

Continued.

NANDA Approved Nursing Diagnostic Categories—cont'd

7.3.1	Hopelessness
7.3.2	Powerlessness
8.1.1	Knowledge Deficit (specify)
8.3	Altered Thought Processes
9.1.1	Pain
9.1.1.1	Chronic Pain
9.2.1.1	Dysfunctional Grieving
9.2.1.2	Anticipatory Grieving
9.2.2	Potential for Violence: Self-directed or directed at others
9.2.3	Post-Trauma Response
9.2.3.1	Rape-Trauma Syndrome
9.2.3.1.1	Rape-Trauma Syndrome: Compound Reaction
9.2.3.1.2	Rape-Trauma Syndrome: Silent Reaction
9.3.1	Anxiety
9.3.2	Fear

*as published in the Summer 1988 NANDA Nursing Diagnosis Newsletter.
Pattern 1: Exchanging
Pattern 2: Communicating
Pattern 3: Relating
Pattern 4: Valuing
Pattern 5: Choosing
Pattern 6: Moving
Pattern 7: Perceiving
Pattern 8: Knowing
Pattern 9: Feeling
*New diagnostic categories approved 1988.
**Revised diagnostic categories approved 1988.
Categories with modified label terminology.

ities, prevent illness, identify acute or chronic needs/problems, or support the client in meeting death with dignity, identification and analysis of the strengths of the client is imperative to provide comprehensive, meaningful nursing care. Almost every client, no matter how critically or chronically ill, has strengths. This health aspect of client functioning must be recognized, identified and mobilized to assist the client in reaching the highest possible level of functioning or in meeting death with dignity.

The Neuman Systems Model uses nursing diagnosis as the first step in its nursing process format, as shown in Table 4-2. Nursing diagnosis includes the synthesis of Neuman's system theory with the family assessment data. One purpose of this synthesizing effort is to determine the wellness level of family systems based on selected relevant client data and theory. "Health for the family is equated with optimal family system stability, that is, the best possible wellness state at any given time (Neuman, 1989, p. 33). Health is also equated with wellness (Neuman, 1989). Stability can be described as the condition in which all family member variables (physiological, psychological, sociocultural, developmental, and spiritual) are in balance or harmony with the whole of the family system (Neuman, 1989). Families strive to achieve this wellness state; it is the goal of health-promoting behaviors. Additional purposes for the synthesizing efforts include identification of the availability of resources to accomplish desired wellness outcomes and the strategies by which a family can use its strengths to facilitate this process. Nursing diagnosis involves a data base regulated by the family and the nurse's identification and evaluation of potential or actual stressors that pose a threat to the stability of the family unit. This diagnosis is determined by analyzing the following: the family's basic structure and energy resources; its lines of defense, lines of resistance, and potential reaction; the family's possibilities for reconstitution; and the identification of potential or actual intrafamily, interfamily, and extrafamily stressors that influence the family's interactive patterns and relationship processes. Nurses also need to identify past, present, and potential coping strategies that contribute to family stability; identify and evaluate internal and external resources that contribute to family health; identify and evaluate family strengths that contribute to family system balance and reconstitution; and clarify perceptual differences that occur between the family's interpretation of the problem and the nurse's impressions. If differences exist, a plan needs to be developed to help resolve the perceptual differences.

According to Neuman (1989, p. 44), diagnostic statements are written in terms of variance from wellness at the lines of defense and resistance. "Once a meaningful and comprehensive diagnostic statement of the overall situation can be made, major areas for goal setting and subsequent intervention can logically be determined and defended as required."

Nursing Goals

When working with families, the goals of intervention are to attain or maintain the maximum level of wellness by maintaining family stability. Therefore, all nursing intervention strategies are designed with this goal in mind. How the goal is accomplished is negotiable. The nurse and family decide together what prescriptive changes are necessary, based on the nursing diagnosis and the family's strengths, problems, needs, and resources.

After these changes are identified, a nursing contract is set up with the family. Sloan and Schommer (1975) define a family nursing contract as any working agreement continuously renegotiable between the family and the nurse. These parties share an understanding of the desired prescriptive changes and how these changes might be accomplished. Contracts can be formal (written) or informal (verbal), depending on the family's needs (Spradley, 1981; Stanhope and Lancaster, 1984). They identify the responsibilities of both family and nurse. Contracting encourages families to act for themselves in self-care rather than become passive recipients of health care (Blair, 1971). It also encourages collaborative participation between the family and the nurse in the development, implementation, and evaluation of the process (Stanhope and Lancaster, 1984).

The contract is a concept that uses basic principles of adult education, including mutual negotiation, self-direction, and mutual evaluation (Gustafson, 1977). These principles become both the means and the ends of the contract since families are able to assess their situation and help plan interventions, then work to implement them and evaluate the process.

Nursing Outcomes

Nursing outcomes are determined by instituting a health promotion mode within one of the three prevention-as-intervention modes described in Table 4-4. *Primary prevention/intervention* mode focuses on the actions necessary to retain system stability (Neuman, 1989) and on the movement of the family/family system toward a positively balanced state of increased health (Pender, 1987). The *secondary prevention/intervention* mode addresses actions that are necessary to attain system stability, and the *tertiary prevention/intervention* mode encompasses those actions instituted to maintain system stability (Neuman, 1989). Evaluation of the outcome goals confirms whether the goals were accomplished and/or documents the need for goal reformation. Nurses wanting to consider intermediate and long-range goals for the family system need to structure their actions in relation to having short-term goals and outcomes.

Table 4-4   Format for prevention as intervention

Primary Prevention	Secondary Prevention	Tertiary Prevention
1. Classify stressors that threaten stability of the client/client system; prevent stressor invasion	1. Following stressor invasion, protect basic structure	1. During reconstitution, attain and maintain maximum level of following treatment
2. Provide information to retain or strengthen existing client/client system strengths	2. Mobilize and optimize internal/external resources to attain stability and energy conservation	2. Educate, re-educate, and/or reorient as needed
3. Support positive coping and functioning	3. Facilitate purposeful manipulation of stressors and reactions to stressors	3. Support client/client system toward appropriate goals
4. Desensitize existing or possible noxious stressors	4. Motivate, educate, and involve client/client system in health care goals	4. Coordinate and integrate health service resources
5. Motivate toward wellness	5. Facilitate appropriate treatment and intervention measures	5. Provide primary and/or secondary preventive intervention as required
6. Coordinate and integrate interdisciplinary theories and epidemiological input	6. Support positive factors toward wellness	
7. Educate or re-educate	7. Promote advocacy by coordination and integration	
8. Use stress as a positive intervention strategy	8. Provide primary preventive intervention as required	

From Neuman, B. (1989). *The Neuman systems model* (2nd ed). Norwalk, CT: Appleton and Lange. Copyright © 1980 by Betty Neuman; revised 1987 by Betty Neuman.

Neuman Systems Model Operationalized

The Neuman Systems Model gives structure and substance to nursing actions (Neuman, 1989). It provides nurses with a blue-print for systematic family assessment and intervention. This model, depicted in Fig. 4-1, addresses activities related to family wellness/stability and prevention as intervention.

Nurses considering prevention activities must remember that potential and actual problem situations confront families each day, jeopardizing the stability of the family unit. When faced with these stressors, families develop and use coping strategies to prevent any decrease in family function. This action is di-rected toward protection of the family's basic structure and en-ergy resources. The basic structure encompasses family charac-teristics, family functions, and patterns of interaction that are in-fluenced by the physiological, psychological, developmental, and spiritual characteristics of the individual members. If the in-tegrity of the basic structure is not preserved, then system viabil-ity ceases.

Family system stability is the common goal of families and nurses. Frequently they work together in therapeutic partnerships to preserve the family system. This alliance occurs when fami-lies, faced with potential or actual situations that could lead or contribute to family instability, are unable to resolve their issues without outside assistance. Depending on the stressful situation, families may have the resources to take their problems in stride and adapt easily. If so, family functioning is only temporarily impaired. However, there are situations that families perceive as overwhelming and they are unable to summon sufficient internal or external resources to deal with them. When this occurs, fam-ily system stability is in jeopardy.

Families facing potential or actual stressful circumstances ex-perience varying amounts of tension and react with varying de-grees of restorative or adaptive ability. The amount of tension and/or stress that the family experiences depends on their per-ception of the situation. The degree of reconstitution/adaptation is based on the family's ability to restore impaired family func-tions (Neuman, 1989). Some families have difficulty mobilizing their energy resources to focus on system reconstitution. The reasons for this vary. Some lack information; others have at-tempted to use their usual coping strategies, which fail to work

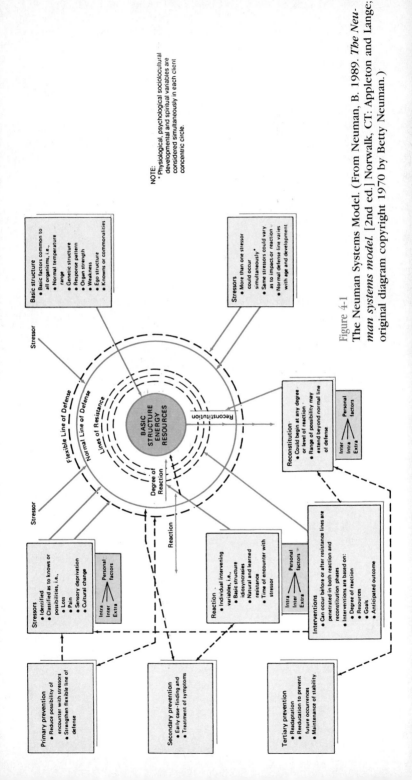

NOTE:
* Physiological, psychological, sociocultural, developmental and spiritual variables are considered simultaneously in each client concentric circle.

Figure 4-1

The Neuman Systems Model. (From Neuman, B. 1989. *The Neuman systems model.* [2nd ed.] Norwalk, CT: Appleton and Lange; original diagram copyright 1970 by Betty Neuman.)

Basic structure
- Basic factors common to all organisms, i.e.,
- Normal temperature range
- Genetic structure
- Response pattern
- Organ strength
- Weakness
- Ego structure
- Knowns or commonalities

Stressors
- More than one stressor could occur simultaneously*
- Same stressors could vary as to impact or level of reaction
- Normal defense line varies with age and development

Stressor

Flexible Line of Defense
Normal Line of Defense
Lines of Resistance

BASIC STRUCTURE ENERGY RESOURCES

Reconstitution

Degree of Reaction

Reaction

Reconstitution:
- Could begin at any degree or level of reaction
- Range of possibility may extend beyond normal line of defense

Inter
Intra
Extra
Personal factors

Stressors
- Identified
- Classified as to knows or possibilities, i.e.,
- Loss
- Pain
- Sensory deprivation
- Cultural change

Intra
Inter
Extra
Personal factors

Reaction
- Individual intervening variables, i.e.,
- Basic structure idiosyncrasies
- Natural and learned resistance
- Time of encounter with stressor

Intra
Inter
Extra
Personal factors

Interventions
- Can occur before or after resistance lines are penetrated in both reaction and reconstitution phases
- Interventions are based on:
- Degree of reaction
- Resources
- Goals
- Anticipated outcome

Primary prevention
- Reduce possibility of encounter with stressors
- Strengthen flexible line of defense

Secondary prevention
- Early case-finding and
- Treatment of symptoms

Tertiary prevention
- Readaptation
- Reeducation to prevent future occurrences
- Maintenance of stability

in new situations, and some perceive the problems as unsolvable.

The term *line of defense* refers to the protective strategies that families institute to guard their basic structural unit from the stressful situation (Hoffman, 1982; Neuman, 1982). The *flexible line of defense* refers to the dynamic level of health that families attain following a temporary response to a stressor impinging on the system (Johnson and others, 1982; Neuman, 1989). Examples of situations that may impinge on the flexible line of defense are career changes, marriage, retirement, and children entering the family (Reed, 1989).

Inside the flexible line of defense is the *normal line of defense,* which refers to the family's state of wellness over time (Neuman, 1982, 1989). It includes the family's process of adaptation and/or reconstitution. Families respond to situations in ways they consider to be "normal" for them (Venable, 1980). Examples of stressful situation or problems that may impact ways of coping and behaving considered "normal" for the family unit are spousal difficulty, unemployment, and the death of a family member (Reed, 1989).

The *lines of resistance* are found within the circle of the normal line of defense, and they protect the family's basic structure (Neuman, 1989). These lines of resistance are forces within the family system that can be activated to protect and preserve the stability and energy resources of the basic family unit. These forces are brought into play when problems or stressful situations penetrate the family's normal line of defense (Neuman, 1989). Stressors not successfully dealt with at the normal line of defense have the potential of breaking through the lines of resistance, thus threatening the viability of the system's basic structure (Neuman, 1989). Examples of stressors that cross the normal line of defense and threaten the viability of the family structure are substance abuse by a family member, family violence, chronic physical or mental illness, and loss of a family member's physical abilities.

Basic family structure and energy resources refers to the characteristics, functions, and survival skills common to the family system. The physiological, psychological, sociocultural, developmental, and spiritual variables of the individual family members influence these characteristics and functions. They are also influenced by how the family variables are operationalized via the psychosocial characteristics, physical status, developmental characteristics, and spiritual influence of the family system. This core of the family must be diligently protected if the family unit is to remain healthy, stable, and functional.

Prevention as Intervention

Neuman (1989) provides a systematic method of identifying interventions that are appropriate for use in assisting families with restoration of family functions. Nursing interventions can be implemented in families at any level of functioning and with any degree of instability. As nurses assist families in maintaining their stability and normal family functions, they focus on different areas of the assessment and intervention process. However, family nurses realize that the assessment and intervention are not discrete; their work with the family involves moving from one area to another.

There are three broad areas of concentration: (1) wellness and assessment of the stressors at the lines of defense and resistance with institution of interventions to prevent invasion, (2) family reactions and the degree of instability at the lines of defense and resistance with interventions to reduce the degree of reaction to stressors, and (3) restoration of family stability and family function at levels of prevention as intervention with interventions to support internal or external resources for reconstitution.

Prevention as intervention: primary.   The primary prevention/intervention mode, described in Fig. 4-2, focuses the family's and nurse's attention on three areas: (1) identification of actual or potential family stressors, (2) assessment of family stressors to anticipate the possible consequences of potential illness, and (3) prevention intervention measure to prevent stressor invasion.

In Format 1, primary prevention/intervention mode, Neuman (1989) begins to operationalize the strategy of prevention as intervention. The nurse identifies the behaviors that families use to increase their health-promoting activities and in turn their level of wellness. Engaging in health-promoting activities enables the family to move toward higher levels of stability. The family, in this case, is acting on its environment rather than reacting to potential threats that the environment imposes on it (Pender, 1987). Activities germane to health promotion and primary prevention are, in part, the playing out of the family's health belief system. This belief system includes an understanding of (1) the definition of health to which the family subscribes, (2) the importance and valuing of health, (3) perceived control of family

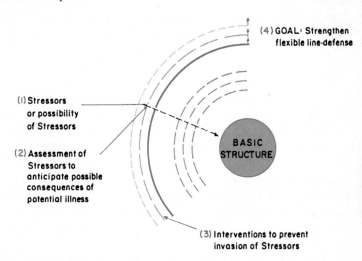

Figure 4-2
Format for primary prevention as intervention mode. (From Neu-
man, B. 1989. *The Neuman systems model.* [2nd ed.] Norwalk, CT:
Appleton and Lange; copyright 1980 by Betty Neuman.)

member health and family system health, (4) the desire for competence in the family's ability to interact or transact effectively
with the environment, (5) family member and family system
awareness of health-promoting behaviors, (6) self-esteem of
family members, (7) perceived family health status, which contributes to the frequency and intensity of health-promoting behaviors, and (8) perceived benefits of instituting intrafamily
health-promoting behaviors (Pender, 1987).

Intervention activities at the primary prevention/intervention
level include coping strategies initiated by families, family members, or nurses before or after encountering a problem or stressful situation (Gilliss, Highley, Roberts, and Martinson, 1989;
Neuman, 1983). It encompasses actions that families undertake
to decrease the possibility of encountering potential or actual
stressors, as well as those that strengthen the flexible line of defense in the presence of stressors (Neuman, 1983). Neuman
(1982) cites additional intervention strategies nurses that can use:
(1) provide the family with information about its strengths, (2)
support the family's coping and functioning capabilities, (3) de-
sensitize existing or potential harmful stressors in the family, (4)
encourage the family's attempts toward achieving wellness, and

(5) educate and/or reeducate family members. Examples of intervention measures at this level are classes on growth and development of children and adults, premarital counseling, first aid classes, and parenting classes.

The goal in this primary prevention/intervention mode is to strengthen the flexible line of defense. Nurses can accomplish this by supporting behaviors that the families use to increase their health-promoting activities and by enhancing the strengths that families already possess.

Prevention as intervention: secondary.   The secondary prevention/intervention mode, described in Fig. 4-3, focuses the family's and nurse's attention to three areas: (1) the family's reaction to stressors, (2) assessing the degree of family reaction to stressors, and (3) family interventions to reduce the degree of reaction to stressors.

Nurses and families accomplish secondary prevention/intervention by identifying and treating problem situations early (Gilliss, Highley, Roberts, and Martinson, 1989). Various degrees of reaction can occur within a family member, family members, or between the family and society when stressors impinge on the family system. Reactions are demonstrated by the degree of instability occurring at the lines of defense and/or resistance. Instability at the flexible line of defense can be assessed by being alert to the dynamic state of the family as it manages the ongo-

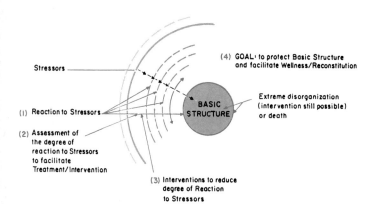

Figure 4-3
Format for secondary prevention as intervention mode. (From Neuman, B. 1989. *The Neuman systems model.* [2nd ed.] Norwalk, CT: Appleton and Lange; copyright 1980 by Betty Neuman.)

ing encounter with stressful situations. The dynamic state of the family includes such elements as conflict-resolution mechanisms, decision making, task allocation, family bonding patterns, instituting family roles, and family rules (Miller and Janosik, 1980).

Nurses can further assess instability or reactions occurring at the normal line of defense by being cognizant of how families normally respond to stressful situations. "This line of defense acts as a wellness standard against which to determine health variance from a more immediate or situational condition" (Neuman, 1989, p. 19). The term *normal* is defined by the families themselves. The nurse can determine the degree of reaction by assessing the following elements: communication patterns, problem-solving measures, mechanisms instituted to meet family member needs for intimacy and affection, and ways of dealing with loss and change (Reed, 1989).

Neuman (1989) conceptualizes as "normal" stressors those situations or problems creating instability for the family unit or its members and controlled by the flexible and normal lines of defense. They include events surrounding the family's activities of daily living or the "nitty gritty" business of family life (Reed, 1989).

The elements found within both the flexible and the normal lines of defense also comprise the family's normal coping mechanisms. When stressors are of such an intensity that prescribed coping mechanisms from the two lines of defense prove ineffective, the level of family instability increases and family lines of resistance are called into operation.

The lines of resistance are composed of internal factors that the family can mobilize to control or defend its basic structure against stressors (Neuman, 1989). These lines are arranged in such a way that stressors must break through the family's normal coping mechanisms at the lines of defense to strike the family's basic energy resources (Neuman, 1982). Assessment of the amount of family reaction at the lines of resistance includes evaluation of internal factors found in the family's basic structure. They are interrelatedness, interdependence, values, and beliefs (Reed, 1989). Each family member may view these internal factors differently, and therefore extreme reaction and instability may result when stressors penetrate this resistance line. The intensity of reaction is related to how family members perceive the stressor. The variable characteristics that the dyad initially brought to the beginning family structure from their families of origin often form the basis for how the family perceives and resolves problems. Both members of the couple bring certain beliefs, values, and ways of relating that were learned in their family of origin. As the new family structure (family of procreation) begins to develop, the couple must mesh their different belief systems, value judgments, and patterns of relating and dependence. This results in the creation of new family system characteristics. How the young family grows and matures is based in part on the interrelatedness of these internal elements. Eventually, not all family members may continue to support the original couple beliefs. As such, the way that each perceives stressors or problems attempting to penetrate the lines of resistance may vary. Excessive instability and disorganization of the family system may prevail.

Intervention strategies designed for this mode include actions initiated after the family encounters stressors. These encompass early case finding by the nurse and treatment of family instability following its reaction to the stressor. Neuman (1982) recommends additional strategies: (1) protect the basic family structure, (2) mobilize and maximize both internal and external family resources toward family stability and energy conservation, (3) facilitate the family's purposeful manipulation of problems or stressful conditions and their reaction to them, (4) educate families and assist them in developing their own health care goals, (5) help families use appropriate treatment and intervention measures, (6) support the family's positive reaction toward illness, (7) facilitate family attempts to use means for dealing with the situation by assisting them with health care service coordination, and, (8) provide primary prevention/intervention as needed. Examples of intervention measures at this level include family crisis intervention, treatment of a family member illness, marital counseling, employment counseling, and grief work (Reed, 1989).

Prevention as intervention: tertiary.   The tertiary prevention/intervention mode, described in Fig. 4-4, focuses the family's and nurse's attention on two areas: (1) the family's ability to restore its functions following secondary intervention and (2) assessment of the degree of reconstitution achieved following secondary intervention for reaction to stressors.

All families attempt to cope with stressful situations at some level, and each family reacts in its own way. Stressors vary in

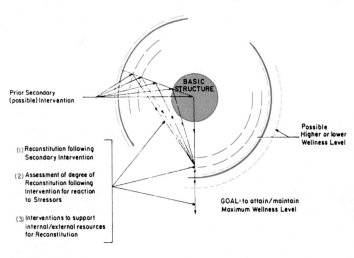

Figure 4-4

Format for tertiary prevention as intervention mode. (From Neuman, G. 1989. *The Neuman systems model.* [2nd ed.] Norwalk, CT: Appleton and Lange; copyright 1980 by Betty Neuman.)

their potential to disturb the family's equilibrium or normal line of defense (Neuman, 1989). Moreover, the relationship of physiological, psychological, sociocultural, developmental, and spiritual variables of the individuals contributing to the family systems categories (psychosocial characteristics, physical status, developmental characteristics, spiritual influence) can at any time affect the degree to which the family system is able to mobilize its flexible line of defense against the stressors (Neuman, 1989).

Intervention strategies at the tertiary prevention/intervention level are those initiated after treatment has been completed. Nurses and families focus on reconstitution, rehabilitation, and reeducation of the family unit and/or its individual members. Nursing actions are directed toward (1) maintaining the maximum level of family wellness and stability, (2) educating, reeducating, and/or reorienting the family as appropriate, (3) supporting the family unit in its effort to set realistic health goals and institute needed changes, (4) coordinating health service resources for families, and (5) providing families with primary and/or secondary prevention/intervention as needed (Neuman, 1989). Examples of tertiary preventive measure are family counseling, support groups of all types, and rehabilitation groups (Reed, 1989).

Although the central focus of the tertiary format is on restoration of family functions and reconstitution of family stability, nurses frequently encounter families with compromised basic structures. This is due, in part, to the continuation of stressor penetration into the heart of the family. Reconstitution efforts at the family's normal line of defense following secondary intervention have somehow failed. We support the notion that stressors can penetrate the lines of resistance and contribute to system demise. When this occurs, attaining or maintaining maximum wellness level requires immediate nursing intervention. Nurses perceive families encountering stressors that have not been contained at the normal lines of defense and moving close to system demise as being at the tertiary level on the Family Systems Stressor Strength Inventory, presented in Chapter 5.

"In using this prevention as intervention typology, the client condition in relation to environmental stressors, becomes readily apparent. One or all three of the prevention modalities give direction to, or may be simultaneously used, for nursing action, with possible synergistic benefits" (Neuman, 1989, pp. 37-38). Chapter 5 considers material relative to families, the nursing process, and the Neuman Systems Model, along with the stressors and strengths affecting family systems. A family systems stressor-strength inventory has been designed for nurses to use in their family focused practice.

Family Systems Stressor-Strength Inventory (FS³I)

5

Family Systems Stressor-Strength Inventory Overview

The purpose of this chapter is to describe an inventory that will assist nurses in their efforts to assess families.

The Family Systems Stressor-Strength Inventory (FS³I), grounded in the Neuman Systems Model, provides a mechanism by which nurses are able to assess family health and stability. It begins with an overview of selected situations influencing family stability and progresses to an assessment of specific concerns that family members deem significant. The inventory takes into account a broad range of intrafamily, interfamily, and extrafamily forces that have the potential of affecting a family's functioning capacity and hence its health and stability. Termed stressors, problem situations, or areas of concern, these forces occur either within and between the family's internal environment or its external milieu.

The inventory process begins with the nurse presenting individual family members with a list of 45 situations dealing with some aspect of normal family life. The nurse asks them to numerically quantify the amount of stress that each situation creates. Presenting family members with a list of situations that are common to most families appears to decrease family defensiveness. With a lessening of defensiveness comes increased family system openness to the nurse and to examination of the areas of concern. The 45 stressors listed in Table 5-1 have been culled from the research contributions of Curran (1985). We have designated them as intrafamily, interfamily, and extrafamily system forces.

The second portion of the assessment inventory addresses specific family concerns, or areas of stress, in a straightforward manner. The inventory asks family members to identify their

Table 5-1   Intrafamily, interfamily, and extrafamily system stressors

Intrafamily System Stressors	Interfamily System Stressors	Extrafamily System Stressors
Family member(s) feeling unappreciated	Communication with children	Economics/finances/budgets
Guilt for not accomplishing more	Housekeeping standards	Unhappiness with work situation
Insufficient "me" time	Insufficient couple time	Overvolunteerism
Self-image/self-esteem/feelings of unattractiveness	Insufficient family playtime	Neighbors
Perfectionism	Children's behavior/discipline/sibling fighting	Unemployment
Dieting	Television	Nuclear and environmental fears
Health/illness	Overscheduled family calendar	Church/school activities
Drugs/alcohol	Lack of shared responsibility in the family	Unsatisfactory housing
Widowhood	Moving	Organized sports activities
Retirement	Spousal relationship (communication, friendship, sex)	Change in work patterns
Homework/school/grades	Holidays	Two-paycheck family
	In-laws	
	Teen behavior	
	New baby	
	Houseguests	
	Family vacations	
	Remarriage	
	Relationship with former spouse	
	Summer	
	Weekends	
	Religious differences	
	Predinner hour	
	Older parents	

From Curran, D. (1985). *Stress and the healthy family*. Minneapolis, MN: Winston Press, Inc.; reprinted by permission of Harper & Row, Publishers, Inc., New York, NY.

major problems and/or areas of concern and describe, by way of a series of questions and answers, the extent to which they affect the family system. For example, the inventory asks how much of an effect a particular stressful situation has on the family's usual pattern of living, its ability to work together as a unit, or on its potential future functioning; or to the extent to which the family expects assistance from with its current concerns. This portion of the assessment inventory attempts to filter out a specific family stressor from the family's general problem areas.

After identifying the family's general areas of concern and a description of any specific stressors affecting system health, nurses rivet their attention on determining family unit strengths. The purpose of identifying these strengths is to examine the family's potential and actual problem-solving abilities. For example, are families using their strengths to deal with stressful situations and/or their areas of concern, and if so, to what extent? Nurses elicit the answers to these questions and others by presenting the family with a list of 20 family traits that are known to exist in well-functioning family systems (Curran, 1983). Each trait involves some aspect of family life, and each is considered a strength (see the box).

Family members identify the extent to which each of the strengths or traits mentioned is operationalized in their family system. Their numerical response and general description pinpoint the extent to which family members exhibit these traits. We strongly believe that awareness of family strengths facilitates and gives direction to the prevention/intervention process. Families and nurses work together to identify stressful situations occurring in the family system and the family strengths available to support prevention and intervention activities. Family strengths can prevent family instability and wellness variances by enhancing the family's problem-solving and reconstitution/adaptation ability.

Nurses take into account both their own and family member perceptions of stressors and strengths during and after the assessment and intervention process. They accomplish this first by asking family members to complete a self-administered assessment questionnaire apart from the nurse. Upon completion of this task the nurse rephrases the questions and asks family members to elaborate on their responses. This additional information facilitates greater awareness of how stressful situations or areas of concern influence family system stability.

Family Systems Strengths

Communicates with and listens to one another	Has a shared religious core
Affirms and supports one another	Respects the privacy of one another
Teaches respect for others	Respects the privacy of one another
Has a sense of play and humor	Values service to others
Exhibits a sense of shared responsibility	Fosters family table time and conversation
Teaches a sense of right and wrong	Shares leisure time
Has a strong sense of family in which rituals and traditions abound	Admits to and seeks help with problems
	Honors its elders
Has a balance of interaction among members	Accepts and encourages individual values
	Values work satisfaction
	Is financially secure
	Able to let go of grown children

From Curran, D. (1985). *Stress and the healthy family*. Minneapolis, MN: Winston Press, Inc.; reprinted by permission of Harper & Row, Publishers, Inc., New York, NY.

Family Systems Stressor-Strength Inventory Sections

The Family Systems Stress-Strength Inventory and scoring keys are divided into two assessment sections. *Section One* (Family Form) focuses on family member perceptions of situations and concerns that influence their family's health and the strengths that the family uses to deal with the identified stressors (see Appendix).

Section Two (Nurse Form) concentrates on the nurse's perceptions of the family's areas of concern and areas of strength.

Each of the two sections is broken down into three parts: (1) Family Systems Stressors: General, (2) Family Systems Stressors: Specific, and (3) Family Systems Strengths. Part 1, Family Systems Stressors: General, identifies the overall stressors affecting the family system and the potential source of family member involvement: intrafamily system, interfamily system, and extrafamily system. Part 2, Family Systems Stressors: Specific, identifies a specific stressor or problem situation that has a high family priority and elicits information germane to its effect on the family system. Part 3, Family Systems Strengths, identifies strengths incumbent in the system and examines how these strengths are being used to retain, attain, and maintain family stability.

Family members can complete Section One before the nurse interviews them. The nurse completes Section Two during and after nurse and family member review and elaboration on family member responses given in Section One. The instrument is designed to be completed by individual family members. The rationale for using this approach is that each family member may perceive problems, stress areas, or areas of concern differently (Curran, 1985). A composite score would not reflect individual member concerns and could alter the assessment findings, so the quantitative summary sheet shows a separate graph for each family member score.

We are in the process of establishing inventory reliability and validity. A jury of experts and a thorough review of the literature and family instrumentation determined the validity of the initial construct and content. A larger field testing projects of the inventory is underway, after which reliability will be established.

The nurse enters all numerical and descriptive data on two summary forms: the (1) Family Systems Stressor-Strength Inventory: Quantitative Summary, and the (2) Family Systems Stressor-Strength Inventory: Qualitative Summary. A demographic face sheet precedes these summary materials and includes information such as name, family member completing assessment, ethnic group(s), referral source, interviewer, family members, relationship in family, religious and ethnic background, age, marital status, education, occupation, and current reason(s) for seeking health care assistance.

Section One, Family Form: Family Systems Stressor-Strength Inventory

Section One, as previously mentioned, contains three parts: Family Systems Stressors: General, Family Systems Stressors: Specific, and Family Systems Strengths.

Part 1, Family Systems Stressors: General. Part 1, Family Systems Stressors: General, is based on the family research of Curran (1985) and the systems work of Neuman (1982, 1983, 1989). The classification of stressors, situations, and areas of concern was selected from Curran's research (1985) with families; the designations for prevention/intervention modes were drafted from Neuman's work (1983). Curran (1985) identified 45 areas of concern that influence the health of married and single family units. Each situation has the potential to create varying amounts of stress for the family system. We incorporated the 45 situations into Part One of the assessment instrument. The 45 questions, written as identified areas of concern, require the respondent to answer in a Likert scale format. The nurse requests that family members circle the amount of stress they experience. The answers can range from little or no stress (wellness/health and stability) to very much family stress (greatest variance from wellness and stability). A column designating nonapplicability accompanies each item. The inventory focuses on amounts of stress in terms of the family's actions or reactions to situations penetrating their lines of defense and resistance. The defense and resistance lines designate the prevention/intervention modes for initiation of therapeutic activities.

The inventory also requests selected demographic data: name, age, sex, marital status, education, occupation, religious preference, referral source, ethnic background, and family member relationship.

Scoring Format Part 1, Family Systems Stressors: General.
The scoring format for Part 1 of the inventory uses lines of defense, lines of resistance, and intrafamily, interfamily, and extrafamily system stressors (Neuman, 1982, 1989). The scores on the Likert rating scale range from 1 (wellness/health and stability) to 5 (greatest variance from wellness and stability). The scores for the family member are added together, and a general family system stressor scores is calculated. This score designates the amount of stress that has penetrated the family system (from the family member's perspective) and produced the family reaction. The scores are then matched with the appropriate lines of defense and resistance. The identified lines of defense and resistance determine the family system prevention/intervention mode: primary, secondary, and tertiary. Intervention is to be initiated at the identified mode. There are three subscales: (1) intrafamily system stressors, (2) interfamily system stressors, and (3) extrafamily system stressors. The purpose of the subscales is to identify the family member's involvement with wellness and stability. The subscale scores are aligned with the appropriate lines of defense and resistance, thereby identifying the recommended prevention/intervention mode. Nurses begin their therapeutic actions at the designated mode and use the information to make

nursing diagnoses and write goal statements. Nurses always develop goal statements in concert with families.

Part 2, Family Systems Stressors: Specific.   Part 2, Family Systems Stressors: Specific, is based on Neuman's Systems Model. The questions have been modified to incorporate a family focus (Neuman, 1983). Family members begin Part 2 by identifying the major stressful situation, problem, or area of concern that is influencing the health of their family unit. This requires a brief written response. Next, the inventory asks family members nine closed-ended questions with a choice of answers ranging from "little or no influence on family health" to "very much." A "non-applicable" column is provided. Family members select their answers using a Likert scale. Seven of these questions pertain to the stressor or problem situation that the family member initially identified, and two questions relate to the overall health of family members.

Scoring Format Part 2, Family Systems Stressors: Specific. The nurse records the family members' brief, written responses identifying family concerns and problems and integrates them into the qualitative summary. The Likert numerical rating scale is the means provided for family members to describe the amount of family stress produced by specific stressor(s). The scores range from 1 (wellness/health and stability) to 5 (greatest variance from wellness and stability). The nurse adds the scores for the family members interviewed, and calculates a specific family stressor score. This score designates the amount of stressor penetration and family reaction. Matching the score with the appropriate lines of defense and resistance, determines whether to initiate prevention activities and intervention modes at the primary, secondary, or tertiary level. Nurses note the prevention level at which the nursing intervention mode is to be initiated. Nurses are then able to determine their diagnoses and begin establishing goals. As previously noted, nurses always develop goals in concert with families.

Part 3, Family Systems Strengths.   Part 3 is based on Curran's (1986) research with healthy families. The nurse presents each family member with a list of 20 family traits, each considered a strength, that contribute to the health and functioning ability of family systems. The family then designates the extent to which family members use the traits. The numerical responses indicating frequency of use are placed on a Likert rating scale.

Scoring Format Part 3, Family Systems Strengths. The scoring format for Part 3 uses lines of defense and lines of resistance. The scores on the Likert rating scale range from 1 ("seldom or not at all") to 5 ("always"), and the scale includes a column for nonapplicability. The nurse adds the scores for the family members and obtains a family system strength score. Separate family member scores designate the extent to which family system members are operationalizing their strengths for purposes of retaining, attaining, and maintaining system stability. These strengths also represent the prevention/intervention resources available to the family and serve as a foundation for the development of nursing therapeutic actions.

Section Two, Nurse Form: Family Systems Stressor-Strength Inventory

Section Two of the assessment inventory is a conversational rephrasing of questions found in Section One, Family Form: Family Systems Stressor-Strength Inventory. Its purpose is to compare the family perceptions with those of the nurse. Neuman (1989) recommends that perceptions of nurses as well as families be obtained for comparison, clarification, comprehensiveness, and identification of relationships. The nurse brings a substantial theoretical and experiential family knowledge base to the process of forming perceptions about the family.

The content of each item in Section Two remains identical to those of Section One; however, the question format in Section Two accommodates the rephrasing of questions. Since the questions are reworded and personalized for the family, the nurse uses an open-ended format instead of the closed-ended format. The nurse records the family member's response and writes a brief note, then assesses the family's attempts toward wellness/ health, and stability, and the effects of wellness variance on the family system. The nurse uses the written information as documentation of their reaction and computes the degree of family action or reaction into a number on the Likert scale. If discrepancies of perceptions occur between the family and the nurse, then the nurse and family must reconcile their perceptual differences before a nursing diagnosis can be made (Neuman, 1989). **Scoring Format Parts 1, 2, and 3: Family Systems Stressor-Strength Inventory.** Assessment data relative to Section Two (Nurse Form), Part 1 (Family Systems Stressors: General) are summarized on The Family Systems Stressor-Strength Inventory: Qualitative Summary form. They include a summary of assessment data relative to Section Two (Nurse Form), Part 1 Family Systems Stressors: General), and qualitative information obtained in Parts 2 and 3 of Section One.

The quantitative scoring procedure for Section Two (Nurse Form), Parts 2 and 3 (Family Systems Stressor: Specific and Family Sysatems Strengths) is the same as the procedure used for scoring Section One (Family Form).

Family Systems Stressor-Strength Inventory: Quantitative Summary

Following compilation of objective scores for each of the two sections—Family Form: Family Systems Stressor-Strength Inventory and Nurse Form: Family Systems Stressor-Strength Inventory (FS^3I)—the nurse enters the scores on the summary form, *Family Systems Stressor-Strength Inventory (FS^3I): Quantitative Summary*. This graphic form gives a visual representation of the variations of family stability/family health and designates the appropriate level for instituting prevention/intervention measures. These measures, and the activities contained therein, are based on the lines of defense and resistance. Family member/family system concerns are grouped according to family member involvement: intrafamily (within the individual family member), interfamily (between or among family members/family system and/or relatives and friends in close proximity), and extrafamily (between the family/family system and those in distant proximity to family). Family strengths are plotted separately using prevention/intervention modes based on lines of defense and resistance. However, in this instance the lines of defense and resistance designate the range of family strengths available for use at the points of stressor penetration. For example, if the family strength assessment score falls within the range of the normal line of defense, then the family possesses strengths that can facilitate problem resolution at the secondary prevention/intervention level. The same rationale applies for scores designated at the flexible line of defense and the lines of resistance (primary and tertiary prevention/intervention levels). This graphic representation facilitates a comparison of scores between family member perceptions and nurse perceptions. Differences and/or discrepancies between perceptions are described in the qualitative summary.

Family Systems Stressor-Strength Inventory: Qualitative Summary

Qualitative information generated from Sections One and Two is summarized and entered on the summary form: Family Systems Stressor-Strength Inventory (FS³I): Qualitative Summary. This form includes three parts: (1) Family Systems Stressors: General, (2) Family Systems Stressors: Specific, and (3) Family Systems Strengths. Part 1, Family Systems Stressors: General, facilitates the recording of descriptive data germane to general family stressors and asks the nurse to prioritize the areas of concern in order of importance to the family.

Part 2, Family Systems Stressors: Specific, aids in recording of the specific tension-producing situation/problem/concern that is influencing family stability. The form provides columns for describing the specific qualitative system data in a manner that reflects the family member's perceptions, the nurse's perceptions, and any apparent discrepancies or differences between perceptions. The nurse records significant family health data for each family member using the five variables: physiological, psychological, developmental, sociocultural, and spiritual. The form summarizes family system category materials according to the major areas: psychosocial, physical status, developmental characteristics, and spiritual influence.

Part 3, Family Systems Strengths, records the nurse's perceptions of existing family strengths and documents how these traits are operationalized in the family system. Part 3 documents the identification of specific strengths supportive of prevention/intervention activities.

Family Systems Stressor-Strength Inventory (FS³I) Family Care Plan

The family care plan was formulated using the Neuman Systems Model (1989) and the Neuman College Nursing Process Tool (1987). The broad areas of nursing diagnosis, nursing goals, and nursing outcomes are divided into six sections: (1) nursing diagnosis, (2) family strengths, (3) prioritized family goals, (4) predesignated activities, and (5) outcomes including evaluation and replanning.

Nursing diagnosis.   Formulating nursing diagnoses requires the nurse to carry out several functions: (1) analyze all data collected from the quantitative and qualitative summaries, (2) identify the actual and potential family concerns and prioritize them, (3) state the nursing diagnosis based on the causative stressor(s) in family system, and (4) incorporate the family's response to stressor(s) using subjective and objective data which support the nursing diagnosis. Following integration or synthesis of this material, nurses are able to make comprehensive nursing diagnostic statements based on the family's system variance from wellness.

Family strengths.   The nurse records the strengths and/or the supportive resources available within the family's internal and external environment on the family care plan. The identified strengths and/or resources contribute to family unity and solidarity and foster the development of inherent family potential. All strengths facilitate the retention, attainment, and/or maintenance of family stability and health. Families with limited strengths may need to incorporate additional strengths to master specific family skills (e.g., communicating with children or balancing interactions between members). When this is the case, the additional strengths needed can be listed as a family goal and a plan for its attainment developed.

Family and nurse goals.   The purpose of goal setting is to correct the wellness variance and stabilize the family system. Goals are designed by the nurse and family members. Goal consideration includes stressor identification, family strengths, and the internal and external environmental resources available for family system use. The nurse negotiates with the family to formulate appropriate prevention as intervention strategies. The prevention and intervention strategies focus on retaining, attaining, and/or maintaining family system stability and optimal health.

Type of prevention/intervention mode with designated activites.   The numerical ranking on the Likert scale, in concert with supportive descriptive family data, designates the type of preventive mode that needs to be considered for instituting treatment measures. The prevention/intervention modes are primary, secondary, and tertiary.

Following the formulation of nursing diagnoses, family strengths, family goals, and prevention/intervention modes, the nurse and family members develop a plan for accomplishing system goals. This plan incorporates selected prevention/intervention activities to carry out at the primary, secondary, and tertiary prevention/intervention levels. These include specific action directed toward (1) actions to retain family system stability (primary prevention as intervention); (2) actions to attain family system stability (secondary prevention as intervention), and (3) actions to maintain family system stability (tertiary prevention as intervention). The intervention activities assist the family in meeting its identified health goals. Appropriate theoretical and experiential principles must support all prevention activities.

Nursing outcomes. Evaluating outcomes for the established family care plan requires that both nurse and family reexamine the prioritized goals previously set and determine whether they were achieved. This evaluation process centers on analyzing the effectiveness of the nursing prevention/intervention activities facilitating goal attainment. A new plan needs to be made if goals were not achieved.

Replanning of family goals is necessary when the outcome goals have not been met. The nurse and family consider the effectiveness of previous nursing interventions and make alterations where deemed appropriate. Reassessment of the family/family system and designing new plans is important when any of the following conditions exist: (1) changes in the nature of the family stressors or areas of concern, (2) changes in the family member variables: intrafamily, interfamily, and extrafamily, and/or changes in the family system variables based on the major categories: psychosocial relationship characteristics, physical status, developmental characteristics, and spiritual influence, and (3) changes in priorities of goals in relation to the primary, secondary, and tertiary prevention modes. The nurse needs to add a statement of replanning actions to the Family Care Plan, for example: "change intervention to . . . ."; "continue present intervention"; "distcontinue, goal met"; "redefine nursing diagnosis" (Neuman, 1987).

The Family Systems Stressor-Strengths Inventory will be applied to selected case studies in Chapter 6. Nurses will be able to evaluate the inventory's usefulness and applicability to nursing practice settings.

Family Systems Stressor-Strength Inventory (FS³I) Applied to Family Case Studies

6

Use of a theoretical framework as the foundation for family systems assessment and clinical intervention increases the professionalism of nurses. "The Neuman Systems model has proven its utility as a most effective framework for unique and comprehensive approaches to the individual, the family, or the community as client" (Lillis and Cora, 1989, p. 51). We have expanded the use of this model by developing an assessment inventory that analyzes family systems both qualitatively and quantitatively. All data are synthesized and reformulated into a family care plan that reflects Neuman's nursing process format and family systems strengths.

This chapter demonstrates the use of the Family Systems Stressor-Strength Inventory (FS³I) by describing the instrument's application to actual clinical situations. Three families, are given as examples, and accompanying assessment data and family care plans are given. These examples demonstrate the instrument's effectiveness and versatility. Quantitative and qualitative summary data forms for each family can be found in the Appendix.

The three case studies focus on the following situations: (1) a blended childrearing family with a preschool child suffering from recurrent episodes of otitis media, (2) a nuclear family experiencing the loss of the children's father and the wife's husband, and (3) a nuclear middlescent family involved in a health crisis of one of their aging parents. Each example begins with a brief description of the family's current situation and state of wellness. Identification of general and specific stressors affecting the family system and documentation of existing family strengths available for system use follow. Subsequently a nursing diagnosis is made; family and nurse goals established; primary, secondary, or tertiary prevention/intervention activities developed; and nursing outcomes postulated.

Clinical Example 1: Blended Childbearing Family and Health Promotion
Background

The Cobb family consists of the marital couple, Kent and Merlene; one child from this marriage, Mallory (3 years); and two children from previous marriages, Kurtis (11 years) and Erin (11 years). Kurtis is a child from Kent's first marriage and Erin a child from Merlene's first marriage. This blended family is a yours, mine, and ours family system arrangement.

The family came in contact with the health care system as a result of a school nurse's routine health promotion visit to a day care center. The preschool teacher reported that one of the regular preschoolers had frequent episodes of otitis media and that the family was very concerned. Since the family knew that a school nurse made frequent visits to the day care center, the family asked the director to arrange an appointment for them to meet with the nurse. As part of the school district's family health assessment and screening process, Mr. and Mrs. Cobb were asked to complete the FS³I.

Summary of Cobb Family Systems Stressor Strength Inventory

Family systems stressors (general). The family systems stressors (general) were ranked by the marital dyad at ranges encompassing the flexible and normal lines of defense (see sample FS³I at end of chapter). Kent's general systems stressors were in the range of the flexible line and Merlene's were in the normal line of defense. Merlene reported higher levels of intra-, inter-, and extrafamily stress than did Kent. For example, Merlene's intrafamily stressor score was higher on situations involving feelings of not being appreciated, guilt for not accomplishing more, unattractiveness, and dieting. Her interfamily stressors scores were higher on areas encompassing communication with children, housekeeping standards, insufficient couple/family play time, lack of shared responsibility, holidays, inlaws, weekends, religious differences, and predinner hour. Kent had lower interfamily stressors scores on situations involving insufficient family playtime, television, overloaded family calendar, and new baby (Mallory). Extrafamily stressors were ranked by both Kent and Merlene at similar levels: the flexible line of defense. The extrafamily situations included economics, church-school activities, change in work patterns, two-paycheck family, and neighbors.

In reviewing the family systems stressors with Merlene and Kent, the nurse was able to identify the perceptions of stressors held by each. Similarities and differences were explored. This information contributed to an understanding of the specific family problems identified by family members in the subsequent assessment sections. Frequently individual family members identify and/or perceive general and specific family systems stressors differently.

Family systems stressors (specific).   The Cobb family identified five specific family systems stressors or problem situations: (1) overscheduled calendar, (2) remarried/blended family and its many complications, (3) health concerns for youngest child and weight for mother, (4) parenting concerns (primarily the stepchild of each parent), and (5) maintaining standards such as housekeeping and economics. The nurse and family agreed that the five identified areas were affecting family stability and health. However, the stressors were not strong enough to break through the lines of resistance, so the family's basic core or basic structure was not being threatened. Over the past 3 years the family structure and function,—including family member composition, roles, rules, responsibilities, boundaries, goals, and ability to work together—had not significantly changed.

The family member variables (physiological, psychological, developmental, sociocultural, and spiritual) and the four major family categories) psychological relationships, physical status, developmental characteristics, and spiritual influences) demonstrated some variance from wellness at the lines of defense as documented by their assessment inventory scores. Reconstitution effects to restore optimal system stability focused on therapeutic actions derived from the primary and secondary prevention/intervention modes.

Family systems strengths.   The mother and father identified personalized family systems strengths that combined, in part, many of the specific strengths mentioned in the strength assessment section. These were husband and wife communication, equally shared responsibility by parents, role flexibility, work appreciation, caring about their family, and cognitive recognition of their problems. Indeed, both the family and the nurse agreed on what they perceived as family strengths, and it was believed that the strengths were capable of improving the family system instability. These strengths supported the prevention/intervention activities for the primary and secondary levels.

Primary prevention strategies focused on activities to identify potential general stressors that could further affect family stability and designing measures to prevent stressor penetration. Factors influencing the family's flexible line of defense involved parental roles, family rules, decision-making and task allocation, bonding of family members from two families, and conflict resolution. Primary prevention measures for this family included informative classes on blended families, child and adolescent development, parenting, and healthy lifestyles. Secondary prevention strategies focused on reducing the symptoms of stressors that had penetrated the flexible line of defense. Factors influencing the family's normal line of defense involved communication patterns among spouses, ex-spouses, and children; marital couple differences on how money should be spent; varied family member needs for intimacy and affection; Merlene's weight problem; and Mallory's otitis media. Measures designed to deal with these factors focused on ways to reduce the existing symptoms and attain system stability. Examples include marital counseling for issues encompassing money and family blend, focused family time for avocational activities, fun communication exercises to inhance the family's verbal and nonverbal message system, innovative weight management programs for Merlene, and appropriate treatment for Mallory's otitis media.

Family Care Plan

The family care plan included the following categories: (1) the nursing diagnosis based on general and specific family systems stressors, (2) identification of family systems strengths supporting prevention/intervention activities, (3) nursing goals for family and nurse, (4) modes of prevention and intervention (primary, secondary, and tertiary) with designated activities, and (5) nursing outcomes.

Each nursing diagnosis presented reflected a parameter of family system health variance. Examples include (1) compromised family coping at the normal line of defense due to blended family status, (2) impaired communication between mother/son at the normal line of defense due to differences in parenting styles (mother and stepmother), and (3) deficient avocational activities at the flexible line of defense due to spousal vocational responsibilities. The nursing diagnoses reflected the strength of stressor penetration by designating the lines of defense and/or resistance. The existing reconstitution measures used by the family, which were built on family strengths, were developed by the family and nurse.

Nursing goals focused on retaining and attaining system stability using the primary and secondary intervention modes. Therapeutic activities were individually designed for the family's use. Nursing outcomes, which are determined by nursing interventions, evaluation of outcome goals following intervention, and goal replanning, were not yet determined, since the care plan was just being put into motion at the time of this writing.

Summary

The system stability for this family, on a continuum of health and illness, demonstrates wellness variance at or between the flexible and normal lines of defense. Nursing interventions focused on retaining and attaining optimal system stability, that is, the best possible wellness state at this time.

Clinical Example 2: Nuclear Childbearing Family and the Death of the Husband/Father
Background

On Friday Ann Brooks came into Dr. Johnson's office for her annual allergy visit. The nurse noticed that she looked preoccupied and very sad. In the process of updating Ann's records, she asked if there had been any changes in her address, insurance coverage, or health status since her last visit. Ann said that "everything had changed and everything was different." The nurse asked her to explain what she meant.

Four months prior to this office visit, Ann's 46-year-old father died of a heart attack. Ann, age 18, was home at the time, as was her 16-year-old sister, Jane, and their mother, Judy, age 42. The two girls began CPR and were later joined by the paramedics. However, they could not revive their father. Mr. Brooks had no history of heart disease; however, he did have high cholesterol and blood pressure levels for which he was being treated. His weight was kept within normal limits by daily exercise. Mr. Brooks had smoked cigarettes in the past but had stopped doing so on advice of his physician. Mr. Brooks consulted the family physician 3 days before his death because of a fainting spell and chest pain. He was examined and nitroglycerin prescribed. The physician told Mr. Brooks to "take it easy." An appointment for a complete heart workup was scheduled 4 days later, but he died before he could keep the appointment.

Ann reported that the last 4 months had been emotionally and physically exhausting for the whole family. She said she came home from college on weekends to help her mother and sister with household activities. At times she felt she had to parent her mother and sister in order for them to cope with the many changes that have occurred in the family system. She described her sister, Jane, as being angry and uncooperative. Jane often refused to do what her mother said. For example, she would not come home from school on time, refused to help around the house, and argued at length with her mom. Jane was unable to talk about her father's death and when pressed withdrew to her room. Ann said Jane did not cry at her father's funeral and had not expressed her grief openly to any family members.

Ann described her mother as not being able to function as she had before her husband's death, even though her mother had returned to her teaching position. Her mother cried for long periods of time, had episodes of impulsivity and moodiness, and could not concentrate on any particular subject except her husband's death. Ann reported that her mother called people in the middle of the night to talk about her husband's needless death. She did not believe he had to die so young. One particular male friend, whom Ann referred to as her mother's new "boyfriend," was over at the house "all the time." He took their mother out, leaving Ann and Jane alone. Ann said that she and her sister, Jane, dislike him because he is so different from their dad. Ann described how much she and her sister had loved their dad and what great times they had had together. One of their special treats was to go out for breakfast with him on Saturday mornings. He would take each girl out on alternate Saturdays so that they could discuss whatever was on their minds. "I got to know my dad as a real friend during those times," she said. "We spent quality time together."

Ann reported that her parents had a good marriage and the

family was "close knit." They had many friends, as was evident at her father's funeral. Over 700 people came to the funeral, which was held at the church they regularly attended, and the company that he worked for closed for the day. The major source of emotional support has come from the maternal and paternal grandparents, numerous aunts and uncles, cousins, and friends. Ann told the nurse that she wanted her home to be a happy place once again, but she did not know how to make that happen. The office nurse asked Ann if she and the other family members would be interested in filling out a family assessment form (FS³I) so that she could help her family through this difficulty.

Summary of Brooks Family Systems Stressor Strength Inventory

Family systems stressors (general). The family systems stressors (general) were documented by family members at the flexible line of defense. This was also true for situations occurring within and between family members (intra- and interfamily) and between the family and society (extrafamily). Jane marked 18 of the 45 stressors as not being applicable to her. For example, Jane cited widowhood, retirement, communication with children, insufficient couple time, family play time, moving, spousal relationship, new baby, etc. as not being applicable to their family life. Ann agreed with this ranking except for the category of widowhood. Ann ranked widowhood as a high stressor for the family unit as did her mother.

The family members agreed on the general stress areas. Each of the following situations was ranked as a high stress situation: teen behaviors, homework/school grades (Jane high school, Ann college, and Judy graduate school), family vacations, holidays, economics, children's behavior/discipline/sibling fighting, change in work patterns (Ann worked while attending college, Jane had a part-time job, and Judy was a full-time teacher). The general stressors as ranked by Jane and Judy were within the range of the flexible line of defense, while Ann thought the stressful areas were penetrating the normal line of defense.

In reviewing general stressors with the family members, the nurse was able to identify the perceptions held by each. This included recognition of perceptual similarities and differences. Initiating this kind of dialogue helped establish a common ground for the selection of specific stressors, clarified individual points of view, and facilitated communication between family members. It also provided an opportunity for the nurse to observe family interaction patterns.

Family systems stressors (specific).   Judy (mother) and Ann (older daughter) identified the specific stressor as death of husband and father, while Jane (younger daughter) cited fighting with her mother as her major concern. The death of Mr. Brooks was a potent stressor that had penetrated the family's normal line of defense. The instability it generated had the potential for disrupting the family core. The lines of resistance were busily engaged in stabilizing the family structure and family functions. Family member composition, roles, rules, responsibilities, boundaries, goals, and their ability to work together had been significantly altered by the death of Mr. Brooks. The mother's grieving process was affecting her ability to listen, communicate, and interact with her children. The daughters' expectations of how their mother should behave did not include their mom seeking refuge and solace from a male they considered a potential father replacement. Therefore, Ann and Jane expressed feelings of anger and loneliness. The abrupt change in parental authority, responsibility, and power appeared to aggravate an already existing conflict between Jane and her mother. Some of the mother-daughter differences were maturational and developmental in nature and began when Jane entered adolescence.

The death of Mr. Brooks affected all family members individually and collectively. The family member variables (physiological, psychological, developmental, sociocultural, spiritual) and the four major family categories (psychological relationship, physical status, developmental characteristics, spiritual influence) exhibit a variance from wellness at the normal line of defense with potential disruption of the family core. Reconstitution required the initiation of therapeutic activities that used the primary, secondary, and tertiary prevention/intervention modes.

Family system strengths.   System strengths identified by the three family members quantitatively support selected prevention/intervention activities at the primary and secondary levels. The mother's perception of family strengths also support the tertiary prevention/intervention mode. Family system strengths contributing to the three prevention intervention modes are respect for others and sense of trust, shared religious core, respect of privacy, sharing of time together, table talk, admitting to and seeking help with problems, and a desire to cope together as a family system. These strengths are the building blocks for therapeutic actions directed at retaining, attaining, and maintaining system stability. They can be woven together into therapeutic patterns that facilitate and restore family health and well-being.

Family Care Plan

The family care plan includes the following: (1) the nursing diagnosis based on general and specific family systems stressors, (2) identification of family systems strengths supporting prevention/intervention activities, (3) nursing goals for family and nurse, and (4) modes of prevention and intervention (primary, secondary, and tertiary) with designated activities and nursing outcomes. Each nursing diagnosis reflected a parameter of family system instability at the lines of defense and resistance. Examples include (1) compromised family coping at normal line of defense due to the death of spouse and father, (2) impaired communication, interaction, and obedience patterns at normal line of defense due to family loss, and (3) significant alteration in daughter age/stage behavioral patterns at flexible and normal lines of defense due to death of father. The nursing diagnoses reflected the potency of stressor penetration by designating the lines of defense and resistance. The family systems strengths were able to support the nursing goals of attaining and maintaining system stability at the primary and secondary levels. Additional family strengths that could contribute to the maintenance of system stability at the lines of resistance, if greater variance from wellness occurred, were identified, including talking over feelings of loss and pain, listening to and respecting the ways each member was handling her own grief, and respect for different value systems.

The nursing goals established by nurse and family were delineated along with the prevention/intervention mode that would direct therapeutic activities, namely, the primary and secondary modes. The goals focused on retaining and attaining system balance and prevention of stressor penetration through lines of resistance.

Therapeutic outcomes are dependent on selecting the appropriate intervention measures that facilitate the family's reconstitution efforts. These are yet to be determined for this family.

Summary

This real-life situation offered an opportunity for a nurse working in a primary care setting to make a difference in the life of a family. The office nurse expanded the traditional role that nurses have held in physician's offices by taking responsibility for conducting a family assessment. Nurses must be cognizant that individual clients are usually members of family systems; and as such, the health of one member affects the well-being of all members.

Clinical Example 3: Nuclear Middlescent Family and Aging Parents
Background

The home health nurse (HHN) became acquainted with the Harmon/Gardner family through a discharge planning conference at the local community hospital. Mrs. Harmon, age 83, had recently undergone an exploratory laparotomy where the diagnosis of ovarian cancer was confirmed. A large tumor was debulked and a permanent colostomy performed. Mrs. Harmon had many unforeseen complications following her operations, but she was able to weather them well. Now she was being discharged home, where she lived with her 82-year-old blind husband. The hospital team was concerned that Mrs. Harmon's spousal and household responsibilities would interfere with her recovery. Mrs. Harmon needed to rest in order to prepare for upcoming chemotherapy treatments.

The Harmons had six children, five of whom were living but in different parts of the United States. Four daughters, two of them nurses, had previously shared in family caregiving. Peggy Gardner, the youngest of the four daughters, attended the discharge conference with her husband, Robert. The team observed Mrs. Harmon's anxiety over the meaning of the diagnosis and prognosis. She felt uncomfortable with the care of the colostomy and with the future chemotherapy treatments. Mr. Harmon, blinded by glaucoma complicated by previous strokes, was "fearful about his ability to care for his wife." Mrs. Harmon had been his primary caregiver for many years.

Peggy was concerned about both of her parents. She did not know how she was going to provide long-term care for them since she had a demanding career as a college professor and lived in any adjoining state. The home health nurse asked the Gardner family if they would take part in a family assessment, since the nurse recognized that caring for Mrs. Harmon would place additional stress on the Gardner family unit. The nurse wanted to promote optimal health and wellness for both family systems. If caring for the Harmon family caused a high degree of stress for the Gardners, some primary prevention and intervention activities could be initiated. The Gardners agreed to complete and FS³I, which is found at the end of this chapter.

Summary of Gardner Family Systems Stressor Strength Inventory

Family systems stressors (general). The general family systems stressors were rated by the two family caretakers, Peggy and Robert Gardner, at ranges encompassing the flexible lines and normal lines of defense. Those ranked as high stress areas by both included insufficient "me" time, perfectionism, insufficient couple time, insufficient family playtime, overscheduled family calender, lack of shared responsibility in the family, overvolunteerism, spousal relationship, older parents, and two-paycheck family. Peggy also considered moving back and forth between her home and her parents' home as a highly stressful area while her husband did not. Robert ranked several stressors at a higher level than did Peggy: inlaws, change in work patterns, self-image/self-esteem, and feelings of unattractiveness. They agreed that several situations on the FS³I did not apply to their family situation—for example, teen behaviors, new baby, houseguests, remarriage, and relationships with former spouses.

In reviewing general stressors ranked at the flexible and normal lines of defense, the nurse was able to identify individual family members' perceptions acknowledging similarities and differences between Peggy and Robert. They were aware of some stressful areas but did not know how their family unit would be affected by a long-term commitment to care for the Harmons. The home health nurse was alert to the fact that there was some degree of instability within the Gardner family system that would be increased by the additional responsibilities of caring for Mrs. Harmon.

Family systems stressors specific. The Gardners identified the specific stressor as caretaking of ill and elderly parents. Peggy and Robert's major concerns centered around (1) the crisis surgery of Peggy's mother, (2) the diagnosis of ovarian cancer and what that means to the family over time, (3) the dependency of a blind father, and (4) the overloaded schedule that Peggy and Robert would have as caretakers of aging parents. Peggy, in particular, was concerned about her ability to take on this role in addition to her professional responsibilities. As a college teacher it was difficult for her to take a family medical leave in the middle of an academic quarter. This was particularly true since she had just returned from a year's leave of absence.

Peggy felt a major responsibility for caring for her parents, whereas her husband, Robert, did not. He had not been helpful in her previous caretaking efforts. The home health nurse was more optimistic about the Harmon family's ability to handle their own stressors than were the Gardners. This was the only discrepancy between the family and nurse's specific stressor perceptions.

Mrs. Harmon's illness had the potential of disrupting the Harmon family's structure and function. Spousal roles and responsibilities would have to change. Since the cancer was malignant, the chances for a shortened life span were great. The Harmon and Gardner families, plus Peggy's siblings, expressed anger, fear, and sadness over the diagnosis and prognosis as well as the subsequent treatments that were necessary.

The illness of Mrs. Harmon affected all extended family members individually and collectively. The family member variables (physiological, psychological, developmental, sociocultural, spiritual) and the four major family categories (psychological relationships, physical status, developmental characteristics, spiritual influence) demonstrated a variance from wellness at the normal line of defense for the Gardners and the lines of resistance for the Harmons. Reconstitution necessitated the initiation of therapeutic activities that focused on all three prevention/intervention modes: primary, secondary, and tertiary.

Family systems strengths.   Family systems strengths were identified by Peggy and Robert Gardner as well as the nurse. These strengths supported the prevention/intervention activities at the primary and secondary levels. The nurse believed that the Gardner and Harmon families had sufficient family strengths to also support tertiary intervention strategies. Family systems strengths included values service to others, admits to and seeks help with problems, values work satisfaction, ability to let go, honors its elderly, respects privacy of others, accepts and encouraged individual values and financial security. One major strength that will assist the Garners and Harmons through this crisis will be the help provided by the extended family. All six of the Harmon children and/or their families will take turns staying with their ill and aging parents and grandparents. Different family members have cared for them in the past and they have promised to care for them now. With their help, which will augment the Gardner contribution, the Harmon family equilibrium should return to a somewhat normal state with time.

Family Care Plan

The family care plan included the following categories: (1) the nursing diagnosis based on specific family systems stressors, (2) identification of family systems strengths supporting prevention/ intervention activities, (3) nursing goals for family and nurse, (4) modes of prevention and intervention (primary, secondary, tertiary), and (5) nursing outcomes. Each nursing diagnosis was based on the specific family stressors identified by the Gardners. Three diagnoses were appropriate for this situation: (1) altered family processes at the normal line of defense due to illness of maternal parent and disability of paternal parent, (2) intermittent grieving at the normal line of defense due to cancer diagnosis and postoperative complications, and (3) compromised family coping at the flexible and normal lines of defense due to role overload.

The nursing diagnosis reflected the level of wellness variance. The existing reconstitution measures used by the family were designed by the Gardners, the Harmons, and the home health nurse. They focused on retaining and attaining system stability. The families' strengths were viewed as being able to facilitate therapeutic efforts directed at the primary and secondary prevention/intervention levels. The nursing goals established by the nurse and family were delineated along with the prevention as intervention mode that would direct therapeutic activities. Primary prevention/intervention strategies included reducing the possibility of further stressors, preventing burnout of any one family caretaker, and retaining sufficient rest and nutrition for all family members. Secondary prevention as intervention activities focused on meticulous nursing care to enhance Mrs. Harmon's full physical and psychological recovery, thoughtful family communication among all family member systems (the Harmons and the families of their six children), supporting Mrs. Harmon in the care of her colostomy, and assisting Mr. Harmon with changes in spousal responsibilities. These goals focused on retaining and attaining system balance and prevention of stressor penetration through the lines of resistance.

Therapeutic outcomes depend on selecting the appropriate intervention measures that facilitate the family's reconstitution efforts. The outcomes of intervention for this family are yet to be determined.

Summary

This real-life situation afford nurses working in home health care settings the ability to make a difference in the lives of patients and their caretakers once they leave the inpatient acute care setting. This scenario is played out daily in numerous places across the United States and it is often the discharge nurse (either inpatient nurse or community health nurse) who is responsible for assessing families and planning interventions. The FS³I is a valuable and potent tool for looking at family stressors and how these stressors can be reduced through family strengths to restore families back to health.

Family Systems Stressor-Strength Inventory (FS³I) Family Form

Family Name ___Cobb___   Date ___March 1___

Family Member Completing Assessment ___Merlene___

Ethnic Background ___Caucasian___

Referral Source ___School nurse___   Interviewer ___N. Nurse___

Family Members	Relationship in Family	Age	Marital Status	Education (highest degree)	Occupation
1. Kent	father/husband	40	M	HS + 3 yrs	farmer/truck driver
2. Merlene	mother/wife	37	M	HS + 1 yr	office manager
3. Kurtis	paternal son	11½	N/A	grade 6	
4. Erin	maternal daughter	11½	N/A	grade 6	
5. Mallory	daughter	3	N/A	preschool	
6.					

What is your current reason(s) for seeking health care assistance?

___Preschool physical___

Part 1: Family Systems Stressors (General)

DIRECTIONS: Each of the 45 situations listed here deal with some aspect of normal family life.[a] They have the potential for creating tension within family members, between family members, or between families and external environment. We are interested in your overall impression of how these situations affect your family life. Please circle a number (1 through 5) that best describes the amount of stress or tension they create for you. Thank you for cooperation.

	N/A	Little Stress		Medium Stress		High Stress
1. Family member(s) feeling un-appreciated	0	1	2	3	4	(5)
2. Guilt for not accomplishing more	0	1	2	3	4	(5)
3. Insufficient "me" time	0	1	2	(3)	4	5
4. Self-image/self-esteem/feelings of unattractiveness	0	1	2	3	4	(5)
5. Perfectionism	0	1	2	(3)	4	5
6. Dieting	0	1	2	3	4	(5)
7. Health/illness	0	(1)	2	3	4	5
8. Drugs/alcohol	(0)	1	2	3	4	5
9. Widowhood	(0)	1	2	3	4	5
10. Retirement	(0)	1	2	3	4	5
11. Homework/school grades	(0)	1	2	3	4	5
12. Communication with children	0	1	2	3	4	(5)
13. Housekeeping standards	0	1	2	3	4	(5)
14. Insufficient couple time	0	1	2	3	4	(5)
15. Insufficient family playtime	0	1	2	3	4	(5)
16. Children's behavior/discipline/sibling fighting	0	1	2	3	4	(5)
17. Television	0	1	(2)	3	4	5

18. Overscheduled family calendar   0   1   2   (3)   4   5

19. Lack of shared responsibility in the family   0   1   2   3   4   (5)

20. Moving   0   (1)   2   3   4   5

21. Spousal relationship (communication, friendship, sex)   0   1   (2)   3   4   5

22. Holidays   0   1   2   3   4   (5)

23. Inlaws   0   1   2   3   4   (5)

24. Teen behaviors (communication, music, friends, church, school)   0   1   2   3   (4)   5

25. New baby   (0)   1   2   3   4   5

26. Houseguests   (0)   1   2   3   4   5

27. Family vacations   0   (1)   2   3   4   5

28. Remarriage   0   1   (2)   3   4   5

29. Relationship with former spouse   0   1   2   (3)   4   5

30. Summer   0   1   2   3   4   (5)

31. Weekends   0   1   2   3   4   (5)

32. Religious differences   (0)   1   2   3   4   5

33. Predinner hour   0   1   2   3   4   (5)

34. Older parents   0   (1)   2   3   4   5

35. Economics/finances/budgets   0   1   2   3   4   (5)

36. Unhappiness with work situation   0   1   (2)   3   4   5

37. Overvolunteerism   0   (1)   2   3   4   5

38. Neighbors   0   (1)   2   3   4   5

39.	Unemployment	(0)	1	2	3	4	5
40.	Nuclear and environmental fears	0	(1)	2	3	4	5
41.	Church-school activities	0	1	2	3	4	(5)
42.	Unsatisfactory housing	(0)	1	2	3	4	5
43.	Organized sports activities	(0)	1	2	3	4	5
44.	Change in work patterns	0	1	2	3	4	(5)
45.	Two-paycheck family	0	1	2	3	4	(5)

Part II: Family Systems Stressors (Specific)

DIRECTIONS: The following 10 questions are designed to provide specific information about tension producing situations, problems, or areas of concern influencing your family's health.[b] Please circle a number (1 through 5) that best describes the influence this situation has on your family's life.

What do you consider your major stressful situation, problem, or concern at this time?

<u>Time for family after working all week and on</u>

<u>weekends.</u>

<u>Weight problem</u>

	N/A	Little or None		Medium		Very much
1. To what extent is your family bothered by this problem or stressful situation?	0	1	2	3	4	(5)
2. How much of an effect does this stressful situation have on your family's usual pattern of living?	0	1	2	(3)	4	5
3. How much has this situation affected your family's ability to work together as a family unit?	0	1	2	3	(4)	5

Has your family ever experienced a similar concern in the past?

YES ___✔___ If YES, complete question 4

NO _____ If NO, proceed to question 5

	N/A	Little or None		Medium		Very much
4. How successful was your family in dealing with this situation/problem/concern in the past?	0	1	(2)	3	4	5
5. How strongly do you feel this current situation/problem/concern will affect your family's future?	0	1	2	(3)	4	5
6. To what extent are family members able to help themselves in this present situation/problem/concern?	0	(1)	2	3	4	5
7. To what extent do you expect others to help your family with this situation/problem/concern?	0	(1)	2	3	4	5

	N/A	Poor	Satisfactory		Excellent
8. Rate the overall health status of your family as a whole.	0	1	2	(3) 4	5

9. Rate the overall health status of each family member by name.

	N/A	Poor		Satisfactory		Excellent
Kent	0	1	2	3	(4)	5
Merlene	0	1	(2)	3	4	5
Kurtis	0	1	2	3	4	(5)
Erin	0	1	2	3	4	(5)
Mallory	0	1	(2)	3	4	5

Part III: Family Systems Strengths

DIRECTIONS: Each of the twenty traits/attributes listed below deals with some aspect of family life.[c] Each one contributes to the health and well-being of family members as individuals and to the family as a whole. Please circle a number (1 through 5) that best describes the extent to which family members use these traits.

My Family:	N/A	Seldom		Usually		Always
1. Communicates and listens to one another	0	1	2	(3)	4	5
2. Affirms and supports one another	0	1	2	(3)	4	5
3. Teaches respect for others	0	1	2	3	4	(5)
4. Develops a sense of trust in members	0	1	2	(3)	4	5
5. Has a sense of play and humor	0	1	(2)	3	4	5
6. Exhibits a sense of shared responsibility	0	1	2	3	4	(5)
7. Teaches a sense of right and wrong	0	1	2	3	4	(5)
8. Has a strong sense of family in which rituals and traditions abound	0	1	2	3	4	(5)

9. Has a balance of interaction among members   0   1   2   ③   4   5

10. Has a shared religious core   ⓪   1   2   3   4   5

11. Respects the privacy of one another   0   1   2   3   4   ⑤

12. Values service to others   0   1   2   ③   4   5

13. Fosters family table time and conversation   0   1   2   3   4   ⑤

14. Shares leisure time   0   1   2   ③   4   5

15. Admits to and seeks help with problems   0   1   2   ③   4   5

16. Honors its elders   0   1   2   ③   4   5

17. Accepts and encourages individual values   0   1   2   ③   4   5

18. Values work satisfaction   0   1   2   3   4   ⑤

19. Is financially secure   0   1   ②   3   4   5

20. Is able to let go of grown children   ⓪   1   2   3   4   5

[a]Based on Curran, D. 1985. Stress and the healthy family. Minneapolis: Winston Press.

[b]Based on Neuman's Systems Model. Neuman, B. 1989. The Neuman systems model. Norwalk, CT: Appleton-Lange.

[c]Based on Curran, D. 1983. Traits of a healthy family. Minneapolis: Winston Press.

Family Systems Stressor-Strength Inventory (FS³I)
Family Form

Family Name ___Cobb___   Date ___March 1___

Family Member Completing Assessment ___Kent___

Ethnic Background ___Western European/English, Danish,___
_____Spanish___
Referral Source ___School nurse___   Interviewer ___N. Nurse___

Family Members	Relationship in Family	Age	Marital Status	Education (highest degree)	Occupation
1. Kent	father/ husband	40	M	HS + 3 yr	farmer/ truck driver
2. Merlene	mother/ wife	37	M	HS + 1 yr	office manager
3. Kurtis	paternal son	11½	NA	grade 6	
4. Erin	maternal daughter	11½	NA	grade 6	
5. Mallory	daughter	3	NA	preschool	
6.					

What is your current reason(s) for seeking health care assistance?

___Preschool physical___

Part 1: Family Systems Stressors (General)

DIRECTIONS: Each of the 45 situations listed here deal with some aspect of normal family life.[a] They have the potential for creating tension within family members, between family members, or between families and external environment. We are interested in your overall impression of how these situations affect your family life. Please circle a number (1 through 5) that best describes the amount of stress or tension they create for you. Thank you for cooperation.

	N/A	Little Stress		Medium Stress		High Stress
1. Family member(s) feeling un-appreciated	0	1	2	3	(4)	5
2. Guilt for not accomplishing more	0	1	2	3	(4)	5
3. Insufficient "me" time	0	1	2	3	(4)	5
4. Self-image/self-esteem/feelings of unattractiveness	0	1	(2)	3	4	5
5. Perfectionism	0	1	2	3	(4)	5
6. Dieting	0	1	2	(3)	4	5
7. Health/illness	0	1	(2)	3	4	5
8. Drugs/alcohol	(0)	1	2	3	4	5
9. Widowhood	0	(1)	2	3	4	5
10. Retirement	0	(1)	2	3	4	5
11. Homework/school grades	(0)	1	2	3	4	5
12. Communication with children	0	(1)	2	3	4	5
13. Housekeeping standards	0	1	2	(3)	4	5
14. Insufficient couple time	0	1	2	3	(4)	5
15. Insufficient family playtime	0	1	2	3	4	(5)
16. Children's behavior/discipline/sibling fighting	0	1	2	3	(4)	5
17. Television	0	1	2	3	4	(5)

18. Overscheduled family calendar   0   1   2   3   4   ⑤

19. Lack of shared responsibility in the family   0   1   ②   3   4   5

20. Moving   ⓪   1   2   3   4   5

21. Spousal relationship (communication, friendship, sex)   0   1   ②   3   4   5

22. Holidays   0   1   2   3   ④   5

23. Inlaws   0   ①   2   3   4   5

24. Teen behaviors (communication, music, friends, church, school)   0   ①   2   3   4   5

25. New baby   0   1   2   3   4   ⑤

26. Houseguests   0   ①   2   3   4   5

27. Family vacations   ⓪   1   2   3   4   5

28. Remarriage   ⓪   1   2   3   4   5

29. Relationship with former spouse   0   1   ②   3   4   5

30. Summer   0   ①   2   3   4   5

31. Weekends   ⓪   1   2   3   4   5

32. Religious differences   ⓪   1   2   3   4   5

33. Predinner hour   ⓪   1   2   3   4   5

34. Older parents   0   1   ②   3   4   5

35. Economics/finances/budgets   0   1   2   3   4   ⑤

36. Unhappiness with work situation   0   1   2   ③   4   5

37. Overvolunteerism   0   1   2   3   ④   5

38. Neighbors   0   1   2   3   4   ⑤

39. Unemployment	0	(1)	2	3	4	5
40. Nuclear and environmental fears	0	1	2	(3)	4	5
41. Church-school activities	0	(1)	2	3	4	5
42. Unsatisfactory housing	(0)	1	2	3	4	5
43. Organized sports activities	(0)	1	2	3	4	5
44. Change in work patterns	0	(1)	2	3	4	5
45. Two-paycheck family	0	1	2	(3)	4	5

Part II: Family Systems Stressors (Specific)

DIRECTIONS: The following 10 questions are designed to provide specific information about tension producing situations, problems, or areas of concern influencing your family's health.[b] Please circle a number (1 through 5) that best describes the influence this situation has on your family's life.

What do you consider your major stressful situation, problem, or concern at this time?

Confusion and frustration with children

visiting other parent on weekends.

	N/A	Little or None		Medium		Very much
1. To what extent is your family bothered by this problem or stressful situation?	0	1	(2)	3	4	5
2. How much of an effect does this stressful situation have on your family's usual pattern of living?	0	1	(2)	3	4	5
3. How much has this situation affected your family's ability to work together as a family unit?	0	1	(2)	3	4	5

Has your family ever experienced a similar concern in the past?

YES   ✓   If YES, complete question 4

NO   ____   If NO, proceed to question 5

	N/A	Little or None		Medium		Very much
4. How successful was your family in dealing with this situation/problem/concern in the past?	0	(1)	2	3	4	5
5. How strongly do you feel this current situation/problem/concern will affect your family's future?	0	(1)	2	3	4	5
6. To what extent are family members able to help themselves in this present situation/problem/concern?	0	1	2	3	(4)	5
7. To what extent do you expect others to help your family with this situation/problem/concern?	0	1	2	3	4	(5)

	N/A	Poor	Satisfactory		Excellent
8. Rate the overall health status of your family as a whole.	0	1	2	3	(4)	5

9. Rate the overall health status of each family member by name.

	N/A	Poor	Satisfactory		Excellent
Kent	0	1	2	(3)	4	5
Merlene	0	1	2	(3)	4	5
Kurtis	0	1	2	3	4	(5)
Erin	0	1	2	3	(4)	5
Mallory	0	1	(2)	3	4	5

Part III: Family Systems Strengths

DIRECTIONS: Each of the twenty traits/attributes listed below deals
with some aspect of family life.[c] Each one contributes to the health
and well-being of family members as individuals and to the family as
a whole. Please circle a number (1 through 5) that best describes the
extent to which family members use these traits.

My Family:	N/A	Seldom		Usually		Always
1. Communicates and listens to one another	0	1	2	(3)	4	5
2. Affirms and supports one another	0	1	2	3	(4)	5
3. Teaches respect for others	0	1	2	3	(4)	5
4. Develops a sense of trust in members	0	1	2	3	(4)	5
5. Has a sense of play and humor	0	1	2	3	(4)	5
6. Exhibits a sense of shared responsibility	0	1	2	3	(4)	5
7. Teaches a sense of right and wrong	0	1	2	3	4	(5)
8. Has a strong sense of family in which rituals and traditions abound	0	1	2	(3)	4	5

9. Has a balance of interac-   0   1   2   ③   4   5
    tion among members

10. Has a shared religious   0   1   2   ③   4   5
    core

11. Respects the privacy of   0   1   2   ③   4   5
    one another

12. Values service to others   0   1   2   ③   4   5

13. Fosters family table time   0   1   2   3   ④   5
    and conversation

14. Shares leisure time   0   1   2   ③   4   5

15. Admits to and seeks help   0   1   2   ③   4   5
    with problems

16. Honors its elders   0   1   2   ③   4   5

17. Accepts and encourages   0   1   2   ③   4   5
    individual values

18. Values work satisfaction   0   1   2   3   4   ⑤

19. Is financially secure   0   1   2   ③   4   5

20. Is able to let go of grown   0   1   2   3   ④   5
    children

[a]Based on Curran, D. 1985. **Stress and the healthy family.** Minneapolis: Winston Press.

[b]Based on Neuman's Systems Model. Neuman, B. 1989. **The Neuman systems model.** Norwalk, CT: Appleton-Lange.

[c]Based on Curran, D. 1983. **Traits of a healthy family.** Minneapolis: Winston Press.

Family Systems Stressor-Strength Inventory (FS³I) Clinician Form

Family Name   <u>Cobb</u>   Date   <u>March 1</u>

Part I: Family Systems Stressors (General)

Briefly discuss the 45 situations with the family member(s) and ask if there are additional areas of concern. The purpose here is to begin clarifying the family member(s) perceptions of stressful situations and to zero in on their major area of concern.

<u>Merger and hassles of blended family. Custody;</u>

<u>in-laws; former spouse issues.</u>

Part II: Family Systems Stressors (Specific)

DIRECTIONS: The following 10 questions are designed to provide specific information about the particular situation influencing the family's health.[b] Please circle a number (1 through 5) that best describes the influence this situation has on the family's health from your point of view. Record the family response(s) and your perceptions.

What do you consider to be the family's most stressful situation/problem/or areas of concern at this time? (Identify problem area(s))

<u>Time for family rest and togetherness;</u>

<u>Complexity of remarriage/step-parent family;</u>

<u>Confusion over children visiting other parent</u>

on weekends.

	N/A	Little or none	Medium		Very Much
1. To what extent is the family bothered by this situation/problem/concern? (Effects on psychosocial relationships communication, interactions)	0	1	2	3	4	(5)

Family Response

Very bothered. Affects all aspects of family system.

Clinician Perceptions

Stressor affects communication between spouses, parent/child, and siblings; Interaction patterns altered.

	N/A	Little or none		Medium		Very Much

2. How much alteration in the family's usual pattern of living is occurring as a result of this situation/problem/concern? (Identify life-style patterns and developmental tasks)

N/A	Little or none		Medium		Very Much
0	1	2	(3)	4	5

Family Response
Family always feels chaotic.

Clinician Perceptions
Wife's former spouse precipitated most recent move to farm. Present mother-in-law controlling. Weekdays stable; weekend unstable.

3. How much has this situation affected the family's ability to work together as a family unit? (Identify roles and tasks and how these are being altered.)

N/A	Little or none		Medium		Very Much
0	1	2	(3)	4	5

Family Response
Mother reports effects are great.
No long-term task planning taking place.
No couple time. No family vacation.

Clinician Perceptions
Husband and wife are learning how to work together but parenting appears to be troublesome area. Mother is disciplinarian and father plays role of children's friend. Spouse avocational activities limited.

		Little			Very
	N/A	or none	Medium		Much

4. Has the family ever experienced similar situations in the past? If so describe what the family did. How successful were they in resolving the situation/problem/concern? (Identify past coping patterns, adaptive strategies, and what success means to family.)

Circled: 3 (on scale 0 1 2 ③ 4 5)

Family Response
Family believes they have not been in the situation before as this is second marriage for both.

Clinician Perceptions
Merlene's parents divorced. Both were alcoholics and she had to parent them. Kent's parents divorced and his mother abandoned kids as soon as they reached adolescence.

		Little			Very
	N/A	or none	Medium		Much

5. How strongly do you think the present situation/problem/concern will affect the family and family members in the future? What effects do you expect? What are the anticipated consequences? (Identify current and potential coping patterns.)

Circled: 5 (on scale 0 1 2 3 4 ⑤)

Family Response
Family situation is unlikely to change until children are out of home.

Clinician Perceptions
Problem will get worse before it gets better as the children go through their teen years. Future role confusion and loyalty problems for two children from previous marriages. Family coping 1 day at a time to maintain stability.

	N/A	Little or none		Medium		Very Much
6. To what extent are family members able to help themselves in the present situation/problem/concern? Identify self-assistive behaviors, family expectations, and spiritual influence.	0	1	2	3	(4)	5

Family Response
Family members attempting to deal with blended family arrangement.

Clinician Perceptions
Parents are able to cope. Merlene may be overfunctioning perfectionist which compounds problems children have in complying with two standards of family behaviors, e.g. chores, discipline, play.

	N/A	Little or none		Medium		Very Much
7. To what extent does the family expect others to assist them with their present situation? What roles do family members expect others to play? (Describe roles and availability of extrafamily resources.)	0	1	(2)	3	4	5

Family Response
No one else from within family system can help. Mother has support from female friend. Has seen counselor on one occasion.

Clinician Perceptions
Family may benefit from outside help from external resources. Parent—blended and teenaged family classes may be of assistance.

	N/A	Poor		Satisfactory		Excellent
8. Describe the overall health status of the family system. Consider four major categories: physical status, psychosocial characteristics, developmental characteristics, and spiritual influence	0	1	2	3	(4)	5

Family Response

Health is basically good. Some ear problems with younger child.

Clinician Perceptions

Members overall health status good.

9. Rate the overall health status of each family member using 5 variables as reference points: physiological, psychological, developmental, sociocultural, and spiritual influence.

		N/A	Poor		Satisfactory		Excellent
a.	Kent	0	1	2	3	(4)	5
b.	Merlene	0	1	2	3	4	(5)
c.	Kurtis	0	1	2	3	4	(5)
d.	Erin	0	1	2	3	4	(5)
e.	Mallory	0	1	2	(3)	4	5

Family Response

Merlene rated own health as less than satisfactory. Other family members health good.

Clinician Perceptions

Overall family health status quite good. Seek doctor care for acute illnesses. Merlene is overweight and Mallory has frequent otitis media. Family unit at different developmental levels because of blend.

Part III: Family Systems Strengths

DIRECTIONS: Each of the 20 trait and/or attributes listed here deal with some aspect of family life.[c] Each one contributes to the health and well-being of family members as individuals and to family as a whole. Briefly describe your perception of how these strengths are operationalized in this family and circle the number (1 through 5) that best describes the extent to which they are used.

	N/A	Seldom or not at all		Usually		Always
This Family:						
1. Communicates and listens to one another	0	1	2	(3)	4	5

Clinician Perceptions
    Family members attempting to do this

2. Affirms and supports one another	0	1	2	3	4	(5)

Clinician Perceptions
    Supportive unit

3. Teaches respect for others	0	1	2	3	4	(5)

Clinician Perceptions

4. Develops a sense of trust in members	0	1	2	3	4	(5)

Clinician Perceptions

5. Has a sense of play and humor	0	1	(2)	3	4	5

Clinician Perceptions
    Need to learn and schedule play times

6. Exhibits a sense of shared responsibility	0	1	2	3	(4)	5

Clinician Perceptions

7. Teaches a sense of right   0   1   2   3   4   ⑤
    and wrong

Clinician Perceptions

8. Has a strong sense of   0   1   ②   3   4   5
    family in which rituals
    and traditions abound

Clinician Perceptions

9. Has a balance of interac-   0   1   2   ③   4   5
    tion among members

Clinician Perceptions

10. Has a shared religious   0   1   2   ③   4   5
    core

Clinician Perceptions

11. Respects the privacy of   0   1   2   3   ④   5
    one another

Clinician Perceptions

12. Values service to others   0   1   2   ③   4   5

Clinician Perceptions

13. Fosters family table time   0   1   2   3   4   ⑤
    and conversation

Clinician Perceptions
    One time family unites each day

14. Shares leisure time   0   1   2   (3)   4   5

Clinician Perceptions

15. Admits to and seeks help   0   1   2   (3)   4   5
    with problems

Clinician Perceptions

16. Honors its elders   0   1   2   3   (4)   5

Clinician Perceptions

17. Accepts and encourages   0   1   2   (3)   4   5
    individual values

Clinician Perceptions

18. Values work satisfaction   0   1   2   3   4   (5)

Clinician Perceptions
    Merlene and Kent extremely responsible at work

19. Is financially secure   0   1   2   (3)   4   5

Clinician Perceptions

20. Is able to let go of grown (0)   1   2   3   4   5
    children

Clinician Perceptions

[a]Based on Curran, D. 1985. **Stress and the healthy family.** Minneapolis: Winston Press.
[b]Based on Neuman's Systems Model. Neuman, B. 1989. **The Neuman systems model.** Norwalk, CT: Appleton–Lange.
[c]Based on Curran, D. 1983. **Traits of a healthy family.** Minneapolis: Winston Press.

Family Systems Stressor-Strength Inventory (FS³I)
Summary Form

Family Name <u>Cobb</u>   Date <u>March 1</u>

Family Member(s) Completing Assessment <u>Kent & Merlene</u>

Ethnic Background(s) <u>Western European/English, Danish,</u>
                      <u>Spanish Caucasion</u>
Religious Background(s) <u>Roman Catholic</u>

Referral Source <u>School Nurse</u>   Interviewer <u>N. Nurse</u>

Family Members	Relationship in Family	Age	Marital Status	Education (highest degree)	Occupation
1. Kent	father/ husband	40	M	HS + 3 yrs	farmer/ truck driver
2. Merlene	mother/ wife	37	M	HS + 1 yr	office manager
3. Kurtis	paternal son	11½	NA	grade 6	
4. Erin	maternal daughter	11½	NA	grade 6	
5. Mallory	daughter	3	NA	preschool	
6.					

Family's current reason for seeking health care assistance?

  Preschool physical

Scoring Key

Family Member Perceptions
Section 1: Family Form

Part I Family Systems Stressors (General)

Add scores from questions 1 to 45 and calculate an overall score for Family Systems Stressors (General). Ratings are from 1 (most positive) to 5 (most negative). Subscale scores range from 45 to 225.

Family Systems Stressors (General) Score

$$\frac{(\quad)}{45} \times 1 = \underline{\hphantom{xxxxx}}$$

Kent   96/45 = 2.1

Merlene   128/45 = 2.8

Graph subscale score on Quantitative Summary Form: Family Systems Stressors: General, Family Member Perceptions.

A. Intrafamily Systems Subscale Score:

Add scores from questions 1-11 and calculate a subscale score. Ratings are from 1 (most positive) to 5 (most negative). Subscale scores range from 11 to 55.

Intrafamily Systems Stressors Score

$$\frac{(\quad)}{11} \times 1 = \underline{\hphantom{xxxxx}}$$

Kent   25/11 = 2.3

Merlene   34/11 = 3.1

Graph score on Quantitative Summary Form: Family Systems Stressors (Intrafamily), Family Member Perceptions.

Family Member Perceptions
Section 1: Family Form

B. Interfamily Systems Subscale Score:

Add scores from questions 12-34 only and calculate a subscale score. Ratings are from 1 (most positive) to 5 (most negative). Scores range from 23 to 115.

Interfamily Systems Stressors Score

$$\frac{(\quad)}{23} \times 1 = \underline{\qquad}$$

Kent   49/23 = 2.1

Merlene   69/23 = 3.0

Graph subscale score on Quantitative Summary Form. Family Systems Stressors (Interfamily). Family Member Perceptions.

C. Extrafamily Systems Subscale Score:

Add scores from questions 35-45 and calculate a subscale score. Ratings are from 1 (most positive) to 5 (most negative). Scores range from 11 to 55.

Extrafamily Systems Stressors Score

$$\frac{(\quad)}{11} \times 1 = \underline{\qquad}$$

Kent   24/11 = 2.2

Merlene   25/11 = 2.3

Graph subscale score on Quantitative Summary Form: Family Systems Stressors (Extrafamily). Family Member Perceptions.

Part II Family Systems Stressors (Specific)

Add scores from questions 1 to 8 only and calculate a score for Family Systems Stressors (Specific). Ratings are from 1 (most positive) to 5 (most negative). Questions 4, 6, 7, and 8 are reverse scored.* Scores range from 8 to 40.

Family Systems Stressors (Specific) Score

$$\frac{(\quad)}{8} \times 1 = \underline{\hspace{2cm}}$$

Kent   16/8 = 2

Merlene 32/8 = 4.0

Graph score on Quantitative Summary Form: Family Systems Stressors (Specific) Family Member Perceptions. Scores for question 9 are recorded on Qualitative Summary Form 2D: Family Systems Stressors (Specific).

Part III Family Systems Strengths

Add scores from questions 1 to 20 and calculate a score for Family Systems Strengths. Ratings are from 1 (seldom used) to 5 (always used). Scores range from 20 to 100.

Family Systems Strengths Score

$$\frac{(\quad)}{20} \times 1 = \underline{\hspace{2cm}}$$

Kent   71/20 = 3.6

Merlene 66/20 = 3.3

Graph score on Quantitative Summary Form: Family Systems Strengths.

*Reverse Scoring:

Question answered as **one** is scored as 5 points
Question answered as **two** is scored as 4 points
Question answered as **three** is scored as 3 points
Question answered as **four** is scored as 2 points
Question answered as **five** is scored as 1 point

Clinician Perceptions
Section 2: Clinician Form

Part I Family Systems Stressors (General)

Identify predominant tension producing situations from list of 45 situations/problems/concerns and prioritize them in order of importance to family. Record on Qualitative Summary Form: Family Systems Stressors (General).

Additional Comments:

General Stressors: time for individuals, couple, and play

Intrafamily: Feeling unappreciated, guilt for not accomplishing more, dieting

Interfamily Communication with children, housekeeping standards, insufficient group and family time. Lack of shared responsibility, use of holiday time & child visitation, in-laws

Extrafamily:

Summers, weekends, predinner hours, economics, church-school activities, change in work patterns, two-paycheck family

Part II Family Systems Stressors (Specific)   26/8 = 3.25

Calculate quantitative scores for questions 1 to 8 in same manner as for Section 1, Part II. Family Member Perceptions. Graph on Quantitative Summary Form for Family Systems Stressors (Specific), Clinician Perceptions.

Identify specific tension producing situation/problem/concern that is influencing family health and record on Qualitative Summary Form 2A: Family Systems Stressors (Specific).

Part III Family Systems Strengths   70/20 = 3.5

Calculate quantitative scores for questions 1 to 20 in same manner as for Section 1, Part III. Family Member Perceptions. Graph on Quantitative Summary Form for Family Systems Strengths, Clinician Perceptions.

Identify Family Systems Strengths that contribute to family stability, health and can serve as a basis for prevention/intervention activities. Record on Qualitative Summary Form Part III: Family Systems Strengths.

Quantitative Summary

DIRECTIONS: Graph the scores from each family member inventory by placing an "X" at the appropriate location and connect with a line. (Use first name initial for each line.)

Key: Kent ●———
        Merlene X----

Sum of strengths available for prevention/intervention mode	Family Systems Strengths	
	Family Member Perceptions	Clinician Perceptions

5.0		
4.8		
4.6		
4.4		
4.2		
4.0		
3.8		
3.6	●	
3.4		◉
3.2		
3.0	✗	
2.8		
2.6		
2.4		
2.2		
2.0		
1.8		
1.6		
1.4		
1.2		
1.0		

*PRIMARY Prevention Intervention Mode: Flexible Line   ) 1.0-2.3
*SECONDARY Prevention Intervention Mode: Normal Line) 2.4-3.6
*TERTIARY Prevention Intervention Mode: Resistance Lines) 3.7-5.0
*Breakdown of numerical scores for stressor penetration are suggested values

Qualitative Summary*
(Family and Clinician Perceptions)

Part I: Family Systems Stressors: General

Identify predominant tension producing situation(s) in family and list them in order of importance to the family.

Situation/Problem/Concern	Priority for Family
1. Overscheduled calendar	high
2. Remarriage/blended family	high
3. Health concerns	high
4. Parenting concerns	high
5. Housekeeping standards	high
Economics	high

Comments:

Discrepancy between husband and wife on general stressors regarding volunteerism, communication with children, self-image.

*Combines information from Family Form and Clinician Form.

Part II: Family Systems Stressors: Specific

Identify specific tension producing situation/problem/concern
influencing family health.

Integrating blended families. Chaos on

weekends/holidays in regard to custody and

visitation. Time for family activities.

Weight control for wife.

Comments:

Part II: Family Systems Stressors: Specific
B. Summarize perceptions of the specific family situation/problem/
concern and identify discrepancies between family and clinician
perceptions.

Stressor (Situation)	Family Perception
1. Extent family bothered by situation/problem/concern: effects on psychosocial relationships, communications, and interactions	All aspects of family functioning affected by blended family structure.
2. Alterations in usual life-style patterns and family developmental tasks	Parents feel out of control of family activities and functions.
3. Effects on family's ability to work together: alteration in roles and tasks	Usual way of functioning since their marriage. Long-term planning difficult.
4. Similar situations, problems, concerns: family's past coping patterns; what "success" means to family	Family states that this has not occurred before, since this is first remarriage.
5. Effects of present situation on family health in future: anticipated consequences: current and potential coping patterns	Family situation will not change until children leave home. Coping patterns remain constant.
6. Family's ability to help themselves in situation: self-assistive behaviors; family expectations and spiritual influence	Family good at helping self.
7. Family expectations of others and their role in helping family; extrafamily resources and their role	No one will help.

Clinician Perception	Discrepancies
Stressors of blended families. Affects couple, children, in-laws, previous spouses	None
Alterations in routine lifestyle patterns and developmental tasks due to blended status.	None
Roles fluid. Boundaries permeable. Responsibilities shared.	None
Repeating some family interaction patterns from family of origin, e.g. Merlene's need to parent spouse.	Discrepancy. Family will learn about intergenerational patterns.
Interaction patterns may get worse during teen years. Cope 1 day at a time. Can learn new coping and communication patterns.	Probably will not totally resolve even when children leave.
Family good with self-help. Could benefit from outside assistance on occasional basis, e.g. counseling.	Could benefit from outside help.
Difficulty in asking for help.	Not able to ask for or afford help.

C. Summarize significant health status data for each family member using five variables.

	Family Member Kent [1]	Family Member Merlene [2]	Family Member Kurtis [3]
Physiological	Presence of risk factors, i.e., aneurysm, absence of disease	Good health. 50 lbs overweight	Good
Psychological	High tolerance Stable Ability to cope	High tolerance. Stable; able to cope. Expresses feelings.	Behavior difficult with biological mother.
Developmental	Age-appropriate for task and stage	Age-appropriate for task and stage.	Age-appropriate for task and stage.
Sociocultural	Job stability? Self-employed	Job stable. Responsible socially.	Child of divorce and remarriage. Sibling rivalry.
Spiritual	Belief in higher power. Attends Catholic church	Belief in higher power "spiritual, not religious."	Knows right from wrong. Sense of trust.

Family Member Erin 4	Family Member Mallory 5	Family Member 6
Good health	Chronic otitis media	
No symptoms	Strong willed and hard to discipline.	
Age-appropriate for task and stage.	Age-appropriate for task and stage.	
Child of divorce and remarriage.	Child of blended family.	
Knows right from wrong. Sense of trust.	Musical, creative.	

D. Using the four major categories of the family system, combine significant health status data from family member variables.

Major Category	Family System
Psychological Relationship	Relationships flexible Boundaries permeable Interaction predominates Effective coping
Physical Status	Optimal energy Homeostatic on weekdays Borderline on weekends
Spiritual Influence	Family derives some support from spiritual beliefs and some support from extended family system.
Developmental Characteristics	Age and stage appropriate Childrearing family Blended family

Part III: Family Systems Strengths

Identify family systems strengths that contribute to family stability and support actual and potential prevention/intervention activities.

Family Systems Strengths
1. Spousal communication
2. Equal, shared responsibility by parents
3. Values work satisfaction at home and on the job
4. Care about their family
5. Cognitive recognition of their problem
6.
7.

Part IV: Family Care Plan*

List the three most significant clinician diagnoses (prioritize).

Diagnosis General and Specific Family Systems Stressors	Family Systems Strengths Supporting Family Care Plan	Goals Family and Clinician
1. Compromised family coping at normal line of defense due to blended family arrangement	Good spousal communication Equal sharing of responsibility by parents Commitment to retaining system stability	Retain permeable informational boundaries between adults parenting children.
2. Impaired communication between mother and step-son at normal line of defense due to differences in parenting style (step-mother and mother)	Cognitive recognition of family problems Willingness to seek help with family conflicts	Clarify roles, rules, responsibilities, lines of communication among custodial and noncustodial families.
3. Deficient avocational activities at flexible line of defense due to spousal vocational responsibilities	Values work satisfaction at home and work	Develop workable plan for avocational activities that facilitate couple time and family time.

Prevention/Intervention Mode		Outcomes
Primary, Secondary, or Tertiary	Prevention/Intervention Activities	Evaluation and Replanning
Secondary - Arrange for regular family night meeting for openly discussing children's concerns, assist family members to make contribution to establish selected household rules & roles. Discuss strengths of blended families. Design "fun exercises" for examining problem-solving process.		In process
Secondary - Identify and incorporate meaningful ways by which mother and stepson can discuss areas of conflict and agreement. Play communication games that focus on lines of communication and feedback loops.		In process
Primary — Clarify desired amount of time for couple and family activities, identify activity interests for each family member. Discuss time requirements for work and play. Arrange meeting with non-custodial parent to discuss visitation privileges based on child needs.		In process

Family Systems Stressor-Strength Inventory (FS³I)
Family Form

Family Name ___Brooks___   Date ___Feb 1___

Family Member Completing Assessment ___Judy___

Ethnic Background ___Scandinavian___

Referral Source ___Clinic Nurse___   Interviewer ___N. Nurse___

Family Members	Relationship in Family	Age	Marital Status	Education (highest degree)	Occupation
1. Judy	Mother	42	Widow	MS+	Teacher
2. Ann	Daughter	18	S	HS	College Student
3. Jane	Daughter	16	S		High school student
4.					
5.					
6.					

What is your current reason(s) for seeking health care assistance?

___death of my husband___

Part 1: Family Systems Stressors (General)

DIRECTIONS: Each of the 45 situations listed here deal with some aspect of normal family life.[a] They have the potential for creating tension within family members, between family members, or between families and external environment. We are interested in your overall impression of how these situations affect your family life. Please circle a number (1 through 5) that best describes the amount of stress or tension they create for you. Thank you for cooperation.

	N/A	Little Stress		Medium Stress		High Stress
1. Family member(s) feeling un-appreciated	0	1	2	③	4	5
2. Guilt for not accomplishing more	0	1	2	③	4	5
3. Insufficient "me" time	0	1	2	3	④	5
4. Self-image/self-esteem/feelings of unattractiveness	0	1	②	3	4	5
5. Perfectionism	0	1	2	③	4	5
6. Dieting	0	1	②	3	4	5
7. Health/illness	0	1	②	3	4	5
8. Drugs/alcohol	0	①	2	3	4	5
9. Widowhood	0	1	2	3	4	⑤
10. Retirement	⓪	1	2	3	4	5
11. Homework/school grades	0	1	2	3	④	5
12. Communication with children	0	1	2	3	④	5
13. Housekeeping standards	0	1	2	③	4	5
14. Insufficient couple time	⓪	1	2	3	4	5
15. Insufficient family playtime	0	1	2	③	4	5
16. Children's behavior/discipline/sibling fighting	0	1	2	3	④	5
17. Television	0	①	2	3	4	5

18. Overscheduled family calendar   0   1   (2)   3   4   5

19. Lack of shared responsibility in the family   0   1   2   3   (4)   5

20. Moving   0   1   2   3   (4)   5

21. Spousal relationship (communication, friendship, sex)   (0)   1   2   3   4   5

22. Holidays   0   1   2   3   (4)   5

23. Inlaws   0   (1)   2   3   4   5

24. Teen behaviors (communication, music, friends, church, school)   0   1   2   3   4   (5)

25. New baby   (0)   1   2   3   4   5

26. Houseguests   0   1   2   (3)   4   5

27. Family vacations   0   (1)   2   3   4   5

28. Remarriage   (0)   1   2   3   4   5

29. Relationship with former spouse   (0)   1   2   3   4   5

30. Summer   0   (1)   2   3   4   5

31. Weekends   0   (1)   2   3   4   5

32. Religious differences   0   (1)   2   3   4   5

33. Predinner hour   0   1   2   (3)   4   5

34. Older parents   (0)   1   2   3   4   5

35. Economics/finances/budgets   0   1   2   3   (4)   5

36. Unhappiness with work situation   0   1   (2)   3   4   5

37. Overvolunteerism   0   (1)   2   3   4   5

38. Neighbors   0   (1)   2   3   4   5

39. Unemployment	0	1	2	③	4	5
40. Nuclear and environmental fears	0	①	2	3	4	5
41. Church-school activities	0	1	②	3	4	5
42. Unsatisfactory housing	0	①	2	3	4	5
43. Organized sports activities	0	①	2	3	4	5
44. Change in work patterns	0	①	2	3	4	5
45. Two-paycheck family	⓪	1	2	3	4	5

Part II: Family Systems Stressors (Specific)

DIRECTIONS: The following 10 questions are designed to provide specific information about tension producing situations, problems, or areas of concern influencing your family's health.[b] Please circle a number (1 through 5) that best describes the influence this situation has on your family's life.
What do you consider your major stressful situation, problem, or concern at this time?

The sudden death of my 46-year-old husband from

a heart attack and the effect of this loss on

each family member and on the family as a unit

	N/A	Little or None		Medium		Very much
1. To what extent is your family bothered by this problem or stressful situation?	0	1	2	3	4	⑤
2. How much of an effect does this stressful situation have on your family's usual pattern of living?	0	1	2	3	4	⑤
3. How much has this situation affected your family's ability to work together as a family unit?	0	1	2	3	4	⑤

Has your family ever experienced a similar concern in the past?

YES _____ If YES, complete question 4

NO __✓__ If NO, proceed to question 5

	N/A	Little or None		Medium		Very much
4. How successful was your family in dealing with this situation/problem/concern in the past?	0	1	2	3	4	5
5. How strongly do you feel this current situation/problem/concern will affect your family's future?	0	1	2	3	4	(5)
6. To what extent are family members able to help themselves in this present situation/problem/concern?	0	1	2	(3)	4	5
7. To what extent do you expect others to help your family with this situation/problem/concern?	0	1	2	(3)	4	5

	N/A	Poor	Satisfactory		Excellent
8. Rate the overall health status of your family as a whole.	0	1	2	3	(4)	5

9. Rate the overall health status of each family member by name.

Name	N/A	Poor	Satisfactory		Excellent
Judy	0	1	(2)	3	4	5
Ann	0	1	2	(3)	4	5
Jane	0	1	2	(3)	4	5
	0	1	2	3	4	5
	0	1	2	3	4	5

Part III: Family Systems Strengths

DIRECTIONS: Each of the twenty traits/attributes listed below deals with some aspect of family life.[c] Each one contributes to the health and well-being of family members as individuals and to the family as a whole. Please circle a number (1 through 5) that best describes the extent to which family members use these traits.

My Family:	N/A	Seldom		Usually		Always
1. Communicates and listens to one another	0	1	2	3	(4)	5
2. Affirms and supports one another	0	1	2	3	(4)	5
3. Teaches respect for others	0	1	2	3	(4)	5
4. Develops a sense of trust in members	0	1	2	3	(4)	5
5. Has a sense of play and humor	0	1	2	3	(4)	5
6. Exhibits a sense of shared responsibility	0	1	2	(3)	4	5
7. Teaches a sense of right and wrong	0	1	2	3	4	(5)
8. Has a strong sense of family in which rituals and traditions abound	0	1	2	3	4	(5)

9. Has a balance of interaction among members	0	1	2	(3)	4	5
10. Has a shared religious core	0	1	2	3	(4)	5
11. Respects the privacy of one another	0	1	2	3	(4)	5
12. Values service to others	0	1	2	3	(4)	5
13. Fosters family table time and conversation	0	1	2	(3)	4	5
14. Shares leisure time	0	1	2	(3)	4	5
15. Admits to and seeks help with problems	0	1	2	3	(4)	5
16. Honors its elders	0	1	2	3	(4)	5
17. Accepts and encourages individual values	0	1	2	3	(4)	5
18. Values work satisfaction	0	1	2	3	(4)	5
19. Is financially secure	0	1	(2)	3	4	5
20. Is able to let go of grown children	0	1	2	3	(4)	5

[a]Based on Curran, D. 1985. **Stress and the healthy family.** Minneapolis: Winston Press.

[b]Based on Neuman's Systems Model. Neuman, B. 1989. **The Neuman systems model.** Norwalk, CT: Appleton-Lange.

[c]Based on Curran, D. 1983. **Traits of a healthy family.** Minneapolis: Winston Press.

Family Systems Stressor-Strength Inventory (FS³I)
Family Form

Family Name <u>Brooks</u>   Date <u>Feb 1</u>

Family Member Completing Assessment <u>Ann</u>

Ethnic Background <u>American (Scandinavian)</u>

Referral Source <u>Clinic Nurse</u>   Interviewer <u>N. Nurse</u>

Family Members	Relationship in Family	Age	Marital Status	Education (highest degree)	Occupation
1. Judy	Mother	42	Widow	MS+	Teacher
2. Ann	Daughter	18	S	HS	College student
3. Jane	Daughter	16	S		High school student
4.					
5.					
6.					

What is your current reason(s) for seeking health care assistance?

<u>death of father</u>

Part 1: Family Systems Stressors (General)

DIRECTIONS: Each of the 45 situations listed here deal with some aspect of normal family life.[a] They have the potential for creating tension within family members, between family members, or between families and external environment. We are interested in your overall impression of how these situations affect your family life. Please circle a number (1 through 5) that best describes the amount of stress or tension they create for you. Thank you for cooperation.

	N/A	Little Stress		Medium Stress		High Stress
1. Family member(s) feeling un-appreciated	0	1	2	(3)	4	5
2. Guilt for not accomplishing more	0	1	2	(3)	4	5
3. Insufficient "me" time	0	(1)	2	3	4	5
4. Self-image/self-esteem/feelings of unattractiveness	0	(1)	2	3	4	5
5. Perfectionism	0	1	(2)	3	4	5
6. Dieting	0	1	2	3	(4)	5
7. Health/illness	0	(1)	2	3	4	5
8. Drugs/alcohol	0	(1)	2	3	4	5
9. Widowhood	0	1	2	3	4	(5)
10. Retirement	(0)	1	2	3	4	5
11. Homework/school grades	0	1	2	3	4	(5)
12. Communication with children	(0)	1	2	3	4	5
13. Housekeeping standards	0	1	2	3	4	(5)
14. Insufficient couple time	(0)	1	2	3	4	5
15. Insufficient family playtime	(0)	1	2	3	4	5
16. Children's behavior/discipline/sibling fighting	0	1	2	3	4	(5)
17. Television	0	(1)	2	3	4	5

18. Overscheduled family calendar   0   1   (2)   3   4   5

19. Lack of shared responsibility in the family   0   1   2   (3)   4   5

20. Moving   (0)   1   2   3   4   5

21. Spousal relationship (communication, friendship, sex)   (0)   1   2   3   4   5

22. Holidays   0   1   2   3   4   (5)

23. Inlaws   (0)   1   2   3   4   5

24. Teen behaviors (communication, music, friends, church, school)   0   1   2   3   4   (5)

25. New baby   (0)   1   2   3   4   5

26. Houseguests   (0)   1   2   3   4   5

27. Family vacations   0   1   2   3   4   (5)

28. Remarriage   (0)   1   2   3   4   5

29. Relationship with former spouse   (0)   1   2   3   4   5

30. Summer   0   (1)   2   3   4   5

31. Weekends   0   1   2   (3)   4   5

32. Religious differences   0   (1)   2   3   4   5

33. Predinner hour   (0)   1   2   3   4   5

34. Older parents   (0)   1   2   3   4   5

35. Economics/finances/budgets   0   1   2   3   (4)   5

36. Unhappiness with work situation   (0)   1   2   3   4   5

37. Overvolunteerism   0   (1)   2   3   4   5

38. Neighbors   0   (1)   2   3   4   5

39. Unemployment	0	①	2	3	4	5
40. Nuclear and environmental fears	⓪	1	2	3	4	5
41. Church-school activities	0	①	2	3	4	5
42. Unsatisfactory housing	0	①	2	3	4	5
43. Organized sports activities	0	1	②	3	4	5
44. Change in work patterns	0	1	2	3	④	5
45. Two-paycheck family	0	①	2	3	4	5

Part II: Family Systems Stressors (Specific)

DIRECTIONS: The following 10 questions are designed to provide specific information about tension producing situations, problems, or areas of concern influencing your family's health.[b] Please circle a number (1 through 5) that best describes the influence this situation has on your family's life.

What do you consider your major stressful situation, problem, or concern at this time?

death of my father
_____

_____

_____

		Little or None		Medium		Very much
	N/A					
1. To what extent is your family bothered by this problem or stressful situation?	0	1	2	3	4	⑤
2. How much of an effect does this stressful situation have on your family's usual pattern of living?	0	1	2	3	4	⑤
3. How much has this situation affected your family's ability to work together as a family unit?	0	1	2	3	4	⑤

Has your family ever experienced a similar concern in the past?

YES _____ If YES, complete question 4

NO __✓__ If NO, proceed to question 5

	N/A	Little or None		Medium		Very much
4. How successful was your family in dealing with this situation/problem/concern in the past?	0	1	2	3	4	5
5. How strongly do you feel this current situation/problem/concern will affect your family's future?	0	1	2	3	4	(5)
6. To what extent are family members able to help themselves in this present situation/problem/concern?	0	1	2	(3)	4	5
7. To what extent do you expect others to help your family with this situation/problem/concern?	0	1	(2)	3	4	5

	N/A	Poor	Satisfactory		Excellent
8. Rate the overall health status of your family as a whole.	0	1	2	3	4	(5)

9. Rate the overall health status of each family member by name.

Name	N/A					
Judy	0	1	2	3	4	(5)
Ann	0	1	2	3	4	(5)
Jane	0	1	2	3	4	(5)
_____	0	1	2	3	4	5
_____	0	1	2	3	4	5

Part III: Family Systems Strengths

DIRECTIONS: Each of the twenty traits/attributes listed below deals
with some aspect of family life.[c] Each one contributes to the health
and well-being of family members as individuals and to the family as
a whole. Please circle a number (1 through 5) that best describes the
extent to which family members use these traits.

My Family:	N/A	Seldom		Usually		Always
1. Communicates and listens to one another	0	1	(2)	3	4	5
2. Affirms and supports one another	0	1	2	(3)	4	5
3. Teaches respect for others	0	1	2	3	(4)	5
4. Develops a sense of trust in members	0	1	2	(3)	4	5
5. Has a sense of play and humor	0	1	2	(3)	4	5
6. Exhibits a sense of shared responsibility	0	1	(2)	3	4	5
7. Teaches a sense of right and wrong	0	1	2	3	4	(5)
8. Has a strong sense of family in which rituals and traditions abound	0	1	2	(3)	4	5

9. Has a balance of interaction among members	0	1	(2)	3	4	5
10. Has a shared religious core	0	1	2	(3)	4	5
11. Respects 'the privacy of one another	0	1	2	(3)	4	5
12. Values service to others	0	1	2	(3)	4	5
13. Fosters family table time and conversation	0	1	(2)	3	4	5
14. Shares leisure time	0	1	2	(3)	4	5
15. Admits to and seeks help with problems	0	1	(2)	3	4	5
16. Honors its elders	0	1	2	3	(4)	5
17. Accepts and encourages individual values	0	1	2	(3)	4	5
18. Values work satisfaction	0	1	2	(3)	4	5
19. Is financially secure	0	(1)	2	3	4	5
20. Is able to let go of grown children	0	1	2	3	(4)	5

[a]Based on Curran, D. 1985. **Stress and the healthy family.** Minneapolis: Winston Press.

[b]Based on Neuman's Systems Model. Neuman, B. 1989. **The Neuman systems model.** Norwalk. CT: Appleton-Lange.

[c]Based on Curran, D. 1983. **Traits of a healthy family.** Minneapolis: Winston Press.

Family Systems Stressor-Strength Inventory (FS³I)
Family Form

Family Name ___Brooks___   Date ___Feb 1___

Family Member Completing Assessment ___Jane___

Ethnic Background ___Scandinavian___

Referral Source ___Clinic Nurse___   Interviewer ___N. Nurse___

Family Members	Relationship in Family	Age	Marital Status	Education (highest degree)	Occupation
1. Judy	Mother	42	Widow	MS+	Teacher
2. Ann	Daughter	18	S	HS	College student
3. Jane	Daughter	16	S		High school student
4.					
5.					
6.					

What is your current reason(s) for seeking health care assistance?

___death of my dad___

Part 1: Family Systems Stressors (General)

DIRECTIONS: Each of the 45 situations listed here deal with some aspect of normal family life.[a] They have the potential for creating tension within family members, between family members, or between families and external environment. We are interested in your overall impression of how these situations affect your family life. Please circle a number (1 through 5) that best describes the amount of stress or tension they create for you. Thank you for cooperation.

	N/A	Little Stress		Medium Stress		High Stress
1. Family member(s) feeling un-appreciated	0	1	2	(3)	4	5
2. Guilt for not accomplishing more	0	1	2	(3)	4	5
3. Insufficient "me" time	0	(1)	2	3	4	5
4. Self-image/self-esteem/feelings of unattractiveness	0	1	2	3	(4)	5
5. Perfectionism	0	(1)	2	3	4	5
6. Dieting	0	1	(2)	3	4	5
7. Health/illness	0	1	(2)	3	4	5
8. Drugs/alcohol	0	(1)	2	3	4	5
9. Widowhood	(0)	1	2	3	4	5
10. Retirement	(0)	1	2	3	4	5
11. Homework/school grades	0	1	2	3	4	(5)
12. Communication with children	(0)	1	2	3	4	5
13. Housekeeping standards	0	(1)	2	3	4	5
14. Insufficient couple time	(0)	1	2	3	4	5
15. Insufficient family playtime	(0)	1	2	3	4	5
16. Children's behavior/discipline/sibling fighting	0	1	(2)	3	4	5
17. Television	0	(1)	2	3	4	5

18. Overscheduled family calendar   0   (1) 2 3 4 5

19. Lack of shared responsibility in the family   0   (1) 2 3 4 5

20. Moving   (0) 1 2 3 4 5

21. Spousal relationship (communication, friendship, sex)   (0) 1 2 3 4 5

22. Holidays   0 1 2 3 4 (5)

23. Inlaws   0 (1) 2 3 4 5

24. Teen behaviors (communication, music, friends, church, school)   0 1 2 3 4 (5)

25. New baby   (0) 1 2 3 4 5

26. Houseguests   (0) 1 2 3 4 5

27. Family vacations   (0) 1 2 3 4 5

28. Remarriage   (0) 1 2 3 4 5

29. Relationship with former spouse   (0) 1 2 3 4 5

30. Summer   0 (1) 2 3 4 5

31. Weekends   0 1 2 (3) 4 5

32. Religious differences   (0) 1 2 3 4 5

33. Predinner hour   0 (1) 2 3 4 5

34. Older parents   (0) 1 2 3 4 5

35. Economics/finances/budgets   0 1 2 (3) 4 5

36. Unhappiness with work situation   (0) 1 2 3 4 5

37. Overvolunteerism   (0) 1 2 3 4 5

38. Neighbors   0 (1) 2 3 4 5

39. Unemployment	0	(1)	2	3	4	5
40. Nuclear and environmental fears	0	(1)	2	3	4	5
41. Church-school activities	0	1	(2)	3	4	5
42. Unsatisfactory housing	0	(1)	2	3	4	5
43. Organized sports activities	0	(1)	2	3	4	5
44. Change in work patterns	(0)	1	2	3	4	5
45. Two-paycheck family	(0)	1	2	3	4	5

Part II: Family Systems Stressors (Specific)

DIRECTIONS: The following 10 questions are designed to provide specific information about tension producing situations, problems, or areas of concern influencing your family's health.[b] Please circle a number (1 through 5) that best describes the influence this situation has on your family's life.
What do you consider your major stressful situation, problem, or concern at this time?

fighting with my mother

	N/A	Little or None		Medium		Very much
1. To what extent is your family bothered by this problem or stressful situation?	0	1	2	3	4	(5)
2. How much of an effect does this stressful situation have on your family's usual pattern of living?	0	1	2	3	4	(5)
3. How much has this situation affected your family's ability to work together as a family unit?	0	1	2	3	(4)	5

Has your family ever experienced a similar concern in the past?

YES _____ If YES, complete question 4

NO ___✓___ If NO, proceed to question 5

	N/A	Little or None		Medium		Very much
4. How successful was your family in dealing with this situation/problem/concern in the past?	0	1	2	3	4	5
5. How strongly do you feel this current situation/problem/concern will affect your family's future?	0	1	2	3	4	(5)
6. To what extent are family members able to help themselves in this present situation/problem/concern?	0	1	2	(3)	4	5
7. To what extent do you expect others to help your family with this situation/problem/concern?	0	1	2	(3)	4	5

	N/A	Poor	Satisfactory		Excellent
8. Rate the overall health status of your family as a whole.	0	1	2	(3)	4	5

9. Rate the overall health status of each family member by name.

Member	N/A	Poor		Satisfactory		Excellent
Mother, Judy	0	1	2	(3)	4	5
Ann	0	1	2	(3)	4	5
Jane	0	1	2	(3)	4	5
	0	1	2	3	4	5
	0	1	2	3	4	5

Part III: Family Systems Strengths

DIRECTIONS: Each of the twenty traits/attributes listed below deals with some aspect of family life.[c] Each one contributes to the health and well-being of family members as individuals and to the family as a whole. Please circle a number (1 through 5) that best describes the extent to which family members use these traits.

My Family:	N/A	Seldom		Usually		Always
1. Communicates and listens to one another	0	(1)	2	3	4	5
2. Affirms and supports one another	0	1	2	(3)	4	5
3. Teaches respect for others	0	1	2	3	4	(5)
4. Develops a sense of trust in members	0	1	2	3	(4)	5
5. Has a sense of play and humor	0	1	2	3	(4)	5
6. Exhibits a sense of shared responsibility	0	1	(2)	3	4	5
7. Teaches a sense of right and wrong	0	1	2	3	(4)	5
8. Has a strong sense of family in which rituals and traditions abound	0	1	2	(3)	4	5

9. Has a balance of interaction among members   0   1   2   (3)   4   5

10. Has a shared religious core   0   1   2   (3)   4   5

11. Respects the privacy of one another   0   1   2   (3)   4   5

12. Values service to others   0   1   2   (3)   4   5

13. Fosters family table time and conversation   0   1   2   (3)   4   5

14. Shares leisure time   0   1   (2)   3   4   5

15. Admits to and seeks help with problems   0   1   2   3   (4)   5

16. Honors its elders   0   1   (2)   3   4   5

17. Accepts and encourages individual values   0   1   (2)   3   4   5

18. Values work satisfaction   (0)   1   2   3   4   5

19. Is financially secure   0   1   2   (3)   4   5

20. Is able to let go of grown children   0   1   2   (3)   4   5

[a]Based on Curran, D. 1985. **Stress and the healthy family.** Minneapolis: Winston Press.

[b]Based on Neuman's Systems Model. Neuman, B. 1989. **The Neuman systems model.** Norwalk, CT: Appleton-Lange.

[c]Based on Curran, D. 1983. **Traits of a healthy family.** Minneapolis: Winston Press.

Family Systems Stressor-Strength Inventory (FS³I)
Clinician Form

Family Name   <u>Brooks</u>   Date   <u>Feb 1</u>

Part I: Family Systems Stressors (General)

Briefly discuss the 45 situations with the family member(s) and ask if
there are additional areas of concern. The purpose here is to begin
clarifying the family member(s) perceptions of stressful situations and
to zero in on their major area of concern.

<u>widowhood, teen behavior, sibling disagreements</u>

<u>with widowhood, rebuilding of family system</u>

Part II: Family Systems Stressors (Specific)

DIRECTIONS: The following 10 questions are designed to provide
specific information about the particular situation influencing the
family's health.[b] Please circle a number (1 through 5) that best
describes the influence this situation has on the family's health from
your point of view. Record the family response(s) and your
perceptions.

What do you consider to be the family's most stressful situation/
problem/or areas of concern at this time? (Identify problem area(s))

<u>Mother and Ann: major stressor is widowhood</u>

<u>Jane: fighting with mother</u>

		Little or none		Medium		Very Much
	N/A					
1. To what extent is the family bothered by this situation/ problem/concern? (Effects on psychosocial relationships communication, interactions)	0	1	2	3	4	(5)

Family Response
Family never faced a death as painful or
upsetting as this one. All interactions are
affected.
Clinician Perceptions
Family system extremely upset, unstable, and
vulnerable to additional stressors. Learning
to take one day at a time.

	N/A	**Little or none**		**Medium**		**Very Much**
2. How much alteration in the family's usual pattern of living is occurring as a result of this situation/problem/concern? (Identify life-style patterns and developmental tasks)	0	1	2	3	4	(5)

Family Response
Everything has changed in family since death of Mr. Brooks. Life—style patterns of eating together to not knowing what to do to build a new family system.

Clinician Perceptions
Family system changed. Sibling patterns of communication and relating to each other and to mother has changed.

	N/A	**Little or none**		**Medium**		**Very Much**
3. How much has this situation affected the family's ability to work together as a family unit? (Identify roles and tasks and how these are being altered.)	0	1	2	3	4	(5)

Family Response
Not working together optimally because of role changes and having to assume new and different tasks.

Clinician Perceptions
Beginning to work together. Mother willing to talk about her grief but not necessarily with children. Role of parent has changed. Mother is struggling to control family by exerting power formerly held by husband. Children seem to resent this.

	Little				**Very**
N/A	or none		Medium		Much
⓪	1	2	3	4	5

4. Has the family ever experienced similar situations in the past? If so describe what the family did. How successful were they in resolving the situation/problem/concern? (Identify past coping patterns, adaptive strategies, and what success means to family.)

Family Response

No previous deaths in immediate family

Clinician Perceptions

Deaths in extended family; family able to deal with deaths of aunt and uncle but nuclear unit jeopardized by death event.

	Little				**Very**
N/A	or none		Medium		Much
0	1	2	3	4	⑤

5. How strongly do you think the present situation/problem/concern will affect the family and family members in the future? What effects do you expect? What are the anticipated consequences? (Identify current and potential coping patterns.)

Family Response

Will greatly affect family if it can't move past this event.

Clinician Perceptions

Family system needs assistance in dealing with grieving process. Mother turns to extrafamily support while children look to her for support. Mother able to provide only minimal emotional support at this time.

		Little			**Very**
	N/A	**or none**	**Medium**		**Much**

6. To what extent are family   0   1   2   ③   4   5
members able to help them-
selves in the present
situation/problem/concern?
Identify self-assistive behaviors, family expectations,
and spiritual influence.

Family Response
Taking one day at a time and handling grief that
way. Asking for God's help with the pain and
frustration and loss.

Clinician Perceptions
Talk with extended family, expressing range of
grieving patterns from excessive crying to no
crying. Talking about life beyond death and
how spiritual beliefs are sustaining and
uplifting.

		Little			**Very**
	N/A	**or none**	**Medium**		**Much**

7. To what extent does the   0   1   2   ③   4   5
family expect others to assist
them with their present situation? What roles do family
members expect others to
play? (Describe roles and
availability of extrafamily
resources.)

Family Response
No one can change the situation. Mother will
assume dual parent role.

Clinician Perceptions
Family and friends offer to help with household tasks and work responsibilities. House
mortgage paid off because of insurance policy.
Social Security benefits for younger daughter.

	N/A	Poor		Satisfactory		Excellent
8. Describe the overall health status of the family system. Consider four major categories: physical status, psychosocial characteristics, developmental characteristics, and spiritual influence	0	1	2	3	(4)	5

Family Response
Ann has allergies; other members' health okay.
Mother and daughter conflict

Clinician Perceptions
Mother and Jane: interactional and communication conflict; power conflicts.

9. Rate the overall health status of each family member using 5 variables as reference points: physiological, psychological, developmental, sociocultural, and spiritual influence.

	N/A	Poor		Satisfactory		Excellent
a. Judy	0	1	2	3	(4)	5
b. Ann	0	1	2	3	(4)	5
c. Jane	0	1	2	3	4	(5)
d.	0	1	2	3	4	5
e.	0	1	2	3	4	5

Family Response
Mother has had episodes of depression.

Clinician Perceptions
Episodes of depression are under control. Judy has had psychiatric assistance in the past.

Part III: Family Systems Strengths

DIRECTIONS: Each of the 20 trait and/or attributes listed here deal with some aspect of family life.[c] Each one contributes to the health and well-being of family members as individuals and to family as a whole. Briefly describe your perception of how these strengths are operationalized in this family and circle the number (1 through 5) that best describes the extent to which they are used.

This Family:	N/A	Seldom or not at all		Usually		Always
1. Communicates and listens to one another	0	1	(2)	3	4	5

Clinician Perceptions
Mother-daughter conflict

2. Affirms and supports one another	0	1	(2)	3	4	5

Clinician Perceptions

3. Teaches respect for others	0	1	2	3	4	(5)

Clinician Perceptions

4. Develops a sense of trust in members	0	1	2	(3)	4	5

Clinician Perceptions

5. Has a sense of play and humor	0	1	2	3	(4)	5

Clinician Perceptions
Know how to have fun together; shopping

6. Exhibits a sense of shared responsibility	0	1	(2)	3	4	5

Clinician Perceptions
Ann has increased responsibility for keeping family stable

7. Teaches a sense of right   0   1   2   3   4   ⑤
   and wrong

Clinician Perceptions

8. Has a strong sense of   0   1   2   3   4   ⑤
   family in which rituals
   and traditions abound

Clinician Perceptions

All holidays and birthdays celebrated

9. Has a balance of interac-   0   1   2   ③   4   5
   tion among members

Clinician Perceptions

10. Has a shared religious   0   1   2   3   4   ⑤
    core

Clinician Perceptions

11. Respects the privacy of   0   1   2   ③   4   5
    one another

Clinician Perceptions

12. Values service to others   0   1   2   3   ④   5

Clinician Perceptions

Cards, food, calls to friends who are in need

13. Fosters family table time   0   1   2   ③   4   5
    and conversation

Clinician Perceptions

More so when dad was alive

14. Shares leisure time   0   1   2   (3)   4   5

Clinician Perceptions
More when dad was living

15. Admits to and seeks help   0   1   (2)   3   4   5
    with problems

Clinician Perceptions
Easier for mother than children

16. Honors its elders   0   1   2   3   4   (5)

Clinician Perceptions

17. Accepts and encourages   0   1   2   (3)   4   5
    individual values

Clinician Perceptions
 If not too "far out"

18. Values work satisfaction   0   1   2   3   (4)   5

Clinician Perceptions

19. Is financially secure   0   1   (2)   3   4   5

Clinician Perceptions
 Money will be a problem now--college expenses

20. Is able to let go of grown   0   1   2   3   (4)   5
    children

Clinician Perceptions
 Children want to be independent but not financially able to do so

[a]Based on Curran, D. 1985. **Stress and the healthy family.** Minneapolis: Winston Press.

[b]Based on Neuman's Systems Model. Neuman, B. 1989. **The Neuman systems model.** Norwalk, CT: Appleton–Lange.

[c]Based on Curran, D. 1983. **Traits of a healthy family.** Minneapolis: Winston Press.

Family Systems Stressor-Strength Inventory (FS³I) Summary Form

Family Name <u>Brooks</u>   Date <u>Feb 1</u>

Family Member(s) Completing Assessment <u>Judy, Ann, Jane</u>

Ethnic Background(s) <u>Scandinavian</u>

Religious Background(s) <u>Lutheran</u>

Referral Source <u>Clinic Nurse</u>   Interviewer <u>N. Nurse</u>

Family Members	Relationship in Family	Age	Marital Status	Education (highest degree)	Occupation
1. Judy	Mother	42	widow	MS+	Teacher
2. Ann	Daughter	18	S	HS	College student
3. Jane	Daughter	16	S		High school student
4.					
5.					
6.					

Family's current reason for seeking health care assistance?

<u>death of father and husband</u>

<u>daughter Jane fighting with mother</u>

Scoring Key

Family Member Perceptions
Section 1: Family Form

Part I Family Systems Stressors (General)

Add scores from questions 1 to 45 and calculate an overall score for Family Systems Stressors (General). Ratings are from 1 (most positive) to 5 (most negative). Subscale scores range from 45 to 225.

Family Systems Stressors (General) Score

$$\frac{(\quad)}{45} \times 1 = \underline{\hspace{2cm}}$$

Judy $91/45 = 2.0$

Ann $84/45 = 1.9$

Jane $52/45 = 1.2$

Graph subscale score on Quantitative Summary Form: Family Systems Stressors: General, Family Member Perceptions.

A. Intrafamily Systems Subscale Score:

Add scores from questions 1-11 and calculate a subscale score. Ratings are from 1 (most positive) to 5 (most negative). Subscale scores range from 11 to 55.

Intrafamily Systems Stressors Score

$$\frac{(\quad)}{11} \times 1 = \underline{\hspace{2cm}}$$

Judy $24/11 = 2.2$

Ann $26/11 = 2.4$

Jane $22/22 = 2.0$

Graph score on Quantitative Summary Form: Family Systems Stressors (Intrafamily), Family Member Perceptions.

Family Member Perceptions
Section 1: Family Form

B. Interfamily Systems Subscale Score:

Add scores from questions 12-34 only and calculate a subscale score. Ratings are from 1 (most positive) to 5 (most negative). Scores range from 23 to 115.
Interfamily Systems Stressors Score

$$\frac{(\quad)}{23} \times 1 = \underline{\quad\quad\quad}$$

Judy 32/23 = 1.4
Ann 45/23 = 2.0
Jane 22/23 = 1.1

Graph subscale score on Quantitative Summary Form, Family Systems Stressors (Interfamily), Family Member Perceptions.

C. Extrafamily Systems Subscale Score:

Add scores from questions 35-45 and calculate a subscale score. Ratings are from 1 (most positive) to 5 (most negative). Scores range from 11 to 55.
Extrafamily Systems Stressors Score

$$\frac{(\quad)}{11} \times 1 = \underline{\quad\quad\quad}$$

Judy 17/11 = 1.5
Ann 16/11 = 1.5
Jane 10/11 - 1.1

Graph subscale score on Quantitative Summary Form: Family Systems Stressors (Extrafamily), Family Member Perceptions.

Part II Family Systems Stressors (Specific)

Add scores from questions 1 to 8 only and calculate a score for Family Systems Stressors (Specific). Ratings are from 1 (most positive) to 5 (most negative). Questions 4, 6, 7, and 8 are reverse scored.* Scores range from 8 to 40.

Family Systems Stressors (Specific) Score

$$\frac{(\quad)}{8} \times 1 = \underline{\qquad}$$

Judy 28/8 = 3.5

Ann   28/8 = 3.5

Jane 28/8 = 3.5

Graph score on Quantitative Summary Form: Family Systems Stressors (Specific) Family Member Perceptions. Scores for question 9 are recorded on Qualitative Summary Form 2D: Family Systems Stressors (Specific).

Part III Family Systems Strengths

Add scores from questions 1 to 20 and calculate a score for Family Systems Strengths. Ratings are from 1 (seldom used) to 5 (always used). Scores range from 20 to 100.

Family Systems Strengths Score

$$\frac{(\quad)}{20} \times 1 = \underline{\qquad}$$

Judy 76/20 = 3.8

Ann 58/20 = 2.9

Jane 57/20 = 2.7

Graph score on Quantitative Summary Form: Family Systems Strengths.

*Reverse Scoring:

Question answered as **one** is scored as 5 points

Question answered as **two** is scored as 4 points

Question answered as **three** is scored as 3 points

Question answered as **four** is scored as 2 points

Question answered as **five** is scored as 1 point

Clinician Perceptions
Section 2: Clinician Form

Part I Family Systems Stressors (General)

Identify predominant tension producing situations from list of 45 situations/problems/concerns and prioritize them in order of importance to family. Record on Qualitative Summary Form: Family Systems Stressors (General).

Additional Comments:

General Stressors: General systems stressors are at flexible and normal lines of defense.

Intrafamily: Individual family members have range of variability about their individual stressors, e.g., widowhood, self-image/self-esteem, holidays.

Interfamily Teen behavior, mother-daughter conflict, feelings of not being appreciated by family members.

Extrafamily: Economics, finances, budgets

Part II Family Systems Stressors (Specific)

Calculate quantitative scores for questions 1 to 8 in same manner as for Section 1, Part II. Family Member Perceptions. Graph on Quantitative Summary Form for Family Systems Stressors (Specific), Clinician Perceptions. 28/8 = 3.5

Identify specific tension producing situation/problem/concern that is influencing family health and record on Qualitative Summary Form 2A: Family Systems Stressors (Specific).

Part III Family Systems Strengths

Calculate quantitative scores for questions 1 to 20 in same manner as for Section 1, Part III. Family Member Perceptions. Graph on Quantitative Summary Form for Family Systems Strengths, Clinician Perceptions.

Identify Family Systems Strengths that contribute to family stability, health and can serve as a basis for prevention/intervention activities. Record on Qualitative Summary Form Part III: Family Systems Strengths.
64/20 = 3.2

Respect for each other's values and beliefs.
Shared religious core, desire to work
through grieving process as a family system,
but need distance to do so.

Quantitative Summary

DIRECTIONS: Graph the scores from each family member inventory by placing an "X" at the appropriate location and connect with a line. (Use first name initial for each line.)

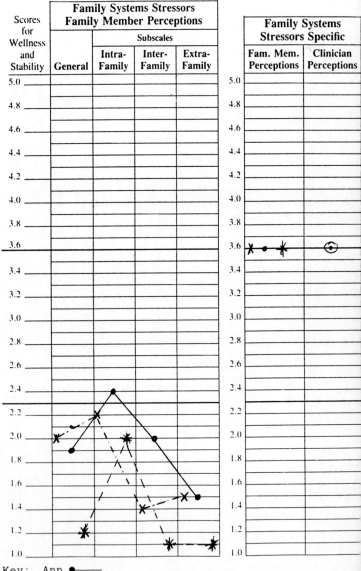

Key: Ann ●———
     Judy X—·—·—·—
     Jane *———

Key: Ann ●— Judy X—·— Jane ✳

Sum of strengths available for prevention/ intervention mode	Family Systems Strengths	
	Family Member Perceptions	Clinician Perceptions
5.0		
4.8		
4.6		
4.4		
4.2		
4.0		
3.8	X	
3.6		
3.4		
3.2		⊙
3.0		
2.8	●	
2.6	✳	
2.4		
2.2		
2.0		
1.8		
1.6		
1.4		
1.2		
1.0		

*PRIMARY Prevention Intervention Mode: Flexible Line   ) 1.0-2.3
*SECONDARY Prevention Intervention Mode: Normal Line   ) 2.4-3.6
*TERTIARY Prevention Intervention Mode: Resistance Lines) 3.7-5.0
*Breakdown of numerical scores for stressor penetration are suggested values

Qualitative Summary*
(Family and Clinician Perceptions)

Part I: Family Systems Stressors: General

Identify predominant tension producing situation(s) in family and list
them in order of importance to the family.

Situation/Problem/Concern	Priority for Family
1. Grieving over death of husband and father	Grieving process
2. Widowhood	Adjustment to changes in family structure, function
3.	
4. Mother-daughter conflict	Power conflict
5. Economics	Economics

Comments:

*Combines information from Family Form and Clinician Form.

Part II: Family Systems Stressors: Specific

Identify specific tension producing situation/problem/concern
influencing family health.

Death of father and spouse
_____

Mother-daughter conflict
_____

_____

_____

_____

_____

Comments:

Part II: Family Systems Stressors: Specific

B. Summarize perceptions of the specific family situation/problem/ concern and identify discrepancies between family and clinician perceptions.

Stressor (Situation)	Family Perception
1. Extent family bothered by situation/problem/concern: effects on psychosocial relationships, communications, and interactions	Communication & interaction different, mother-daughter conflict, problem-solving process new
2. Alterations in usual life-style patterns and family developmental tasks	Must learn new roles. Mother assumes more roles. No longer a balanced family.
3. Effects on family's ability to work together: alteration in roles and tasks	Learning how to work together again & assume new roles; not working well currently
4. Similar situations, problems, concerns: family's past coping patterns; what "success" means to family	Never experienced death of spouse before. Teen behavior was small problem before father's death—not larger.
5. Effects of present situation on family health in future: anticipated consequences; current and potential coping patterns	Coping on day-by-day basis. Don't know overall effects except life will never be the same.
6. Family's ability to help themselves in situation: self-assistive behaviors; family expectations and spiritual influence	Spiritual belief in God is sustaining for all. Daughter trying to work together but dislikes mother's gentleman friend interfering.
7. Family expectations of others and their role in helping family: extrafamily resources and their role	Help from paternal and maternal grandparents, relatives, and friends.

Clinician Perception	Discrepancies
Family structure altered functions rearranged. Change in roles, goals, boundaries, subsystems, and sharing of responsibilities. Much problem-solving done by father.	Daughter wants more time with mother.
Total alteration in life style patterns	None
Trying out new roles. Mother dislikes total responsibility for family & financial adjustments. Ability to work together taxed.	None
Family wants to be happy again and function as well as it had before	None
Family basic structure intact despite loss of a member. Coping as totally changed unit. Jane needs to express feelings about dad's death.	Focus on coping together as a family system. Jane doesn't want to work together; isolates herself.
Daughters banding together more with each other than with mother.	None
Mother more dependent on extended family than daughters. Wants outside help to "make them feel better."	Mother seems more dependent on help from others than daughters

C. Summarize significant health status data for each family member using five variables.

	Family Member 1 Judy	Family Member 2 Ann	Family Member 3 Jane
Physiological	Minimal emotional & physical energy; not able to carry out daily tasks as before	Feels physically drained, tired. Allergies under control. High BP, chol	Eating poorly, sleeping poorly
Psychological	Cries often; sad; angry that husband died & that it could have been prevented; may be grieving	Feels she could have saved dad if she did CPR "better"; sad, quiet, in pain; controls emotions	Acts out anger, hostility; fights with mom; doesn't express sadness in typical grief patterns. Idolized dad as friend, parent
Developmental	Family with teens, but tasks now on hold	Assumes parent role of mother and sister	Teenage behavior; acting out; looking for security
Sociocultural	Many friends; help from friends, LOA from work with pay. Economics a problem (college tuition)	Grandparents & relatives major supports; mom not as supportive as she wants, needs	Grandparents major source of strength, not mother
Spiritual	Belief in God sustaining during period of grief	Prayer & belief in God help to focus on fact that she "will see dad again"	Wonders why God allowed this to happen

Family Member 4	Family Member 5	Family Member 6

D. Using the four major categories of the family system, combine significant health status data from family member variables.

Major Category	Family System
Psychological Relationship	Interaction patterns stressful. Individual family member needs unmet. Family trying to adjust to loss of family & stabilize system. Decision making, coping styles, role relationships, communication styles, and power changed in family system.
Physical Status	All members in good physical health except for feelings surrounding grieving; i.e., emotional and physical energy drain.
Spiritual Influence	Family in developmental phase of family with teenagers. Family system tasks changed: ways of gettig money, communicating not as open; ways of expecting teen behavior not predictable.
Developmental Characteristics	Belief in God & recognition of "His help in time of trouble" sustaining theme. Extended family shares Christian orientation & can support family with grief process.

Part III: Family Systems Strengths

Identify family systems strengths that contribute to family stability and support actual and potential prevention/intervention activities.

Family Systems Strengths
1. Respect and sense for others. Trusts family members.
2. Shared religious core.
3. Trust each other and respect privacy of others.
4. Share time together; leisure time; table talk.
5. Admit to and seek help with problems.
6. Desire to cope together as a family system.
7.

Part IV: Family Care Plan*
List the three most significant clinician diagnoses (prioritize).

Diagnosis General and Specific Family Systems Stressors	Family Systems Strengths Supporting Family Care Plan	Goals Family and Clinician
1. Compromised family coping at normal lines of defense & resistance due to death of spouse, father	Respect for self and others Trust in family members Respect for privacy of others	Facilitate grieving process.
2. Impaired communication, interaction, & obedience patterns at normal lines of defense exacerbated by family loss.	Share time together Admit to & seek help with problems Desire to cope as family unit	Clarify role relationship & interaction
3. Significant alteration in daughter age/stage behavioral patterns at lines of defense due to death of dad.		Provide information to adolescent, i.e., appropriate, acceptable, & reasonable behaviors

| Prevention/Intervention Mode | | Outcomes |
Primary, Secondary, or Tertiary	Prevention/Intervention Activities	Evaluation and Replanning
Secondary and tertiary: Support & respect family's coping measures by providing therapeutic environment for expression of grief. Assist family to use internal resources to stabilize system, i.e., spiritual influence, caring time. Build therapeutic relationship based on caring concept. Teach family members about grieving process.		In process
Secondary: Assist family to clarify roles, rules, lines of communication, feedback loops. Develop measures that involve family members in decision making & shared power. Identify ways by which affection & intimacy needs can be met.		In process
Primary and secondary: Encourage use of family counseling. Discuss "normal" adolescent behavior & what it means in family context. Practice ways by which open dialogue can be maintained with family unit.		In process

Family Systems Stressor-Strength Inventory (FS³I)
Family Form

Family Name ___Gardner___   Date ___Feb.22___

Family Member Completing Assessment ___Robert___

Ethnic Background ___English/Swedish___

Referral Source Community health Interviewer ___N. Nurse___
                 nurse

Family Members	Relationship in Family	Age	Marital Status	Education (highest degree)	Occupation
1. Robert	husband	56	M	PhD	teacher
2. Peggy	wife	51	M	PhD	teacher
3. Betty Harmon	maternal mother	82	M	HS	retired housewife
4. Kenny Harmon	maternal father	81	M	HS	retired railroad
5.					
6.					

What is your current reason(s) for seeking health care assistance?

Betty diagnosed with ovarian cancer. Surgical
debulkment of tumor. Discharge planning to
home.

Part 1: Family Systems Stressors (General)

DIRECTIONS: Each of the 45 situations listed here deal with some aspect of normal family life.[a] They have the potential for creating tension within family members, between family members, or between families and external environment. We are interested in your overall impression of how these situations affect your family life. Please circle a number (1 through 5) that best describes the amount of stress or tension they create for you. Thank you for cooperation.

	N/A	Little Stress		Medium Stress		High Stress
1. Family member(s) feeling unappreciated	0	1	2	(3)	4	5
2. Guilt for not accomplishing more	0	1	2	(3)	4	5
3. Insufficient "me" time	0	1	2	3	(4)	5
4. Self-image/self-esteem/feelings of unattractiveness	0	1	2	3	(4)	5
5. Perfectionism	0	1	2	3	(4)	5
6. Dieting	0	(1)	2	3	4	5
7. Health/illness	0	(1)	2	3	4	5
8. Drugs/alcohol	0	(1)	2	3	4	5
9. Widowhood	(0)	1	2	3	4	5
10. Retirement	(0)	1	2	3	4	5
11. Homework/school grades	(0)	1	2	3	4	5
12. Communication with children	0	1	2	(3)	4	5
13. Housekeeping standards	0	(1)	2	3	4	5
14. Insufficient couple time	0	1	2	3	4	(5)
15. Insufficient family playtime	0	1	2	3	4	(5)
16. Children's behavior/discipline/sibling fighting	(0)	1	2	3	4	5
17. Television	0	(1)	2	3	4	5

18. Overscheduled family calen-   0   1   2   3   4   (5)
    dar

19. Lack of shared responsibility   0   1   2   3   (4)   5
    in the family

20. Moving   0   (1)   2   3   4   5

21. Spousal relationship (commu-   0   1   2   3   4   (5)
    nication, friendship, sex)

22. Holidays   0   1   (2)   3   4   5

23. Inlaws   0   1   2   3   4   (5)

24. Teen behaviors (communica-   (0)   1   2   3   4   5
    tion, music, friends, church,
    school)

25. New baby   (0)   1   2   3   4   5

26. Houseguests   (0)   1   2   3   4   5

27. Family vacations   0   1   2   (3)   4   5

28. Remarriage   (0)   1   2   3   4   5

29. Relationship with former   (0)   1   2   3   4   5
    spouse

30. Summer   0   1   2   3   (4)   5

31. Weekends   0   1   2   3   (4)   5

32. Religious differences   0   1   (2)   3   4   5

33. Predinner hour   0   (1)   2   3   4   5

34. Older parents   0   1   2   3   4   (5)

35. Economics/finances/budgets   0   1   2   (3)   4   5

36. Unhappiness with work situa-   0   1   (2)   3   4   5
    tion

37. Overvolunteerism   0   1   2   3   (4)   5

38. Neighbors   0   (1)   2   3   4   5

39. Unemployment	(0)	1	2	3	4	5
40. Nuclear and environmental fears	0	1	(2)	3	4	5
41. Church-school activities	(0)	1	2	3	4	5
42. Unsatisfactory housing	0	1	2	(3)	4	5
43. Organized sports activities	(0)	1	2	3	4	5
44. Change in work patterns	0	1	2	3	(4)	5
45. Two-paycheck family	0	1	2	3	(4)	5

Part II: Family Systems Stressors (Specific)

DIRECTIONS: The following 10 questions are designed to provide specific information about tension producing situations, problems, or areas of concern influencing your family's health.[b] Please circle a number (1 through 5) that best describes the influence this situation has on your family's life.

What do you consider your major stressful situation, problem, or concern at this time?

Help to provide care for Peggy's aging and ill

parents who live in another state. Peggy is

worried and is gone a lot.

	N/A	Little or None		Medium		Very much
1. To what extent is your family bothered by this problem or stressful situation?	0	1	2	3	4	(5)
2. How much of an effect does this stressful situation have on your family's usual pattern of living?	0	1	2	3	4	(5)
3. How much has this situation affected your family's ability to work together as a family unit?	0	1	2	3	(4)	5

Has your family ever experienced a similar concern in the past?

YES ⟋ If YES, complete question 4

NO _____ If NO, proceed to question 5

	N/A	Little or None		Medium		Very much
4. How successful was your family in dealing with this situation/problem/concern in the past?	0	1	2	3	(4)	5
5. How strongly do you feel this current situation/problem/concern will affect your family's future?	0	1	2	3	4	(5)
6. To what extent are family members able to help themselves in this present situation/problem/concern?	0	1	2	3	(4)	5
7. To what extent do you expect others to help your family with this situation/problem/concern?	0	1	2	3	(4)	5

	N/A	Poor	Satisfactory		Excellent
8. Rate the overall health status of your family as a whole.	0	1	2	3	4	(5)

9. Rate the overall health status of each family member by name.

Name	N/A	Poor		Satisfactory		Excellent
Robert	0	1	2	3	(4)	5
Peggy	0	1	2	(3)	4	5
Betty	0	(1)	2	3	4	5
Kenny	0	(1)	2	3	4	5
_____	0	1	2	3	4	5

Part III: Family Systems Strengths

DIRECTIONS: Each of the twenty traits/attributes listed below deals with some aspect of family life.[c] Each one contributes to the health and well-being of family members as individuals and to the family as a whole. Please circle a number (1 through 5) that best describes the extent to which family members use these traits.

My Family:	N/A	Seldom		Usually		Always
1. Communicates and listens to one another	0	1	(2)	3	4	5
2. Affirms and supports one another	0	1	2	(3)	4	5
3. Teaches respect for others	0	1	2	3	(4)	5
4. Develops a sense of trust in members	0	1	2	3	(4)	5
5. Has a sense of play and humor	0	1	2	(3)	4	5
6. Exhibits a sense of shared responsibility	0	1	(2)	3	4	5
7. Teaches a sense of right and wrong	0	1	2	3	(4)	5
8. Has a strong sense of family in which rituals and traditions abound	0	1	2	(3)	4	5

9. Has a balance of interac-   0   1   2   (3)   4   5
tion among members

10. Has a shared religious   0   (1)   2   3   4   5
core

11. Respects the privacy of   0   1   2   3   4   (5)
one another

12. Values service to others   0   1   2   3   4   (5)

13. Fosters family table time   0   1   2   (3)   4   5
and conversation

14. Shares leisure time   0   1   (2)   3   4   5

15. Admits to and seeks help   0   1   2   3   (4)   5
with problems

16. Honors its elders   0   1   2   3   4   (5)

17. Accepts and encourages   0   1   2   3   4   (5)
individual values

18. Values work satisfaction   0   1   2   3   4   (5)

19. Is financially secure   0   1   2   (3)   4   5

20. Is able to let go of grown   0   1   2   3   4   (5)
children

[a]Based on Curran, D. 1985. **Stress and the healthy family.** Minneapolis: Winston Press.

[b]Based on Neuman's Systems Model. Neuman, B. 1989. **The Neuman systems model.** Norwalk, CT: Appleton-Lange.

[c]Based on Curran, D. 1983. **Traits of a healthy family.** Minneapolis: Winston Press.

Family Systems Stressor-Strength Inventory (FS³I)
Family Form

Family Name <u>Gardner</u>   Date <u>Feb. 22</u>

Family Member Completing Assessment <u>Peggy</u>

Ethnic Background <u>Czech, English, Irish</u>

Referral Source <u>Community health nurse</u>   Interviewer <u>N. Nurse</u>

Family Members	Relationship in Family	Age	Marital Status	Education (highest degree)	Occupation
1. Robert	husband	56	M	PhD	teacher
2. Peggy	wife	51	M	PhD	teacher
3. Betty Harmon	maternal mother	82	M	H.S.	retired-housewife
4. Kenny Harmon	maternal father	81	M	H.S.	retired-railroad
5.					
6.					

What is your current reason(s) for seeking health care assistance?

<u>Betty diagnosed with ovarian cancer. Surgical debulkment of tumor. Discharge planning to home.</u>

Part 1: Family Systems Stressors (General)

DIRECTIONS: Each of the 45 situations listed here deal with some aspect of normal family life.[a] They have the potential for creating tension within family members, between family members, or between families and external environment. We are interested in your overall impression of how these situations affect your family life. Please circle a number (1 through 5) that best describes the amount of stress or tension they create for you. Thank you for cooperation.

	N/A	Little Stress		Medium Stress		High Stress
1. Family member(s) feeling un-appreciated	0	1	2	(3)	4	5
2. Guilt for not accomplishing more	0	1	2	3	(4)	5
3. Insufficient "me" time	0	1	2	3	4	(5)
4. Self-image/self-esteem/feelings of unattractiveness	0	(1)	2	3	4	5
5. Perfectionism	0	1	2	3	4	(5)
6. Dieting	0	1	(2)	3	4	5
7. Health/illness	(0)	1	2	3	4	5
8. Drugs/alcohol	(0)	1	2	3	4	5
9. Widowhood	(0)	1	2	3	4	5
10. Retirement	(0)	1	2	3	4	5
11. Homework/school grades	(0)	1	2	3	4	5
12. Communication with children	0	(1)	2	3	4	5
13. Housekeeping standards	0	1	2	3	(4)	5
14. Insufficient couple time	0	1	2	3	4	(5)
15. Insufficient family playtime	0	1	2	3	4	(5)
16. Children's behavior/discipline/sibling fighting	(0)	1	2	3	4	5
17. Television	(0)	1	2	3	4	5

18. Overscheduled family calendar   0   1   2   3   4   (5)

19. Lack of shared responsibility in the family   0   1   2   3   4   (5)

20. Moving   0   1   2   3   4   (5)

21. Spousal relationship (communication, friendship, sex)   0   1   2   3   4   (5)

22. Holidays   0   (1)   2   3   4   5

23. Inlaws   (0)   1   2   3   4   5

24. Teen behaviors (communication, music, friends, church, school)   (0)   1   2   3   4   5

25. New baby   (0)   1   2   3   4   5

26. Houseguests   (0)   1   2   3   4   5

27. Family vacations   0   1   (2)   3   4   5

28. Remarriage   (0)   1   2   3   4   5

29. Relationship with former spouse   (0)   1   2   3   4   5

30. Summer   0   1   2   (3)   4   5

31. Weekends   0   1   2   (3)   4   5

32. Religious differences   0   1   (2)   3   4   5

33. Predinner hour   0   1   (2)   3   4   5

34. Older parents   0   1   2   3   4   (5)

35. Economics/finances/budgets   0   1   2   3   (4)   5

36. Unhappiness with work situation   0   1   2   3   (4)   5

37. Overvolunteerism   0   1   2   3   4   (5)

38. Neighbors   0   (1)   2   3   4   5

39. Unemployment	0	(1)	2	3	4	5
40. Nuclear and environmental fears	0	(1)	2	3	4	5
41. Church-school activities	0	(1)	2	3	4	5
42. Unsatisfactory housing	0	1	2	(3)	4	5
43. Organized sports activities	(0)	1	2	3	4	5
44. Change in work patterns	0	(1)	2	3	4	5
45. Two-paycheck family	0	1	2	3	4	(5)

Part II: Family Systems Stressors (Specific)

DIRECTIONS: The following 10 questions are designed to provide specific information about tension producing situations, problems, or areas of concern influencing your family's health.[b] Please circle a number (1 through 5) that best describes the influence this situation has on your family's life.

What do you consider your major stressful situation, problem, or concern at this time?

Betty is terminally ill. Peggy must provide

care to aging and ill parents who live in

another state. Life is too complicated already

without the burden of caregiving.

	N/A	Little or None		Medium		Very much
1. To what extent is your family bothered by this problem or stressful situation?	0	1	2	3	4	(5)
2. How much of an effect does this stressful situation have on your family's usual pattern of living?	0	1	2	3	4	(5)
3. How much has this situation affected your family's ability to work together as a family unit?	0	1	2	3	(4)	5

Has your family ever experienced a similar concern in the past?

YES ✓ If YES, complete question 4

NO _____ If NO, proceed to question 5

		Little			**Very**
	N/A	or None		Medium	much

4. How successful was your family in dealing with this situation/problem/concern in the past?
 0   1   2   3   ④   5

5. How strongly do you feel this current situation/problem/concern will affect your family's future?
 0   1   2   3   4   ⑤

6. To what extent are family members able to help themselves in this present situation/problem/concern?
 0   1   2   3   ④   5

7. To what extent do you expect others to help your family with this situation/problem/concern?
 0   1   2   3   4   ⑤

	N/A	Poor	Satisfactory	Excellent

8. Rate the overall health status of your family as a whole.
 0   1   2   3   4   ⑤

9. Rate the overall health status of each family member by name.

Robert	0	1	2	③	4	5
Peggy	0	1	②	3	4	5
Betty	0	①	2	3	4	5
Kenny	0	①	2	3	4	5
	0	1	2	3	4	5

Part III: Family Systems Strengths

DIRECTIONS: Each of the twenty traits/attributes listed below deals with some aspect of family life.[c] Each one contributes to the health and well-being of family members as individuals and to the family as a whole. Please circle a number (1 through 5) that best describes the extent to which family members use these traits.

My Family:	N/A	Seldom		Usually		Always
1. Communicates and listens to one another	0	1	(2)	3	4	5
2. Affirms and supports one another	0	1	(2)	3	4	5
3. Teaches respect for others	0	1	2	(3)	4	5
4. Develops a sense of trust in members	0	1	2	(3)	4	5
5. Has a sense of play and humor	0	1	(2)	3	4	5
6. Exhibits a sense of shared responsibility	0	1	(2)	3	4	5
7. Teaches a sense of right and wrong	0	1	2	3	(4)	5
8. Has a strong sense of family in which rituals and traditions abound	0	1	2	3	(4)	5

9. Has a balance of interac-   0   1   2   3   (4)   5
   tion among members

10. Has a shared religious   0   1   2   (3)   4   5
    core

11. Respects the privacy of   0   1   2   3   (4)   5
    one another

12. Values service to others   0   1   2   3   4   (5)

13. Fosters family table time   0   1   2   (3)   4   5
    and conversation

14. Shares leisure time   0   1   (2)   3   4   5

15. Admits to and seeks help   0   1   2   3   4   (5)
    with problems

16. Honors its elders   0   1   2   3   4   (5)

17. Accepts and encourages   0   1   2   3   (4)   5
    individual values

18. Values work satisfaction   0   1   2   3   4   (5)

19. Is financially secure   0   1   2   (3)   4   5

20. Is able to let go of grown   0   1   2   3   4   (5)
    children

[a]Based on Curran, D. 1985. **Stress and the healthy family.** Minneapolis: Winston Press.

[b]Based on Neuman's Systems Model. Neuman, B. 1989. **The Neuman systems model.** Norwalk, CT: Appleton-Lange.

[c]Based on Curran, D. 1983. **Traits of a healthy family.** Minneapolis: Winston Press.

Family Systems Stressor-Strength Inventory (FS³I)
Clinician Form

Family Name ___Gardner___   Date ___February 22___

Family Name _____   Date _____

Part I: Family Systems Stressors (General)

Briefly discuss the 45 situations with the family member(s) and ask if there are additional areas of concern. The purpose here is to begin clarifying the family member(s) perceptions of stressful situations and to zero in on their major area of concern.

Very little couple time between Robert and Peggy due

to vocational and family demands. Middlescent family

responding to young adult children and aging parents.

Part II: Family Systems Stressors (Specific)

DIRECTIONS: The following 10 questions are designed to provide specific information about the particular situation influencing the family's health.[b] Please circle a number (1 through 5) that best describes the influence this situation has on the family's health from your point of view. Record the family response(s) and your perceptions.

What do you consider to be the family's most stressful situation/ problem/or areas of concern at this time? (Identify problem area(s))

Acute illness of Peggy's mother. Possibility

of terminal illness and death. Peggy's father

is blind and dependent.

		N/A	Little or none		Medium		Very Much
1.	To what extent is the family bothered by this situation/ problem/concern? (Effects on psychosocial relationships communication, interactions)	0	1	2	3	4	(5)

Family Response

Overwhelmed. Just one more thing.

Clinician Perceptions

Competent family but stressful interactions at present. Crisis

		Little			**Very**
	N/A	**or none**	**Medium**		**Much**

2. How much alteration in the   0   1   2   3   4   ⑤
family's usual pattern of
living is occurring as a result
of this situation/problem/
concern? (Identify life-style
patterns and developmental
tasks)

Family Response
Frequent trips out of town to provide caretaking
to both aging parents.

Clinician Perceptions
Peggy making most of the adjustments.
Robert's daily routine not altered. Robert
not involved in caregiving decisions nor does
he seek out opportunities to help.

		Little			**Very**
	N/A	**or none**	**Medium**		**Much**

3. How much has this situation   0   1   2   ③   4   5
affected the family's ability
to work together as a family
unit? (Identify roles and
tasks and how these are being altered.)

Family Response
Robert and Peggy can both maintain the home.
Robert not upset by illness of mother-in-law.

Clinician Perceptions
Peggy gone a lot; getting further behind with
her own work and career. Role of caregiver for
Peggy would be taxing physically, mentally,
and emotionally.

		Little		Very	
N/A	or none		Medium		Much

4. Has the family ever experi- 0   1   2   3   4   (5)
enced similar situations in
the past? If so describe what
the family did. How suc-
cessful were they in resolving the situation/problem/
concern? (Identify past
coping patterns, adaptive
strategies, and what success
means to family.)

Family Response
Similar problem several times in past when
Peggy's father was ill and when Robert's father
died.   Clinician Perceptions
Using coping skills gained from past illness
episodes. Peggy able to talk about illnesses.
Robert does not talk about his own father's
death, so he is unable to be helpful in this
situation.

		Little		Very	
N/A	or none		Medium		Much

5. How strongly do you think 0   1   2   3   4   (5)
the present situation/
problem/concern will affect
the family and family members in the future? What effects do you expect? What
are the anticipated consequences? (Identify current
and potential coping pat-
terns.)

Family Response
Worried about Betty's health and caregiving
ability. Peggy anxious about long-term
effects of illness for self and for parents.
Clinician Perceptions
Crisis situation. Family could get very
disorganized if Betty's illness continues.
Betty could not care for self or her husband
and external resources would be needed. This
would jeopardize stability of Gardner and
Harmon family units.

		Little				**Very**
	N/A	or none		Medium		Much

6. To what extent are family   0   1   2   3   4   (5)
   members able to help them-
   selves in the present
   situation/problem/concern?
   Identify self-assistive behaviors, family expectations,
   and spiritual influence.

Family Response
With help of large extended family, crisis
situation can be resolved.

Clinician Perceptions
Intelligent family; well networked; able to
find appropriate resources for parents
(financial, spiritual, health) and self (own
counseling support).

		Little				**Very**
	N/A	or none		Medium		Much

7. To what extent does the   0   1   2   3   4   (5)
   family expect others to assist
   them with their present situation? What roles do family
   members expect others to
   play? (Describe roles and
   availability of extrafamily
   resources.)

Family Response
Expect help from large extended family members
to assume caregiving roles.

Clinician Perceptions
Peggy expects other family members to help with
parents' care, e.g. financially, housekeeping,
transportation, and daily care.

	N/A	Poor		Satisfactory		Excellent

8. Describe the overall health status of the family system. Consider four major categories: physical status, psychosocial characteristics, developmental characteristics, and spiritual influence

0   1   2   3   4   (5)

Family Response
Peggy and Robert in good health physically. Emotional strain is apparent.

Clinician Perceptions
Family appears physically and mentally healthy. Strain of caregiving and its effect on Peggy and Robert's marital status can be seen.

9. Rate the overall health status of each family member using 5 variables as reference points: physiological, psychological, developmental, sociocultural, and spiritual influence.

	N/A	Poor		Satisfactory		Excellent
a. Robert _____	0	1	2	3	4	(5)
b. Peggy _____	0	1	2	3	4	(5)
c. Betty _____	0	(1)	2	3	4	5
d. Kenny _____	0	1	(2)	3	4	5
e. _____	0	1	2	3	4	5

Family Response
Robert and Peggy report lower health status than nurse does.

Clinician Perceptions
Chronic illness in aging family may jeopardize emotional health of Gardner family unit.

Part III: Family Systems Strengths

DIRECTIONS: Each of the 20 trait and/or attributes listed here deal with some aspect of family life.[c] Each one contributes to the health and well-being of family members as individuals and to family as a whole. Briefly describe your perception of how these strengths are operationalized in this family and circle the number (1 through 5) that best describes the extent to which they are used.

	N/A	Seldom or not at all	Usually		Always
This Family:					
1. Communicates and listens to one another	0	1	2	(3) 4	5

Clinician Perceptions
```
Long-term marriage.  Don't always listen.
```

| 2. Affirms and supports one another | 0 | 1 | 2 | 3 (4) | 5 |

Clinician Perceptions

| 3. Teaches respect for others | 0 | 1 | 2 | 3 4 | (5) |

Clinician Perceptions

| 4. Develops a sense of trust in members | 0 | 1 | 2 | 3 4 | (5) |

Clinician Perceptions

| 5. Has a sense of play and humor | 0 | 1 | (2) | 3 4 | 5 |

Clinician Perceptions

| 6. Exhibits a sense of shared responsibility | 0 | 1 | 2 | (3) 4 | 5 |

Clinician Perceptions

7. Teaches a sense of right   0   1   2   3   (4)   5
   and wrong

Clinician Perceptions

8. Has a strong sense of   0   1   2   3   4   (5)
   family in which rituals
   and traditions abound

Clinician Perceptions

9. Has a balance of interac-   0   1   2   3   (4)   5
   tion among members

Clinician Perceptions

10. Has a shared religious   0   1   (2)   3   4   5
    core

Clinician Perceptions

11. Respects the privacy of   0   1   2   3   4   (5)
    one another

Clinician Perceptions

12. Values service to others   0   1   2   3   4   (5)

Clinician Perceptions

13. Fosters family table time   0   1   2   (3)   4   5
    and conversation

Clinician Perceptions

14. Shares leisure time   0   1   2   (3)   4   5

Clinician Perceptions

15. Admits to and seeks help   0   1   2   3   4   (5)
     with problems

Clinician Perceptions

16. Honors its elders   0   1   2   3   4   (5)

Clinician Perceptions

17. Accepts and encourages   0   1   2   3   (4)   5
     individual values

Clinician Perceptions

18. Values work satisfaction   0   1   2   3   4   (5)

Clinician Perceptions

19. Is financially secure   0   1   2   3   (4)   5

Clinician Perceptions

20. Is able to let go of grown   0   1   2   3   4   (5)
     children

Clinician Perceptions

[a]Based on Curran, D. 1985. Stress and the healthy family. Minneapolis: Winston Press.

[b]Based on Neuman's Systems Model. Neuman, B. 1989. The Neuman systems model. Norwalk, CT: Appleton–Lange.

[c]Based on Curran, D. 1983. Traits of a healthy family. Minneapolis: Winston Press.

Family Systems Stressor-Strength Inventory (FS³I)
Summary Form

Family Name _Gardner_   Date _February 22_

Family Member(s) Completing Assessment _Robert & Peggy Gardner_

Ethnic Background(s) _Czech, English, Irish; English,_
                                                        Swedish
Religious Background(s) _Lutheran_

Referral Source _Community_   Interviewer _N. Nurse_
                              health nurse

Family Members	Relationship in Family	Age	Marital Status	Education (highest degree)	Occupation
1. Robert Gardner	husband	56	M	PhD	teacher
2. Peggy Gardner	wife	51	M	PhD	teacher
3. Betty Harmon	maternal mother	82	M	HS	retired-housewife
4. Kenny Harmon	maternal father	81	M	HS	retired-railroad
5.					
6.					

Family's current reason for seeking health care assistance?

Betty diagnosed with ovarian cancer.

Underwent surgical debulkment; experiencing

postop complication. Planning home health

care coordination.

Scoring Key

Family Member Perceptions
Section 1: Family Form

Part I Family Systems Stressors (General)

Add scores from questions 1 to 45 and calculate an overall score for Family Systems Stressors (General). Ratings are from 1 (most positive) to 5 (most negative). Subscale scores range from 45 to 225.

Family Systems Stressors (General) Score

$$\frac{(\quad)}{45} \times 1 = \underline{\qquad}$$

Robert 94/45 = 2.17
Peggy   99/45 = 2.20

Graph subscale score on Quantitative Summary Form: Family Systems Stressors: General, Family Member Perceptions.

A. Intrafamily Systems Subscale Score:

Add scores from questions 1-11 and calculate a subscale score. Ratings are from 1 (most positive) to 5 (most negative). Subscale scores range from 11 to 55.

Intrafamily Systems Stressors Score

$$\frac{(\quad)}{11} \times 1 = \underline{\qquad}$$

Robert 21/11 = 1.9
Peggy   20/11 = 1.8

Graph score on Quantitative Summary Form: Family Systems Stressors (Intrafamily), Family Member Perceptions.

Family Member Perceptions
Section 1: Family Form

B. Interfamily Systems Subscale Score:

Add scores from questions 12-34 only and calculate a subscale score. Ratings are from 1 (most positive) to 5 (most negative). Scores range from 23 to 115.

Interfamily Systems Stressors Score

$$\frac{(\quad)}{23} \times 1 = \underline{\hspace{2cm}}$$

Robert 53/23 = 2.3
Peggy 53/23 = 2.3

Graph subscale score on Quantitative Summary Form, Family Systems Stressors (Interfamily), Family Member Perceptions.

C. Extrafamily Systems Subscale Score:

Add scores from questions 35-45 and calculate a subscale score. Ratings are from 1 (most positive) to 5 (most negative). Scores range from 11 to 55.

Extrafamily Systems Stressors Score

$$\frac{(\quad)}{11} \times 1 = \underline{\hspace{2cm}}$$

Robert 23/11 = 2.09
Peggy 26/11 = 2.36

Graph subscale score on Quantitative Summary Form: Family Systems Stressors (Extrafamily), Family Member Perceptions.

Part II Family Systems Stressors (Specific)

Add scores from questions 1 to 8 only and calculate a score for Family Systems Stressors (Specific). Ratings are from 1 (most positive) to 5 (most negative). Questions 4, 6, 7, and 8 are reverse scored.* Scores range from 8 to 40.

Family Systems Stressors (Specific) Score

$$\frac{(\quad)}{8} \cdot \times 1 = \underline{\hspace{3cm}}$$

Robert 26/8 = 3.25
Peggy   25/8 = 3.12

Graph score on Quantitative Summary Form: Family Systems Stressors (Specific) Family Member Perceptions. Scores for question 9 are recorded on Qualitative Summary Form 2D: Family Systems Stressors (Specific).

Part III Family Systems Strengths

Add scores from questions 1 to 20 and calculate a score for Family Systems Strengths. Ratings are from 1 (seldom used) to 5 (always used). Scores range from 20 to 100.

Family Systems Strengths Score

$$\frac{(\quad)}{20} \times 1 = \underline{\hspace{3cm}}$$

Robert 71/20 = 3.55
Peggy   70/20 = 3.50

Graph score on Quantitative Summary Form: Family Systems Strengths.

*Reverse Scoring:
Question answered as **one** is scored as 5 points
Question answered as **two** is scored as 4 points
Question answered as **three** is scored as 3 points
Question answered as **four** is scored as 2 points
Question answered as **five** is scored as 1 point

Clinician Perceptions
Section 2: Clinician Form

Part I Family Systems Stressors (General)

Identify predominant tension producing situations from list of 45 situations/problems/concerns and prioritize them in order of importance to family. Record on Qualitative Summary Form: Family Systems Stressors (General).

Additional Comments:
General Stressors:

General system stressors are at flexible and normal lines of defense.

Intrafamily:

Couple have variability in individual stressors. Both do not have enough time for self, each other, or to play.

Interfamily

Robert reports overscheduled, stressful spousal relationship and stress with aging parents and inlaws. Peggy is overstressed in time, responsibility, travel, and spousal relationship.
Extrafamily:

Robert reports work-related stress. Peggy reports stress from work and overvolunteerism.

Part II Family Systems Stressors (Specific)

Calculate quantitative scores for questions 1 to 8 in same manner as for Section 1, Part II. Family Member Perceptions. Graph on Quantitative Summary Form for Family Systems Stressors (Specific), Clinician Perceptions.   22/8 = 2.75

Identify specific tension producing situation/problem/concern that is influencing family health and record on Qualitative Summary Form 2A: Family Systems Stressors (Specific).

Part III Family Systems Strengths

Calculate quantitative scores for questions 1 to 20 in same manner as for Section 1, Part III. Family Member Perceptions. Graph on Quantitative Summary Form for Family Systems Strengths, Clinician Perceptions.   81/20 = 4.05

Identify Family Systems Strengths that contribute to family stability, health and can serve as a basis for prevention/ intervention activities. Record on Qualitative Summary Form Part III: Family Systems Strengths.

```
Respect for others, trust in members, sense
of right and wrong, respect for privacy. Value
service to others, honors elders, individual
values, seeks help, values work.  Both members
of couple have similar values.
```

Quantitative Summary

DIRECTIONS: Graph the scores from each family member inventory by placing an "X" at the appropriate location and connect with a line. (Use first name initial for each line.)

Key:

Robert ●——   Peggy   ✗ - -

Sum of strengths available for prevention/ intervention mode	Family Systems Strengths	
	Family Member Perceptions	Clinician Perceptions
5.0		
4.8		
4.6		
4.4		
4.2		⊙
4.0		
3.8		
3.6		
3.4	● ✗	
3.2		
3.0		
2.8		
2.6		
2.4		
2.2		
2.0		
1.8		
1.6		
1.4		
1.2		
1.0		

*PRIMARY Prevention Intervention Mode: Flexible Line) 1.0-2.3
*SECONDARY Prevention Intervention Mode: Normal Line) 2.4-3.6
*TERTIARY Prevention Intervention Mode: Resistance Lines) 3.7-5.0
*Breakdown of numerical scores for stressor penetration are suggested values

Qualitative Summary*
(Family and Clinician Perceptions)

Part I: Family Systems Stressors: General

Identify predominant tension producing situation(s) in family and list them in order of importance to the family.

Situation/Problem/Concern	Priority for Family
1. surgery and postop complications of mother	_____
2. care of ill mother and blind father	_____
3. diagnosis of cancer	_____
4. overload of caregiving	_____
5. _____	_____

Comments:

*Combines information from Family Form and Clinician Form.

Part II: Family Systems Stressors: Specific

Identify specific tension producing situation/problem/concern influencing family health.

Caretaking of ill and elderly parents in

addition to many other responsibilities

Comments:

Part II: Family Systems Stressors: Specific

B. Summarize perceptions of the specific family situation/problem/ concern and identify discrepancies between family and clinician perceptions.

Stressor (Situation)	Famiy Perception
1. Extent family bothered by situation/problem/concern: effects on psychosocial relationships, communications, and interactions	Sometimes overwhelmed by added responsibilities. Causes additional stress in couple's relationship.
2. Alterations in usual life-style patterns and family developmental tasks	Wife out of town with parents. Husband needs to assume more responsibility.
3. Effects on family's ability to work together: alteration in roles and tasks	Family working together; more stress on wife.
4. Similar situations, problems, concerns: family's past coping patterns; what "success" means to family	Family has had similar prior experiences with two other aging parents.
5. Effects of present situation on family health in future: anticipated consequences; current and potential coping patterns	Possibility of major readjustment before equilibrium if mother dies.
6. Family's ability to help themselves in situation; self-assistive behaviors; family expectations and spiritual influence	Everything will turn out for the best. Capable of handling situation. Belief in God helpful.
7. Family expectations of others and their role in helping family; extrafamily resources and their role	Comes from large family; most willing to help; parents also have many friends.

Clinician Perception	Discrepancies
Crisis situation for family. Past experience in similar situation.	Clinician more confident than family in its ability to cope.
Traveling and family illness causing change in usual patterns.	None
Wife assuming major responsibility.	None
Family has prior experiences to help them cope with this situation.	None
Mother's death or incapitation a good possibility. Care of aged, blind father also a concern.	None
Family appears to have inner resources to help itself.	None
Family well resourced in community.	None

C. Summarize significant health status data for each family member using five variables.

	Family Member Robert[1]	Family Member Peggy[2]	Family Member Betty[3]
Physiological	In good physical health	In good physical health but tired at times	Health compromised by surgery, age, disease.
Psychological	Somewhat detached from maternal parents	Feels responsible for coordinating and giving parental caregiving	Good state of mind despite complications
Developmental	Time in family life cycle when both sets of parents are having health and aging concerns.		Age and stage appropriate
Sociocultural	Has friends in workplace. Doesn't look to others for help.	Has lots of friends and family. Siblings of special support. Good social skills.	Large network of friends in long-term community. Living in retirement community.
Spiritual	Agnostic. Believes that when you die, that's it.	Belief in God. Member of a church. Parents are also members.	Belief and trust in God gives much comfort and hope.

Family Member Kenny [4]	Family Member 5	Family Member 6
Health compromised by age & chronic diseases (blind)		
Goes from worried to cheerful		
Age and stage appropriate		
Large network of friends in long-term community. Living in retirement community.		
Belief and trust in God gives much comfort and hope.		

D. Using the four major categories of the family system, combine
significant health status data from family member variables.

Major Category	Family System
Psychological Relationship	Interactional patterns between spouses sometimes stressful. Family trying to accommodate for potential loss and loss of equilibrium. Good intellectual capacity.
Physical Status	Couple basically in good health. Aging parents' health extremely precarious.
Spiritual Influence	Most family members share Christian orientation, particularly aging parents. Has helped them throughout.
Developmental Characteristics	Middlescent family sandwiched in between older and younger generation who still depend on them.

Part III: Family Systems Strengths

Identify family systems strengths that contribute to family stability and support actual and potential prevention/intervention activities.

Family Systems Strengths

---

1. Respect for others.
   Honors its elders.

---

2. Admits to and seeks help with problems.

---

3. Strong sense of family.

---

4. Values service to others.

5.

6.

7.

Part IV: Family Care Plan*
List the three most significant clinician diagnoses (prioritize).

Diagnosis General and Specific Family Systems Stressors	Family Systems Strengths Supporting Family Care Plan	Goals Family and Clinician
1. Altered family processes at normal line of defense due to illness of maternal parent & disability of paternal parent	Respect and care for others Honors its elders Admits to and seeks help with problems	Develop measures to stabilize family system functioning - caretaking, household tasks, transportation, economics, etc.
2. Intermittent grieving at normal line of defense due to cancer diagnosis, postop complications, chemotherapy prescriptions.	Strong sense of family; extended family support Values service to others Financial security	Alert family members to steps of grieving process and support them with process
3. Compromised family coping at flexible and normal lines of defense due to role overload		Initiate measures that support existing family coping abilities

Prevention/Intervention Mode		Outcomes
Primary, Secondary, or Tertiary	Prevention/Intervention Activities	Evaluation and Replanning
Secondary - Discuss homecare strategies with Mrs. Harmon and family that facilitate carrying out selected household tasks. Arrange for CHN to make home visits that focus on immediate health care needs, i.e., colostomy. Discuss potential external resources available to family, i.e., home health aide, Meals on Wheels, insurance, social worker, neighbors. Model the caring process.		In process
Secondary - Create therapeutic environment facilitating trust/ confidentiality. Discuss steps in grieving process. Initiate strategies for family dialogue relative to pain, sadness. Discuss information about diagnosis, prognosis, chemotherapy.		In process
Primary and Secondary - Assist family members to make a family health care plan. Arrange for external supports that prevent caretaking burnout.		In process

Family Nursing Assessment/ Measurement Instrumentation

7

The purpose of this book is to present a family assessment pocket guide that can be used by a variety of nurses working in a variety of health care settings. The assessment/intervention model and instrument discussed in the earlier chapters provides an efficient and comprehensive guide to aid nurses in planning, implementing, and evaluating care of individuals and families for whom they are responsible. Chapter 6 presented three case examples, each of which portrayed a family in a different stage of the family life cycle and having different health problems.

This chapter includes a discussion and summary description of other selected family assessment/measurement instruments available to clinicians for practice and research, a criterion for selecting them.

Assessment/Measurement Definitions

The terms *assessment* and *measurement* have often been used interchangeably. Webster defines "assess" as follows: to determine the amount of, importance of, or value of an outcome. In this context, assessment is neither instantaneous nor static but a continuous evolving process (Braden and Herban, 1976). "In theory and practice, assessment is a means by which the assessor, by drawing on the past and the present, is able to predict or plan for the future" (Braden and Herban, 1976, p. 63). On the other hand, Waltz, Strickland, and Lenz (1984, p. 2) defined measurement as the "process of assigning numbers to objects to represent the kind and/or amount of an attribute or characteristic possessed by those objects." This definition includes both qualitative and quantitative measurement. Instrumentation is a component of the measurement process and is defined as the "process of selecting or developing devices and methods appropriate for measuring an attribute or characteristic of interest" (Waltz, Strickland, and Lenz, 1984, p. 1).

According to Grotevant (1989, p. 108), assessment is the process of gathering information used in either research or clinical work. In research, "assessment typically involves the operationalization of theoretical constructs for purposes of hypothesis testing or exploration. In clinical practice, assessment involves the collection of information necessary to diagnose and treat presenting problems and evaluate the success of the intervention." The nurse must assess or evaluate the family to diagnose the family's problem. This evaluation is more useful when it is explicitly guided by theory (Grotevant, 1989), preferably a middle-range theory that is "modest in scope and generality, relatively close to data, easily tested, and easily revised" (Holman and Burr, 1980, p. 733).

In nursing, *assessment* is more typically a nursing practice term used as the initial phase in the nursing process that progresses into some kind of intervention and evaluation. *Measurement* is a word more frequently used in nursing research where a particular attribute is measured, giving some kind of quantitative results that can be used for descriptive or inferential statistical analyses. In this chapter, the terms *assessment* and *measurement* will be used interchangeably in reference to instruments that yield some numerical outcome that can be used for planning care or for research purposes. The family assessment interests of family-oriented scientists—academic and practitioner—overlap considerably (Carlson, 1989). "Assessment and measurement are interchangeable terms from the research perspective. Both imply the identification of specific features of the phenomena and the creation and use of clear rules or procedures for quantification" (Carlson, 1989, p. 161).

Family Instrumentation

The increasing sophistication of the family field over the past half century has increased awareness of the need for assessment/ measurement technology. The development of instruments used in understanding family variables has received major attention only since the mid-1930s (Touliatos, Perlmutter, and Straus, 1990).

The literature describes a number of excellent family and family nursing assessment/measurement instruments (Corcoran and Fischer, 1987; Filsinger, 1983; Forman and Hagan, 1984; Fredman and Sherman, 1987; Grotevant and Carlson, 1989; Holman, 1983; Humenick, 1982; Johnson and Bommarito, 1976; Karoly, 1985; Mangen, Bengtson, and Landry, 1988; McCubbin and Thompson, 1987; McDowell and Newell, 1987; Olson, McCubbin, Barnes, et al, 1985; Sabatelli, 1988; Stangler, Huber, and Routh, 1980; Straus and Brown, 1978; Touliatos, Perlmutter, and Straus, 1990). Approximately 30 books and 15 review articles are dedicated just to the review of family measures (Touliatos, Perlmutter, and Straus, 1990, p. 23), whereas very few speak specifically to family nursing measures.[1] Psychologists, sociologists, social workers, family life professionals, and marriage and family practitioners have developed and used family instruments in their respective fields. Each of these helping professionals uses measurement instruments with specific foci and purposes (Speer and Sachs, 1985). For example, sociologists' primary concern has been marital satisfaction, decision making, and role delineation. Psychologists have focused on the interactional patterns of parents and children (Patterson, 1975). Social workers emphasized parental coping abilities (Hurwitz, Kaplan, and Kaiser, 1965), while marriage and family clinicians focused on marital/family dysfunction (Speer and Sachs, 1985). One specialty often overlooks measures developed in other fields, even though the various specialties may need to measure similar concepts. In many cases, measures are developed and published in the literature of family social studies and tend to be read only by that group. Nurses more often read family literature than family professionals read nursing literature. Thus most family instruments are "non-nursing," and although they may be more psychometrically sound than some of the nursing instruments, they may not demonstrate a clear relevance to family nursing. Either the family assessment perspective has been closely aligned with individual disciplines such as nursing or social work (Speer and Sachs, 1985), or measurement has been used to quantify some aspects of families for research purposes.

Few of the books published related solely to family assessment, screening, or measurement have come from nursing. *Screening Growth and Development of Preschool Children: A Guide for Test Selection* (Stangler, Huber and Routh, 1980) and

Analysis of Current Assessment Strategies in the Health Care of Young Children and Childbearing Families (Humenick, 1982) are two nursing-developed books; both are already outdated. Two books were written specifically for measuring health, albeit they were written by non-nurses: *Measuring Health: A Guide to Rating Scales and Questionnaires* (McDowell and Newell, 1987) and *Measurement Strategies in Health Psychology* (Karoly, 1985). Most of the books published on assessment/intervention have come from a variety of other fields. For example, Holman's *Family Assessment: Tools for Understanding and Intervention* (1983) and Corcoran and Fischer's *Measures for Clinical Practice: A Sourcebook* (1987) came from the social work field. *Family inventories* (Olson, McCubbin, Barnes, et al, 1985), *Measurement of Intergenerational Relations* (Mangen, Bergtson and Landry, 1988), and *Family Assessment Inventories for Research and Practice* (McCubbin and Thompson, 1987) came from family social science or family sociology. Fredman and Sherman's *Handbook of Measurements for Marriage and Family Therapy* (1987) and Filsinger's *Marriage and Family Assessment: A Sourcebook for Family Therapy* (1983) were written for family therapists. Finally, Grotevant and Carlson's book, *Family Assessment: A Guide to Methods and Measures* (1989), was written for family and school psychologists.

The latest and most useful compendium for family professionals is the *Handbook of Family Measurement Techniques* (Touliatos, Perlmutter, and Straus, 1990), which provides abstracts of nearly 1000 instruments. Although this book was not published just for health scientists or nurses, it includes many instruments that can be used by all family professionals. The abstracts in the book offer useful information on the nature of the instrument, variables measured, and reliability and validity studies and provide sample items, published references, and information on obtaining the full instrument. The book organizes instruments into five primary and sixteen secondary areas; the primary areas are (1) dimensions of interactions, (2) intimacy and family values, (3) parenthood, (4) roles and power, and (5) adjustment. This handbook gives clinicians as well as researchers access to up-to-date information on existing instrumentation. Three indexes assist readers in locating appropriate selections: author, title, and classification (variables). Criteria had to be met for the instruments to be included in the book which also informs readers how they can obtain copies of the instruments.

The book categorizes all instruments according to methods used: self-report or observational. Interestingly, no nursing journals were consulted in identifying family-related instruments in use, but some nurse-developed instruments are included in the compendium.

Family Nursing Instrumentation

Some nurse academicians have developed instruments that can be used with families (Clemen-Stone, Eigsti, and McGuire, 1987; Feetham, 1983; Friedman, 1986; Hanson, 1985, 1986; Hymovich, 1983; Stanhope and Lancaster, 1984; Wright and Leahey, 1984). Clemen-Stone, Eigsti, and McGuire (1987) and Stanhope and Lancaster (1984) include their assessment tools in the appendixes of large undergraduate community health nursing textbooks whose major function was not family nursing. In her classic textbook on family nursing, Friedman (1985) used structural functional theory to develop a very good family nursing assessment tool that is comprehensive but long and unwieldy in the clinical setting. Wright and Leahey (1984) developed a model for use in family assessment from the structural, developmental, and functional theories of family analysis and therapy and called the model the Calgary Family Assessment Model (CFAM), but no instrument was developed from it. Hanson (1985, 1986) developed the Family Health Inventory, but this instrument requires further psychometric work and field testing.

Some nurse writers elaborate in a more general way on the integration of theory into practice. Clements and Roberts (1983) present family nursing strategies derived from some of the existing conceptual models of nursing but do not discuss any particular assessment tools. Whall (1986) attempts to link family theories of other disciplines to nursing models and essentially reformulates these theories to "form a logically congruent conceptual/theoretical system of nursing knowledge." However, Whall does not present an assessment instrument per se. Whall and Fawcett (1990) summarized five conceptual models of nursing that they believe can be used to focus on the family; King, Neuman, Orem, Rogers, and Roy are just a few that they address in this book. These analysts of nursing theories do not attempt to move conceptual models of other nursing theorists into the practical world of nurses by the development of assessment or intervention instruments. They indicate that the nursing models are

rather abstract and general but do provide direction for generation and testing of middle-range family theories from a "distinc-
tively" nursing perspective. Further, they believe that King,
Neuman, Rogers, and Roy address the family as a whole-unit-
of-analysis, whereas Orem's model addresses the family-as-con-
text.

Family Nursing Curriculum in the United States and Family Assessment/Measurement

No one has known for sure what nursing schools are teaching
regarding nursing concepts and/or assessment. However, a recently completed, descriptive study has identified both family
nursing content and practical experiences being offered in accredited nursing schools throughout the United States (Hanson,
1988; Hanson and Heims, 1990). Some of the specific questions
answered by this study include: (1) What basic concepts and
skills are baccalaureate and graduate students learning pertaining
to family nursing? (2) Is there nationwide consistency in the
nursing content and clinical skills development emphasized in
family nursing components of baccalaureate and graduate nursing curricula? (3) What are the differences in family nursing theory and practice between baccalaureate only and baccalaureate
plus graduate schools of nursing? A descriptive survey was conducted of all accredited schools of nursing, a random sample of
278 schools was drawn, and 135 schools responded. The questionnaire solicited both quantitative and qualitative data.

One survey question asked for a listing of family assessment
instruments being taught in responding school's curriculum. Of
all of the questions asked in this study, this was the most labori-
ous to interpret and analyze. Answers were short, difficult to
read, and seldom clear. The investigators spent many hours and
used numerous resources trying to understand the responses. Table 7-1 summarizes the results, with instruments listed in order
of frequency of use. The table presents assessment instruments
taught in both baccalaureate and graduate nursing programs together. It also lists sources of the instruments to increase its use-
ability to readers. The family assessment instruments being
taught and used most frequently by reporting schools are as follows:

1. Family Health Assessment Form. This is the assessment
   tool contained in Friedman's textbook (1986). Fifteen
   schools reported using this form or some modification

Table 7-1 Family Nursing Curriculum in the United States: Family Assessment/Measurement Instruments

Name of Instruments and Possible Source(s)	Number
Family Health Assessment Form (actual or modification)	15
Friedman MM. (1986). Family nursing: Theory and assessment (2nd ed.). Norwalk, CT: Appleton-Century-Crofts.	
Family Strengths Assessment	9
Beavers WR. (1981). Healthy families. In Berenson G and White H (eds.). Annual review of family therapy. New York: Human Sciences Press.	
Otto HA. (1963). Criteria for assessing family strength. Family Process 2(2):329-338.	
Stinnett N, Sanders G, and DeFrain J. (1981). Strong families: A national study. In Stinnett N, DeFrain J, K King Knaub P, and Rowe G (eds.). Family strengths 3: Roots of well-being. Lincoln: University of Nebraska.	
Genogram	8
Friedman MM. (1986). Family nursing: Theory and assessment. New York: Appleton-Century-Crofts, p 317.	
McGoldrick M, and Gerson R. (1985). Genograms in family assessment. New York: W. W. Norton & Co.	
Wright LM, and Leahey M. (1984). Nurses and families: A guide to family assessment and intervention. Philadelphia: F.A. Davis Co.	
Calgary Family Assessment Model (CFAM)	6
Wright LM, and Leahey M. (1984). Nurses and families: A guide to family assessment and intervention. Philadelphia: F.A. Davis Co., pp 23-68.	
Faculty-Developed Instruments	6
Faculty-developed tool on communication (1)	
Faculty-developed tool that included structure, function, developmental tasks, and self-care requisites based on Orem (1)	

Feetham Family Functioning Scale (FFFS)   4

Feetham SL, and Humenick SS. (1982). The Feetham family functioning survey. In Humenick SS (ed.). Analysis of current assessment strategies in the health care of young children and childbearing families. Norwalk, CT: Appleton-Century-Crofts, pp 259-268.

Introduce/Teach/Study/Critique Many Instruments   4

Ecomap   3

Wright LM, and Leahey M. (1984). Nurses and families: A guide to family assessment and intervention. Philadelphia: F.A. Davis Co.

Holman AM. (1983). Family assessment: Tools for understanding and intervention. Beverly Hills, CA: Sage, pp 62-68.

Family APGAR   3

Smilkstein G. (1978). The family APGAR: A proposal for a family function test and its use by physicians. Journal of Family Practice 6:1231-1239.

Family Coping Index   3

Choi T, Josten L, and Christensen ML. (1983). Health specific family coping index for noninstitutional care. American Journal of Public Health 73:1275-1279.

McMaster Model of Family Functioning   3

Epstein NE, Bishop DS, and Baldwin LM. (1982). McMaster model of family functioning: A view of the normal family. In Walsh (ed.). Normal family processes. New York: The Guilford Press, pp 115-141.

Continued.

Table 7-1 Family Nursing Curriculum in the United States: Family Assessment/Measurement Instruments—cont'd

Name of Instruments and Possible Source(s)	Number
Family Assessment	2
Johnson SH. (1986). Nursing assessment and strategies for the family at risk: High risk parenting (2nd ed.). Philadelphia: JB Lippincott Co,	
Family Assessment	2
Tinkam C, and Voorhies E. (1984). Community health nursing: Evolution and process in family and community. New York: Appleton-Century-Crofts.	
Family Life Cycle	2
Duvall EM. (1977). Marriage and family development. New York: JB Lippincott Co.	
Duvall EM, and Miller BC. (1985). Marriage and family development. New York: Harper & Row, Publishers.	
Family Environment Scale	2
Moos R. (1974). Family environment scale. Palo Alto, CA: Consulting Psychologists Press.	
Family Functioning Index (FFI)	2
Pless IB, and Satterwhite B. (1973). A measure of family functioning and its application. Social Science and Medicine 7:613-621.	
Family Functioning Levels	2
Tapia JA. (1975). The nursing process in family health. In Spradley (ed.). Contemporary community nursing. Boston: Little, Brown & Co.	
Speer JJ, and Sachs B. (1985). Selecting the appropriate family assessment tool. Pediatric Nursing 11:349-355.	

	2

Family Inventory of Life Events and Changes (FILE)

McCubbin HI, and Thompson AI (eds.). (1987). Family assessment inventories for research and practice Milwaukee: University of Wisconsin, pp 81-98.

	2

Instruments Currently Being Developed

	2

Network Analysis (Family Network Map)

MacElveen PM. (1983). Social networks. Available from C.L. Attneave, 5206 Ivanhoe Place NE, Seattle, WA 98105.

Young RK. (1982). Community nursing workbook: Family as client. Norwalk, CT: Appleton and Lange.

	2

Safety Wellness in the Family's Environments Assessment Tool

Kandzari JH, and Howard JE. (1981). The well family: A developmental approach to assessment. Boston: Little, Brown & Co., pp 11-37.

Wellness of the Family System Assessment Tool (pp 28-37)

Self-Responsibility: Knowledge and Action for Wellness Assessment Tool (pp 58-66)

Psychosocial Development and Mental Wellness Throughout the Life Cycle Assessment Tool (pp 116-126)

Dental Wellness Across the Life Span Assessment Tool (pp 56-164)

Safety Wellness in the Family's Environment (pp 258-270)

	2

Social Readjustment Rating Scale (SRRS) (Life Stress Scale)

(Life Change Questionnaire)

Holmes TH, and Rahe RH. (1967). The social readjustment rating scale. Journal of Psychosomatic Research 11:213-218.

Continued.

Table 7-1 Family Nursing Curriculum in the United States: Family Assessment/Measurement Instruments—cont'd

Name of Instruments and Possible Source(s)	Number
ABCX Model of Family Adjustment and Adaptation	1
McCubbin HI, and Thompson AI (eds.). (1987). Family assessment inventories for research and practice. Madison: The University of Wisconsin-Madison, pp 3-32.	
Abuse Assessment	1
Campbell J, and Humphreys C. (1985). Nursing care for victims of violent families. New York: Harper & Row, Publishers.	
Adapted from Many Instruments	1
Adapted from Neuman	1
Neuman B. (1982). The Neuman systems model: Application to nursing education and practice. Norwalk, CT: Appleton-Century-Crofts, pp 188-195, 217-222.	
Adapted from Olson	1
Olson DH, McCubbin HI, Barnes HL, Larsen AS, Muxen MJ, and Wilson MA. (1983). Families: What makes them work. Beverly Hills, CA: Sage.	
Adapted from Orem	1
Orem DE. (1990). Nursing: Concepts of practice (5th ed.) St. Louis: Mosby–Year Book, Inc.	
Adapted from Roy	1
Roy C. (1980). Conceptual models for nursing practice. New York: Appleton-Century-Crofts.	

Assessment of Parent-Infant Interaction

Barnard K, et al. (1979). Nursing child assessment satellite training project (NCAST). Seattle: University of Washington, Department of Maternal/Child Nursing.

Barnard KE, Hammond MA, Booth CC, Bea HL, Mitchell SK, Spicker SJ. (1989). Measurement and meaning of parent-child intervention. In Morrison F, Lord C, and Keating D (eds). Applied developmental psychology, vol III. New York: Academic Press.   1

Chronicity Impact and Coping Instrument: Parent Questionnaire (CICI:PQ)

Hymovich D. (1983). The chronicity impact and coping instrument: Parent questionnaire. Nursing Research 32:275-281.   1

Circumplex Model

Olson D, Russell C, and Sprenkle D. (1980). Circumplex model of marital and family systems II: Empirical studies and clinical intervention. In Vincent JP (ed.). Advances in family intervention, assessment, and theory, Greenwich, CT: JAI Press, p 128-176.   1

Coping Health Inventory for Parents (CHIP)

McCubbin HI, and Thompson AI. (1987). Family assessment inventories for research and practice. Madison: The University of Wisconsin—Madison.   1

Denver Developmental Screening Test (DDST)

Humenick SS. (1982). Analysis of current assessment strategies in the health care of young children and childbearing families. Norwalk, CT: Appleton-Century-Crofts, pp 230-239.   1

Continued.

Table 7-1   Family Nursing Curriculum in the United States: Family Assessment/Measurement Instruments—cont'd

Name of Instruments and Possible Source(s)	Number
Dyadic Adjustment Scale	1
Roberts CS, and Feetham SL. (1982). Assessing family functioning across three areas of relationships. Nursing Research 31(4) 231-235.	
Spanier G, and Filsinger, EE. (1983). The dyadic adjustment scale. In Filsinger EE (ed.). Marriage and family assessment: A sourcebook for family therapy Beverly Hills, CA: Sage, pp 155-168.	
Speer JJ, and Sachs B. (1985). Selecting the appropriate family assessment tool. Pediatric Nursing 11:349-355.	
FACES II	1
Olson DH, Larsen AS, and McCubbin H. (1982). Development of Faces II. In Olson DH, McCubbin HI, Barnes H, Larsen A, Muxen M, and Wilson M. Family inventories. St. Paul: University of Minnesota, pp 16-20.	
Family Adaptability and Cohesion Scales	1
Olson DH, McCubbin HI, Barnes H, Larsen A, Muxen M, and Wilson M. Family inventories. St. Paul: University of Minnesota, pp 1-46.	
Olson DH, Portner J, and Bell R. (1978). Family adaptability and cohesion evaluation scales (FACES). St. Paul: University of Minnesota, Family Social Science.	
Family Assessment	1
Logan BB, and Dawkins CE. (1986). Family centered nursing in the community. Menlo Park, CA: Addison-Wesley.	
Family Assessment	1
McFarlane J. (1986). Clinical Handbook of Family Nursing. New York: John Wiley & Sons.	

Family Assessment Guide

Clemen-Stone SA, Eigsti DG, and McGuire S. (1990). Comprehensive family and community health nursing. St Louis: Mosby–Year Book, Inc.

Family Assessment Guidelines

Barnard M, and Hymovich D (eds). (1979). Family health care: Developmental and situational crises (Vol. II). New York: McGraw-Hill Book Co.

Edison C. (1979). Family assessment guidelines. In Hymovich, DP, Barnard, MV (eds.). Family health care: General perspectives (2nd ed, Vol I). New York: McGraw-Hill Book Co., pp 264-279.

Family Assessment Model

Spradley BW. (1986). Readings in community health nursing (3rd ed). Boston: Little, Brown & Co.
Spradley BW. (1985). Community health nursing: Process and practice for promoting health. St. Louis: Mosby–Year Book, Inc.

Family Behavioral Snapshot

Meyerstein I. (1979). The family behavioral snapshot: A tool for teaching family assessment. American Journal of Family Therapy 7(1):48-56.

Family Health Assessment Guide

Stanhope M, and Lancaster J. (1984). Community health nursing: Process and practice for promoting health. St. Louis: Mosby–Year Book, Inc.

Family Health Tree/Family Medical Record

March of Dimes Birth Defects Foundation, 1275 Mamaroneck Avenue, White Plains, NY, 10605.

1

1

1

1

1

1

Continued.

Table 7-1 Family Nursing Curriculum in the United States: Family Assessment/Measurement Instruments—cont'd

Name of Instruments and Possible Source(s)	Number
Family Mental Health Assessment	
Sedgwick R. (1981). Family mental health: Theory and practice. St. Louis: Mosby–Year Book, Inc., pp 78-97.	1
Family Nursing Process	
Griffith JW, and Christensen PJ. (1982). Nursing process: Application of theories, frameworks and models (2nd ed). St. Louis: Mosby–Year Book, Inc.	1
Family Strength Assessment	
Olson D. (1982). Family strengths. In Olson D, McCubbin HI, Barnes H, Larsen A, Muxen M, and Wilson M. Family inventories. St. Paul: University of Minnesota, pp 137-151.	1
Functional Health Patterns (Family Assessment)	
Gordon M. (1982). Manual of nursing diagnosis. New York: McGraw-Hill Book Co.	1
Gordon M. (1987). Nursing diagnosis: Process and application. New York: McGraw-Hill Book Co.	
General Nutritional, Spiritual Assessment	1
Historical Analysis of the Family	1
Hareven TK. (1987). Handbook of marriage and the family. New York: Plenum Press, pp. 37-57.	

Home Observation for Measurement of the Environment (HOME)   1

Bradley RH, and Caldwell BM. (1977). Home observation for measurement of the environment: A validation study of
  screening efficiency. American Journal of Mental Deficiency, 81(5):417-420.
Caldwell BM. (1978). Home observation for measurement of the environment. Little Rock: University of Arkansas.

Life-style and Health Habits Assessment   1

Pender NJ. (1982). Health promotion in nursing practice. Norwalk, CT: Appleton-Century-Crofts.

No assessment instruments taught   1

No specific assessment instruments   1

Systems Approach to Family Health   1

Hall JE, and Weaver BR. (1985). Distributive nursing practice: Systems approach to community health (2nd ed.). Philadelphia: J.B. Lippincott Co.

Other

Black Family Strengths Assessment (Hill)   1
Chronicity Coping Scale (Williamson)   1
Family Acuity Assessment Instrument   1
Family Care Perspective Guide   1
Family Developmental Survey   1
Family Health Assessment   1
Family Life Chronology   1
Family Observation and Assessment (Clark)   1
Family Therapy Assessment Tool   1
Guidelines for Family Assessment   1
Structural Family Interaction Scale   1

thereof. This higher usage coincided with the fact that this particular book was also the most frequently used family nursing text among U.S. schools of nursing that responded to the survey.

2. Family Strengths Assessment. Survey responses were unclear as to which family strengths assessment tools the nine respondents were reporting. However, Otto, Beavers, and Stinnet are possibilities.

3. Genograms. Eight schools reported using family genograms as a method of teaching family assessment. The sources most likely to be consulted were Friedman (1986), Wright and Leahey (1984), and McGoldrick (1985).

4. Faculty-developed instruments. Six schools reported using some form of faculty-developed instruments. One school reported using communication as a framework; other schools used family structure, family function, developmental tasks, and self-care frameworks. Four schools did not report the conceptual basis for their faculty-developed instruments.

5. Calgary Family Assessment Model (CFAM). Six schools reported using this instrument. This model is derived from Wright and Leahey's textbook (*Nurses and Families: A Guide to Family Assessment and Intervention,* 1984).

6. Four schools introduced, taught, studied, or critiqued many instruments, and four used Feetham's Family Functioning Scale (Feetham, 1983). Three schools used ecomaps, and three used the Family APGAR. The rest of the instruments listed were used by only one or two schools.

In conclusion, schools did not use a few common family assessment instruments. Rather, they reported using a wide variety of tools from various sources. Several schools indicated that they did not even know what a family assessment tool was. It appears that family nursing educators and clinicians have much work to do in terms of teaching and using systematic family assessment, which can then serve as the foundation for nursing practice and research.

Psychometric Evaluation of Nursing Instruments

One of the major problems in finding family measurement instruments involves reliability and validity. Investigators more often than clinicians require scientifically sound instruments. In most cases, the psychometrics have not been completed or the information is not readily available. Straus (1964) found that 80% of the family measures had been used only once and had not proved themselves in clinical or research arenas.

Nursing assessment tools, like those developed in the social and behavioral sciences, have strengths and weaknesses. However, psychometric validation is one limitation attributed particularly to the nursing tools. Nursing family assessment instruments for the most part are not psychometrically sound, nor have they been thoroughly field tested. For example, in a report about measuring the concept of "health" in nursing research, Reynolds, (1988, p. 29) reported that few researchers offer any evidence on which to conclude that the measures they choose are valid or reliable and that if "confidence is based on reports of reliability and validity presented by nurse researchers, one can place little confidence in many of the measures thus far used as health indicators." Consequently, nurses have looked outside their field for more psychometrically grounded instruments. Waltz, Strickland, and Lenz (1984, p. 3) defined *reliability* as the "consistency with which a device or method assigns scores to subjects. *Validity* refers to the determination of whether or not a device or method is useful for the purpose for which it is intended, that is, measures what it purports to measure." Since both of these concepts are important in selecting family nursing assessment/measurement instruments, the reader may want to refer to other sources listed in the book *Measurement in Nursing Research* (Waltz, Strickland, and Lenz, 1986) as well as the bibliography at the end of this chapter.

Feetham (1984, 1990) wrote about conceptual and methodological issues in family nursing research. In her discussion of instrumentation, she says there is a lack of congruence between conceptual/theoretical frameworks and instrumentation selected in studies. This perception of incongruence is also shared by Oliveri and Reiss (1984), who likewise raised questions about the correlations between instruments supposedly measuring the same concept and the interpretation of these correlations. There is also apparently little evidence of a logical link between the concepts investigators are measuring and the concepts instruments are purported to measure. Sensitization is another problem that Feetham (1984) mentions about family nursing instrumentation.

When families become sensitized, a confounding or misinterpretation of responses takes place. That is, due to the sequencing and content of questionnaires or interviews, family members gain increased awareness of issues and priorities that alter true responses or indeed serve as intervention strategies in and of themselves. The methodological problems inherent in family nursing measurement can be controlled somewhat through the choice of design, instrumentation, and analysis. Feetham (1990) wrote that selection of appropriate, reliable, and valid data-gathering methods, training of data collectors, and debriefing of families following data collection help control the ill effects of administering instrumentation. Much more could be said concerning other methodological issues, such as sources and level of family data, sampling, and data analysis, but this discussion goes beyond the purpose of this book, and the reader may want to study some other authors' writing on this subject (Feetham, 1984, 1990; Schrumm, Barnes, Bollman, et al, 1985; Speer and Sacks, 1985; Thomas, 1987; Uphold and Strickland, 1989).

Measurement Strategies

Researchers and clinicians alike have raised many questions about the validity of measures of family phenomena, especially when measuring the family as a whole. Fisher, Kokes, Ransom, et al (1985) offer three strategies for accomplishing family-centered work and discuss individual, relational, and transactional measurement strategies. That there are three levels of analysis strategies is consistent with the work of nurse Friedemann (1989). She discussed the concept of family nursing using a system-based conceptualization with nursing being practiced on three different systems levels. The first level of individual family members views the family as the context of the individuals. The goals for practice on the individual level are physical health and personal well-being. The second interpersonal level addresses dyads and larger units. The main goals of the family nurse at the interpersonal level are mutual understanding and support of family members. The third family system level includes the structural and functional system components interacting with the environment. The goals for the nurse practicing at a systems level consist of changes in the family system as a whole and increasing harmony between systems and subsystems as well as between system and environment.

Individual strategies. Fisher et al. (1985) elaborate on their three levels as they relate to measurement. First, individual strategies collect data from a single family member. This format constitutes the majority of past assessment and measurement techniques and, in cases of families, usually the mother is interviewed or questioned. Children are sometimes studied but grandparents and fathers are seldom the focus of inquiry. The problem with individual strategies, of course, is that one person is speaking for the family unit and may not represent other members' views. The data may be interviews, questionnaires, or observation and may look at perception of self or perception of other family members. Many examples of individual assessment/measurement are found in family and nursing literature. For example, nurses have used a few common instruments with individual members: Chronicity Impact and Coping Instrument (Hymovich, 1983); the various iterations of the Family Adaptability and Cohesion Evaluation Scales (FACES) (Olson, Bell, and Portner, 1980; Olson, McCubbin, Barnes, et al, 1983, 1985; Olson and Portner, 1983; Olson, Portner, and Lavee, 1985; Olson, Russell, and Sprenkle, 1980, 1983; Olson, Sprenkle, and Russell, 1979). Family APGAR (Smilkstein, 1978, 1980); (McMaster) Family Assessment Device (FAD) (Epstein, Baldwin, and Bishop, 1983); Family Dynamics Measure (Lasky, Buckwalter, Whall, et al., 1985); Family Environment Scale (FES) (Moos, 1974); Family Functioning Index (FFI) (Pless and Satterwhite, 1973); and Feetham Family Functioning Survey (FFFS) (Feetham, 1983; Roberts and Feetham, 1982). (See the section of this chapter on selected family assessment/measurement instruments.) Data derived from individuals have their advantages and disadvantages (Whall and Fawcett, 1990), but what the nurse should note before selecting an instrument is the theoretical perspective of the family they might portray.

Relational strategies. Relational strategies and consequent data "are derived from the contributions of family members combined or contrasted in some way to indicate a characteristic of the unit (Fisher et al., 1985, p. 215). This combined product of individual family members then represents some characteristic of the family as a whole. "They are statements about the family" or the perception of individual members, albeit combined. Usually the information comes from a dyad, such as mother/father, mother/child, or nurse/family member. This kind of data may be generated by obtaining a mean of individual scores, by summing scores, by subtracting the difference to obtain a discrepancy or congruence score, or by employing some other statistical technique. Most of the instruments constructed for individuals and named above can also be used to look at relational data. These are examples of instruments that were not originally developed to measure the family as a whole or as a dyad but that can be used to generate relational data. The Dyadic Adjustment Scale (DAS) (Spanier, 1976), Family Health Inventory (Hanson, 1985, 1986), Enriching and Nurturing Relationship Issues, Communication and Happiness (ENRICH), and Premarital Personal and Relationships Evaluation (PREPARE) (Fournier, Olson, and Bruckman, 1983) are a few instruments that were developed for use with dyads in the family. Relationship data provide more information than individual data, but the findings must be viewed with caution because of all of the methodological and statistical hazards. As indicated before, discussing the advantages and disadvantages of relational data collection versus individual or family-focused strategies goes beyond this discussion, but more elaboration is available elsewhere (Fisher, 1982; Fisher et al., 1985; Whall and Fawcett, 1990; Uphold and Strickland, 1989).

Transactional Strategies. Finally, Fisher et al. (1985, p. 215) discuss transactional strategies yielding data that "reflect some product of the system or behavioral interchange among system members that indicates the transactional unification of the system's whole that is significantly different than the sum of its parts." Apparently, transactional data should not be generated from relational instruments but rather by naturalistic inquiry or observations of a quantitative or qualitative nature. Examples of instrumentation yielding transactional data are few (Whall and Fawcett, 1990) and include the Simulated Family Activity Measure (SIMFAM) (Straus and Tallman, 1971) and Structured Family Interview (Watzlawick, 1966). It has been proposed that these approaches are the only ones that truly yield holistic family systems data. Some instruments designed for use with individuals and dyads have been statistically manipulated for employment in assessing whole family. Many methodological problems are associated with these procedures, however, and there are other points of view on this issue.

Whether to use individual, dyadal, or multiple informant data to hypothesize about the family has been a problem for years. In a recent article on issues related to the family as a unit of analysis (Uphold and Strickland, 1989), the authors discussed factors that nurse researchers should consider when deciding whether to use one informant versus several in family research. They make the point that even one family member's perspective is a valuable source of information about family phenomena and that this can provide important data on the relational properties between family members. There are advantages and disadvantages of using individual, dyadal, or multiple informants in family research, but all approaches are valid. What is most helpful about this work is that the authors discuss the various ways of dealing methodologically and statistically with the results of multiple informant data. Nurses can use strategies and approaches, such as summing the score, deriving the mean score, selecting the maximized family score, difference or congruence score, combining these approaches, or using the topological analysis approach or multivariate analysis. Pros and cons to all of these were summarized drawing on the work of Schrumm (1982) and Schrumm, Barnes, Bollman, et al. (1985).

To summarize, most instruments have been designed to measure individual data and do not always adequately measure family phenomena as a whole. This challenge of generating relational and transactional data occurs at a period when family nursing is expanding rapidly. The goal of family nursing, however, should continue to be means to address the family as a whole. The middle-range nursing systems model of Betty Neuman lent itself to the development of an instrument that not only facilitated the development of a nursing assessment/measurement instrument but also helped to bridge the gap between assessment and intervention strategies. The Family Systems Stressor Strengths Inventory (FS^3I) collects both quantitative and qualitative data through questionnaire and observation. It is intended to obtain transactional data that reflect the system or behavioral interchange among family members as a whole, as well as information that is current with nurse-generated data concurrent with the nurse who is providing their care.

The next section of this chapter summarizes selected nursing and nonnursing assessment instruments that would be useful to nursing clinicians and researchers.[2] The bibliography contains additional references. The box contains criteria for the selection of instruments. Waltz, Strickland, and Lenz (1984) give additional information concerning the selection and use of instruments.

Criteria for Selecting Family Assessment/Measurement Instruments

Nurses need to be cognizant of parameters that contribute to the effectiveness of family assessment or measurement instruments. According to Speer and Sachs (1985), these parameters are (1) understandability, (2) administration and scoring, (3) reliability and validity, (4) client appropriateness, and (5) clinical relevance.

Nurses must select instruments for assessment and measurement of family health that are *easily understood*. The questions should be worded at a sixth-grade level, so that family members with poor reading skills or limited vocabularies can comprehend and can respond with dignity.

Families are more likely to complete assessment instruments, and nurses are more apt to use them, if they can be administered in a *short time*. Fifteen or 20 minutes is generally the maximum amount of time that nurses and families can devote to this process, whether in busy clinics, units or other hospital settings, or the home. Other factors worth considering are ease of scoring and the length of time involved in interpreting results.

Determining the *reliability* and *validity* of a family tool involves judgments about the instrument's consistency and whether the results accurately reflect what the tool is attempting to measure. The tool must be both valid and reliable.

To be effective, an instrument needs to be constructed in such a way that the questions are *appropriate* for the majority of families. The composition of words, phrases, and concepts should be universal, not geared to a particular social class, age group, or ethnic background. They must also address topics that the family deems reasonable and appropriate, or they may hesitate to participate.

The last area to consider is the *clinical relevance* of the instrument. If the tool is easy to understand, administer, and score but not relevant, then it is ineffectual. Family health measurement tools must focus on those areas of need for which nursing interventions may be planned.

Selected Family Assessment/Measurement Instruments[2]

Name: **BEAVERS-TIMBERLAWN FAMILY EVALUATION SCALE (BT)**

Purpose: To assess family health

Source: Beavers (1982)
           Lewis, Beavers, Gossett, and Phillips (1976)

The BT is a fourteen item rating scale designed to assess family health. Its primary purpose is for descriptive classification and research but it can also be used clinically. It is based on a model derived from general systems theory, which holds the view that key family challenges are separation and individuation and that individual and family functioning are related. There are six major scales, each of which has subscales: (1) family structure (overt power, parental coalition, and closeness); (2) mythology; (3) goal-directed negotiation; (4) autonomy (clarity of expression, responsibility, invasiveness, and permeability); (5) family affect (range of feelings, mood and tone, unresolvable conflict, and empathy); and (6) global health/pathology. Interrater reliabilities range from 0.58 to 0.79. This instrument would be useful in family counseling and therapy settings for assessment, as well as for measurement in research purposes (treatment outcomes).

Name: **CALGARY FAMILY ASSESSMENT MODEL (CFAM)**

Purpose: To assess families using family structure, family development, and functional assessment

Source: Wright and Leahy (1984)

The CFAM is more of a model than an assessment or measurement instrument, but it has been included here because of its applicability for family nurses. It is a framework that consists of three major categories: family structural assessment, developmental assessment, and functional assessment. Each category is further delineated into subcategories. For example, the structural category consists of internal household composition and boundary as well as external culture and family of origin. The developmental category addresses stages of the family life cycle, tasks, and adaptive and maladaptive attachments. Finally, the functional category examines task allocation, daily routines, emotional communication, and roles. The authors of this model discuss how it can be used more specifically while interviewing families in the clinical setting. The book, Nurses and families: A guide to family assessment and intervention (Wright and Leahey, 1984) provided no interview guide.

Name: **CHRONICITY IMPACT AND COPING INSTRUMENT: PARENT QUESTIONNAIRE (CICI:PQ)**

Purpose: To examine parental perceptions of stressors, prob-
            lematic situations or resources, and parents' coping
            strategies for managing stressors
Sources: Hymovich (1983)
            Speer and Sachs (1985)
            Feetham (1984)

Hymovich developed the CICI:PQ to examine the effect of children's chronic illness on family developmental tasks and parent coping strategies and to measure the outcome of intervention. More specifically, the instrument measures parental perceptions of stressors, problematic situations or resources, and parents' coping strategies for managing the stressors. It provides a protocol for identifying the needs of families with chronically ill children. Hymovich developed the 48-item, six-area instrument using the critical incident technique from parent interviews: children with chronic conditions, parents, spouses, other children, the hospitalization experience, and others. The self-administered test takes 20 minutes. Content validity has been determined, and internal consistency is 0.93 to 0.94. This instrument is considered to be in developmental stages. Its prime contribution is assessing the information and support needs of chronically ill children and their parents. The CICI:PQ measures factors that nurses could help change through the implementation of care plans.

Name: **THE DYADIC ADJUSTMENT SCALE (DAS)**
Purpose: To measure marital or dyadic adjustment
Sources: Spanier (1976)
            Spanier and Filsinger (1983)
            Kazak, Jarmas, and Snitzer (1988)

The researchers developed the DAS for use with married and cohabitating couples. The self-report measure consists of 32 items comprising four dimensions of adjustment: dyadic satisfaction, dyadic consensus, dyadic cohesion, and affectional expression. The scale and subscales are highly reliable: Cronbach's alpha is 0.96 for the entire scale and from 0.73 to 0.94 for the subscales. A consensus of the judges supported the scale's validity and relevance. The DAS is available in several languages for use with various nationalities and cultural groups. The DAS is built on a sound conceptual foundation and is commonly used in family research. In addition to the references listed above, the DAS is also available in paper-and-pencil and computer versions from Multi-Health Systems, Inc, 95 Thorncliffe Park Drive, Suite 200, Toronto, Ontario, Canada M4H 1L7.

Name: ENRICHING AND NURTURING RELATION-
         SHIPS ISSUES, COMMUNICATION AND HAP-
         PINESS (ENRICH) and PREMARITAL PER-
         SONAL AND RELATIONSHIPS EVALUATION
         (PREPARE)

Purpose: To measure problems related to personal, interper-
         sonal, and external issues in relationships among
         marital (ENRICH) and premarital (PREPARE) cou-
         ples

Sources: Fournier, Olsen, and Bruckman (1983)
         Olson, McCubbin, Barnes, Larsen, Muxen, and Wil-
         son (1985)

   Both ENRICH and PREPARE contain 115 Likert-style self-report questions that use a 5-point response format. The questionnaires are conceptually similar, with each designed to serve as a diagnostic tool in assessing relationship problems. ENRICH assesses idealistic distortion, marital satisfaction, personality issues, communication, conflict resolution, financial management, leisure activities, sexual relationship, children and marriage, family and friends, egalitarian roles, and religious orientation. PREPARE assesses all of the above except marital satisfaction, since it is used with couples before marriage. Cronbach's alpha averaged 0.74, with a range of 0.48 to 0.92 on the subscales. Test-retest reliability is reported to be approximately 0.87. This scale could be used by nurses who are interested in couple relationships and how they set the environment for family life.

Name: FAMILY ADAPTABILITY AND COHESION
         EVALUATION SCALE (FACES)

Purpose: To measure cohesion and adaptability as unifying
         family health dimensions

Sources: Olson, Sprenkle, and Russell (1979)
         Olson, Bell, and Portner (1980)
         Olson, Russell, and Sprenkle (1980)
         Mountain (1982)
         Olson, McCubbin, Larsen, Muxen, and Wilson
         (1983, 1985)
         Olson and Portner (1983)
         Olson (1986)

   FACES, under development since 1978, consists of three versions, each presumably an improvement on the former: FACES I, II, and III. FACES is designed to classify families into three general and sixteen specific types on cohesion and adaptability. It can administered to individuals, couples, and families and is available in four forms that contain items examining perceived and ideal couples or families. FACES III is more usable and includes a shortened, 20-item self-report scale used in obtaining data from adult family members on their perceptions of family cohesion and adaptability. The instrument views cohesion as the emotional bonding among family members and includes bonding, independence, boundaries, coalition formation, use of time and space, relationships with friends, decision making, interests, and recreation. Adaptability is a family's ability to change, including the use of family power, negotiation styles, role relationships, relationship rules, and feedback. Subscores for each variable are obtained. Four levels of family cohesion range from extreme low (disengaged) to extreme high (enmeshed). The two "normal" levels are "separated" and "connected." Additionally, the scale includes four levels of adaptability ranging from low adaptability (rigid) to high (chaotic). Two moderate levels of adaptability are "flexible" and "structured." Scores between family members vary considerably, with correlations in the 0.30 to 0.40 range. Cronbach's alpha is reported to be 0.77 for cohesion, 0.62 for adaptability, and 0.68 for total scale. Test-retest is 0.84; internal consistency is 0.78 to 0.90.

Studies have documented the two major dimensions of adaptability and cohesion, but little support is provided for the subcategories. The tool has been used extensively for diagnosis and treatment purposes, and families have demonstrated change after treatment. The instrument assumes that children and family members must speak for the whole family. The instrument is rated easy to understand and administer and is universally useful. It measures factors relevant to nursing and could guide practice, particularly in the area of family mental health, where cohesion and adaptability are viewed as unifying health dimensions. The conceptual model underlying the instrument helps nurses understand family dynamics.

Name: **FAMILY ADAPTABILITY, PARTNERSHIP, GROWTH, AFFECTION, AND RESOLVE TESTS (FAMILY APGAR)**

Purpose: To assess family functioning: adaptability, partnership, growth, affection, and resolve

Sources: Smilkstein (1978, 1980)
           Good, Smilkstein, Good, Shaffer, and Arons (1979)
           Smilkstein, Ashworth, and Montano (1982)

This five-item test taps five areas of family functioning: adaptability, partnership, growth, affection, and resolve. The Family APGAR was found to correlate with family therapists' ratings of clinic patients. The instrument seems to differentiate maladjusted families from well-adjusted families. It is reported to be influenced by individuals' desire to appear "good" to health professionals. The test-retest is 0.83, the internal consistency 0.24 to 0.67. The questions are global rather than specific. The utility of the tool is limited since it does not have a strong empirical base and does not help nurses identify specific intervention strategies. The Family APGAR is quick to use, however, and can serve as a screening device in a busy clinical setting. It can also assist nurses in determining specific areas to investigate more fully.

Name: **(McMASTER) FAMILY ASSESSMENT DEVICE (FAD)**

Purpose: To assess dimensions of family functioning affecting health: problem solving, communication, roles, affective responsiveness, affective involvement, behavior control, and general functioning

Sources: Epstein, Baldwin, and Bishop (1986)
          Miller, Epstein, Bishop, and Keitner (1986)

The FAD was developed from the McMaster Model of Family Functioning to measure dimensions that ultimately affect family health. This screening tool consists of seven scales that look at problem solving, communication, roles, affective responsiveness, affective involvement, behavior control, and general functioning. It contains 60 items including statements about how the family as a group feels, acts, or communicates. The FAD requires each person to make composite judgments about the family. Cronback's alpha is reported to be 0.92 for general functioning and 0.72 to 0.83 for the six original dimensions. The test-retest figure ranges from 0.66 to 0.76.

The test is moderately successful in discriminating between groups that are known to have significant family problems and others who do not. The FAD is easy to use and understand, although its usefulness with clients of different cultural and social backgrounds or different life stages is uncertain. It does not measure family systems per se but rather an individual's view of the family as a whole. Presumably the FAD identifies areas of concern that nurses can change through care plans.

Name: **FAMILY ASSESSMENT GUIDE**
Purpose: To assess families in the community
Source: Clemen-Stone, Eigsti, and McGuire (1987)

The Family Assessment Guide is just a guide rather than a formalized instrument. The authors list some parameters that nurses should use when assessing families, including structural characteristics (financial resources, educational experiences, family roles, division of labor, distribution of power/authority, cultural influences, and activities of daily living); process characteristics (atmosphere of home, communication patterns, decision-making processes, conflict negotiation, achievement of developmental tasks, adaptation to change, and autonomy); relationships with external systems (boundaries, environment, support, interactions, attitudes, and referral processes); and environmental characteristics (neighborhood, housing). The Family Assessment Guide was intended to be an assessment checklist rather than a measurement device per se, but it is an additional resource available to family nurses.

Name: **(The) FAMILY ASSESSMENT TOOL (FAT)**
Purpose: Assessment guide for school nurses: Family perception, health interview, family history
Source: Holt and Robinson (1979)

The FAT is a health interview guide for school nurses. The FAT assists in collecting and presenting health history data on children and families about the following areas: (1) home and environment, including sociocultural influences, (2) family interaction, (3) growth and developmental history, (4) health history, and (5) family history. The nurse completes the assessment in the child's home following an in-school discussion with the teacher observation of the child. The guidelines are very comprehensive and are available by writing to F.A.T. Kit, Box 4941, Boulder, Colorado 80306.

Name: **FAMILY COPING INDEX**
Purpose: To assess nursing needs of family and determine level of coping
Source: Freeman and Heinrich (1981)

The Family Coping Index is an instrument developed for public health nurses who are determining the family's ability to cope with various situations. Each family is rated on a 5-point scale in terms of how they cope in the following areas: physical independence, therapeutic independence, knowledge of condition, principles of personal hygiene, attitude toward health care, emotional competence, family living patterns, physical environment, and use of community resources. The index was developed in 1964 as a tool for practice, an approach to identifying the family's need for nursing care and assessing the potential for behavioral changes, and a method for determining systematically how nurses can help the family manage.

Name: **FAMILY CRISIS ORIENTATED PERSONAL EVALUATION SCALES (F-COPES)**

Purpose: To assess family coping strategies

Source: McCubbin, Olson, and Larsen (1987)

F-COPES was designed to identify problem-solving and behavioral strategies used by families in difficult situations. The instrument examines coping strategies in terms of reliance on resources both internal and external to the immediate family. F-COPES identifies internal coping patterns as (1) confidence in problem solving, (2) reframing family problems, and (3) family passivity. External strategies include (1) church or religious resources, (2) extended family, (3) friends, (4) neighbors, and (5) community resources. Cronbach's alpha is reported to range from 0.64 to 0.84. Test-retest reliability is reported to be 0.81 for the combined scale. This scale has been used for looking at coping strategies of rural versus urban populations, male and female gender roles, and parents and new babies. Nurses may find F-COPES useful in looking at social support issues during times of family transitions.

Name: **FAMILY ENVIRONMENT SCALE (FES)**

Purpose: To assess family environment: relationships, personal growth; system maintenance and change

Sources: Moos (1974)
          Moos and Moos (1976, 1983a, 1983b)
          Fuhr, Moos, and Dishotsky (1981)
          Moos (1985)

The FES is one of the most widely used family measurements, with over 200 publications describing its applications. It was designed to measure social climates in all types of families. This 90-item, true-false questionnaire has 10 subscales measuring three domains: (1) relationship dimensions (cohesion, expressiveness, and conflict; (2) personal growth or goal orientation dimensions (independence, achievement orientation, moral-religious emphasis, intellectual-cultural, and active recreational orientation); and (3) system maintenance and change dimensions (organization and control). The FES includes three forms: the "real" form, the "ideal" form, and the "expectations" form. In terms of psychometrics, the internal consistency for the 10 scales is 0.61 to 0.78, and the test-retest value is 0.68 to 0.86, with low intercorrelations among items. The FES has been reported to have good construct validity. Family profiles are constructed using standardized scores on each subscale, and incongruency scores can be determined by looking at the disagreement between scores among family members. The discriminatory ability of the tool appears significant, and it distinguishes between families experiencing conflict and those who are not. Research has shown that this instrument may be useful in measuring changes in families undergoing treatment. The FES is considered lengthy for clinical use, and scoring is complex, but it is universally appropriate for all types of families. The FES is available from Consulting Psychologists Press, 577 College Avenue, Palo Alto, California 94306.

Name: **FAMILY FUNCTIONING INDEX (FFI)**
Purpose: To assess multidimensional complexities of family functioning; communication, togetherness, closeness, decision making, child orientation
Sources: Pless and Satterwhite (1973)
          Satterwhite, Zweig, Iker, and Pless (1976)
          Brown, Rawlinson, and Hardin (1982)

The FFI measures multidimensional complexities of family functioning. It was designed to identify families at risk, not to measure the level of risk or distress. The five principal components or subscales are communication, togetherness, closeness, decision making, and child orientation. The instrument assumes the presence of young children in the home, so it should not be used for families without children or those with adult children. The FFI was initially developed for use in both research and clinical settings, primarily with families who have chronically ill children. The instrument does not detect short-term or long-term changes in family dynamics, so it might best be used as a predictive or intervening measure rather than as an outcome measure. The understandable, easy-to-take test is viewed as highly stable: 5-year test-retest value was 0.83. The FFI's internal consistency is unknown, but it has been shown to differentiate between well-functioning families and "troubled" families. Nurses could use this instrument as a screening tool to identify areas for intervention. The FFI is available through the National Auxiliary Publications Services (NAPS-3), PO Box 3513, Grand Central Station, New York, New York 10163-3513; telephone 516-481-2300.

Name: **FAMILY HEALTH ASSESSMENT FORM**
Purpose: To assess families using the structural-functional framework: the developmental stage, family history, family structure, family functions, family coping
Source: Friedman (1986)

The Friedman Family Assessment Model, which is built using the structural/functional framework, consists of six broad categories: (1) identifying data, (2) developmental stage and history, (3) environmental data, (4) family structure, (5) family functions, and (6) family coping. Each category contains numerous subcategories. Nurses must decide which subcategories are particularly relevant to explore during family visits in the home. The guidelines consist of a large number of questions designed to be very comprehensive. The Friedman Family Assessment Model is being taught to undergraduate nursing students in many U.S. nursing schools and represents one of the first and most comprehensive approaches to family assessment.

Name: **FAMILY HEALTH ASSESSMENT GUIDE**
Purpose: To assess families for the purpose of planning health care
Source: Stanhope and Lancaster (1984)

The Family Health Assessment Guide consists of a list of topics recommended for use during family assessment. It is not a measurement tool but rather a comprehensive guideline that addresses a family's sociodemographic profile, environment, structure, processes, functions, coping, and health behavior. It also includes interview questions that focus on family problem identification for problem-solving purposes. The book that contains this assessment guide is *Community Health Nursing: Process and Practice for Promoting Health* (Stanhope and Lancaster, 1984).

Name: **FAMILY HEALTH INVENTORY**
Purpose: To measure the physical and mental health of individuals in families
Source: Hanson (1985, 1986)

The FHI is an instrument developed to assess and measure the physical and mental health of families. Open-ended and closed-ended questions were developed for the self-administered scale.

Health behavior, health attitudes, and health status are three of the subscales derived through factor analysis. A panel of experts determined content and construct validity. The inventory awaits further psychometric testing. This instrument is mentioned here because it represents one of few efforts to date to measure the construct "family health," as opposed to individual health. This is a topic of import to family nursing.

Name: **FAMILY INVENTORY OF LIFE EVENTS (FILE)**

Purpose: To assess normative and nonnormative family stress and strains that the family experiences with respect to traumatic events, changing circumstances, and role identities

Source: McCubbin and Patterson (1987)

FILE is a seventy-one-item questionnaire designed to record life events and changes that families have encountered during the past year. The tool contains "yes" and "no" items that are worded to reflect some adjustment in regular patterns of family member interaction. The emphasis is on positive or negative change. The nurse can score FILE in five different ways, depending on the purpose for and use of the information, whether it be for clinical or research situations. Events fall into nine general categories: interfamily strains, marital strains, pregnancy and childbearing strains, financial and business strains, work-family transitions and strains, illness and family "care" strains, losses, transitions "in and out," and legal. Cronbach's alpha for the overall scale ranges from 0.72 to 0.81. Test-retest reliability ranges from 0.66 to 0.84. The instrument has potential for use in clinical settings and has been used with families in stress who have children with chronic illness and/or are obtaining divorces.

Name: **FAMILY STRENGTHS SCALE**

Purpose: To assess family strengths: pride and accord

Sources: McCubbin and Patterson (1983, 1987)

          Olson, McCubbin, Barnes, Larsen, Muxen, and Wilson (1985)

This scale is a 12-item Likert-style instrument designed to measure positive qualities of families that aid in their ability to negotiate social and familial environmental influences effectively. The tool focuses on the factors of pride and accord in families. Cronbach's alpha values are 0.87 for pride, 0.73 for accord, and 0.83 for the combined scale. The test-retest figure is 0.58. Family members utilize a 5-point Likert Scale in completing this instrument. Nurses could use the Family Strengths Scale to assess families that can successfully negotiate their circumstances.

Name: **FEETHAM FAMILY FUNCTIONING SURVEY (FFFS)**

Purpose: To measure parents' perceptions of relationships among family members and their ability to function in the outside world

Sources: Feetham (1984)
           Roberts and Feetham (1982)
           Feetham and Humenick (1982)
           Speer and Sachs (1985)

Feetham, along with Roberts, developed an instrument to assess family functioning across three areas of relationships between (1) the family and broader social units, (2) the family and subsystems, and (3) the family and each individual. The instrument has been used in studies of families having children with health problems and families with healthy infants. This program of research uses a conceptual model. Scales had moderate-to-high interitem reliability (alpha coefficients of 0.66 to 0.84) and were stable over a 2-week test-retest period (0.85). Content validity was established. The instrument has been used to measure social support as well as family functioning. The FFFS has had extensive field testing with families of children who have myelodysplasia. It is relevant for the assessment of traditional middle class families with children. It determines parents' perceptions of relationship and family function. It is somewhat difficult to understand and rather complicated to score. The clinical relevance of the tool is that it measures factors that nurses could help change through care plans.

Name: **HOME OBSERVATION FOR MEASUREMENT OF THE ENVIRONMENT (HOME)**

Purpose: To measure parameters within the home that nurture the development of infants and children

Sources: Caldwell and Bradley (1970)
           Bradley (1982)
           Calloway (1982)

The HOME inventory is designed to assess the quality and quantity of support for cognitive, social, and emotional development available to children through the home environment. The three versions of HOME address different age groups of children: infant (birth to 3 years), preschool (3 to 6 years), and elementary (6 to 10 years). The three primary intended uses are (1) identification of home environments that pose a risk for children's development; (2) evaluation of programs designed to improve parenting skills, and (3) basic research on the relationship between home environments and children's health and development. Home uses an observational coding system and binary scoring; data are obtained in homes from hour-long semistructured interviews with parents and children. This instrument is easy to learn and administer. Internal consistency for total scores and subscales ranged from 0.38 to 0.93. Additional information is available from the Center for Research on Teaching and Learning, Education 205, University of Arkansas at Little Rock, 2801 South University Avenue, Little Rock, Arkansas 72204.

Name: **INVENTORY OF FAMILY FEELINGS (IFF)**
Purpose: To assess the family's affective structure; delineate patterns of conflict relationships and alliances; reveal positive/negative feelings toward each member
Sources: Lowman (1980)
          Margolin and Fernandez (1983)
          Fredman and Sherman (1987)

The IFF is a self-report questionnaire measuring interpersonal affects or the positive and negative feelings of family members for each other. It outlines a family's affective structure and delineates patterns of conflict relationships and alliances. Family members agree or disagree on 38 items on a unidimensional scale that rates their feelings toward other family members. The IFF can generate five different types of scores: individual, dyad, reception, response, and family unit. It can also be used to develop a graphic representation of a family sociogram. The construct and concurrent validity are reportedly good. The tool has limited clinical use because of its unidimensionality; it is appropriate for measuring only one dimension of interpersonal and family relationships—the strength of positive/negative feelings. The IFF is easily administered and scored. Test-retest reliability is 0.96. This instrument would give nurses some idea of how family members feel toward each other, information that may be useful in designing care.

Name: **NURSING CHILD ASSESSMENT SATELLITE SERIES (NCAST)**
Purpose: To measure multiple variables related to parent-child-environment interaction

Sources: Barnard and Eyres (1979)
             Snyder, Eyres, and Barnard (1979)

The series of scales consists of four widely used instruments for the assessment of the child/parent/environment interactions, beginning at birth: *Home Observation for Measurement of the Environment, Nursing Child Assessment Teaching Scales, Nursing Child Assessment Feeding Scales,* and *Nursing Child Assessment Sleep Activity Record.* Earlier research to determine early predictors of child health and developmental problems showed a pattern of parent/child as an interactive system and provided the conceptual basis for these scales. Although the measures are primarily observational, some interviewing is required to complete the scales. Factor analysis has determined the validity of the parent-child construct. Little information is provided relative to the validity of the tools. The tools have the potential for early diagnosis and management of developmental difficulties. These instruments are helpful in planning care for high-risk families and useful in nursing research.

Name: **STRUCTURAL   FAMILY   INTERACTION SCALE (SFIS)**

Purpose: To use Minuchin's theory of family functioning to measure enmeshment/disengagement, neglect/overprotection, rigidity/flexibility, conflict/avoidance, patient management, triangulation of parent-child coalition, and detouring

Source: Perosa, Hansen, and Perosa (1981)

This 85-item instrument measures Minuchin's concepts of enmeshment/disengagement, neglect/overprotection, rigidity/flexibility, parent conflict/avoidance with and without resolution, parent management, triangulation, parent-child coalition, and detouring. It also includes 10 secondary scales focusing on the respondents' evaluation of parents' actions related to conflict behaviors and strategies and overprotection/neglect behaviors. Most items are moderately consistent (alpha of 0.44 to 0.74), but the scale's internal consistency is low. The validity of the tool rests on interscale correlations and the amount of agreement on which item is being measured. This tool may be helpful for nurses who are counselors and who know Minuchin's constructs (such as psychiatric mental health nurses), but it may be too complex and time consuming for standard nursing clinical settings.

Summary and Conclusions

In summary, this chapter has attempted to develop a broader, more comprehensive picture of family assessment and family measurement than previous chapters provided. After defining assessment and measurement, earlier chapters discussed the status of family instrumentation and current family nursing instrumentation. The issues surrounding psychometric evaluation were noted and criteria for selecting instruments were presented. A study that summarizes family nurses assessment instruments in use in the United States provided a basis for understanding what is being taught to students of nursing during their undergraduate and graduate programs. A summary of individual, relational, and transactional measurement strategies then followed, along with examples of instruments that could be categorized according to these three strategies. Finally, the last chapter presented selected instruments with the hope that this list may be useful to other family nurses, whether researchers or clinicians.

In conclusion, the development of family instrumentation, particularly as it relates to the paradigm of nursing, is in its early stages and evolves as the discipline evolves. Great strides have been made in the past 5 years, however, to organize and present the great variation of instruments available for use by nurse clinicians and researchers. We trust that the information in this volume will advance the knowledge and understanding of family health and family nursing.

Footnotes

1. Some good compendium sources specifically for nurses who are seeking instruments for nursing practice or research are available. The bibliography lists many of them. The reader is also referred to the an article in *Image* (1981) as well as Waltz, Strickland, and Lenz (1984); Ward and Felter (1979); and Ward and Lindeman (1979).

2. Literally thousands of family instruments are available to nurses. See the latest compendium by Touliatos, Perlmutter, and Straus (1990). The selected family assessment/measurement instruments chosen for summarization here are those with whom we have had some acquaintance (Hanson, 1988; Mischke-Berkey, Warner, and Hanson, 1989), those that appear to assess families as units, instruments that seem useful for nursing, and instruments that appear in the nursing literature. The list was meant neither to be all inclusive nor recommended, since the choice of an instrument is contingent on the goal of the investigators/clinicians.

References

Ackerman N. (1966). *Treating the troubled family*. New York: Basic Books.

Ackerman N. (1972). The growing edge of family therapy. In C Sager & H Kaplan (Eds.). *Progress in group and family therapy* (pp 440-456). New York: Brunner/Mazel.

Adams B. (1980). *The family: A sociological interpretation*. Chicago: Rand McNally.

Allmond B, Buckman W, & Gofman H. (1979). *The family is the patient*. St. Louis: Mosby.

American Nurses Association. (1980). *Nursing: A social policy statement*. (Publ. No. NP-63). Kansas City, MO: American Nurses Association.

American Nurses Association. (1985). *Code for nurses with interpretive statements*. (Publ. No G-56). Kansas City, MO: American Nurses Association.

Auger JR. (1976). *Behavioral systems in nursing*. Englewood Cliffs, NJ: Prentice Hall.

Bakal DA. (1979). *Psychology and medicine*. New York: Springer.

Baker J, Borchers D, Cochran D, et al. (1986). Parent-child interaction. In Marriner A (Ed.). *Nursing theorists and their work*. St. Louis: Mosby.

Banks R. (1980). Health and the spiritual dimension: Relationships and implications for professional preparation programs. *Journal of School Health 50*(4), 195-202.

Barnard KE. (1984). The family as a unit of measurement. *Journal of Maternal Child Nursing 9*, 21.

Barnard KE, & Eyres SJ. (Eds.). (1979). *Child health assessment, Part 2: The first year of life*. Washington, DC: US Government Printing Office (DHEW Publication No. HRA 79-25).

Barnard, KE, Hammond, MA, Booth, CL, Bea, HL, Mitchell, SK, & Spicker, SJ. (1989). Measurement and meaning of parent-child interaction. In Morrison, F, Lord, C, & Keating, D. (Eds.). *Applied developmental psychology*, vol III. New York: Academic Press.

Barnard M, & Hymovich D. (Eds.). (1979). *Family health care: Developmental and situational crisis* (Vol. II). New York: McGraw-Hill.

Barnard KE, & Neal MV. (1977). Maternal-child nursing research: Review of the past and strategies for the future. *Nursing Research 26*, 193-198.

Bateson G. (1979). *Mind and nature*. New York: Bantam Books.

Beavers WR. (1981). Healthy families. In G Berenson & H White (Eds.). *Annual review of family therapy* (pp 63-91). New York: Human Sciences Press.

Beavers WR. (1982). Healthy, midrange, and severely dysfunctional families. In F Walsh (Ed.). *Normal family processes* (pp 45-66). New York: Guilford.

Beels C, & Ferber A. (1973). What family therapists do. In A Ferber, M Mendelson, & A Napier (Eds.). *The book of family therapy* (pp. 168-209). New York: Houghton Mifflin.

Belew R, & Buchanan D. (1982). Family therapy origins. In I Clements & D Buchanan (Eds.). *Family therapy: A nursing perspective* (pp 3-12). New York: Wiley.

Belsky J, Lerner RM, & Spanier GB. (1984). *The child in the family*. Reading, MA: Addison-Wesley.

Bertrand A. (1972). Social organization: A general systems and role theory perspective. Philadelphia: FA Davis.

264   References

Blair K. (1971). It's the patient's problem and decision. *Nursing Outlook 19*, 588.

Bomar P. (1989). Family stress. In P Bomar (Ed.). *Nurses and family health promotion: Concepts, assessment, and interventions* (pp 103-114). Baltimore: Williams & Wilkins.

Bowen M. (1971). The use of family theory in clinical practice. In J Haley (Ed.). *Changing families: A family therapy reader* (pp 159-192). New York: Grune & Stratton.

Bowen M. (1976). Theory in the practice of psychotherapy. In P Guerin (Ed.). *Family therapy: Theory and practice* (pp 42-90). New York: Gardner.

Bowen M. (1978). *Family therapy in clinical practice*. New York: Jason Aronson.

Braden C, & Herban N. (1976). *Community health: A systems approach*. New York: Appleton-Century-Crofts.

Bradley RH. (1982). The home inventory: A review of the first fifteen years. In NJ Anastasiow & A Fandal (Eds.). *Identifying the developmentally delayed child* (pp 87-100). Baltimore: University Park Press.

Bradley, RH, & Caldwell, BM. (1977). Home observation for measurement of the environment: A validation study of screening efficiency. *American Journal of Mental Deficiency, 81*(5):417-424.

Broderick CB. (1971). Beyond the five conceptual frameworks: A decade of development in family theory. *Journal of Marriage and the Family 33*, 139-159.

Bronfenbrenner U. (1979). *The ecology of human development*. Cambridge, MA: Cambridge University Press.

Brown JS, Rawlinson ME, & Hardin DM. (1982). Family functioning and health status. *Journal of Family Issues 3*, 91-110.

Buchanan BF. (1987). Human-environment interaction: A modification of the Neuman systems model for aggregates, families and the community. *Public Health Nursing 4*, 52-64.

Burgess E. (1926). The family as a unity of interacting personalities. *The Family 7*, 3-9.

Burr Q, Hill E, Nye I, & Reiss I. (1979). *Contemporary theories about the family* (Vols. 1 & 2). New York: Free Press.

Cain A. (1980). Assessment of family structure. In JW Miller & EH Janosik (Eds.). *Family-focused care* (pp. 115-131). New York: McGraw-Hill.

Caldwell BM. (1978). *Home observation for measurement of the environment*. Little Rock: University of Arkansas.

Caldwell BM, & Bradley RH. (1970). *Home observation for measurement of the environment*. Little Rock: University of Arkansas.

Calloway SJ. (1982). Home observation for measurement of the environment. In S. M. Humenick (Ed.). *Analysis of current assessment strategies in the health care of young children and childbearing families* (pp. 252-258). Norwalk, CT: Appleton-Century-Crofts.

Campbell J, & Humphreys C. (1985). *Nursing care for victims of violent families*. New York: Harper & Row.

Caplan G. (1964). *Principles of preventive psychiatry*. New York: Basic Books.

Carlson CI. (1989). Criteria for family assessment in research and intervention contexts. *Journal of Family Psychology 3*(2), 158-176.

Carlson CI, & Grotevant HD. (1987). A comparative review of family rating scales: Guidelines for clinicians and researchers. *Journal of Family Psychology, 1*(1), 23-47.

Carpenito LJ. (1983). *Nursing diagnosis: Application to clinical practice*. Philadelphia: Lippincott.

Chin R. (1980). The utility of systems models and developmental models for practitioners. In JP Riehl & C Roy (Eds.). *Conceptual models for nursing practice*, (2nd ed., pp. 21-37). New York: Appleton-Century-Crofts.

Chinn P, & Jacobs M. (1983). *Theory and nursing: A systematic approach*. St Louis: Mosby.

Choi T, Josten L, & Christensen ML. (1983). Health specific family coping index for noninstitutional care. *American Journal of Public Health 73*, 1275-1279.

Chrisman M, & Riehl-Sisca J. (1989). The systems-developmental-stress model. In J Riehl-Sisca (Ed.). *Conceptual models for nursing practice* (pp. 277-295). Norwalk, CT: Appleton & Lange.

Christenson H (Ed.). (1964). *Handbook of marriage and the family*. Chicago: Rand McNally.

Clark C. (1978). *Mental health aspects of community health nursing*. New York: McGraw-Hill.

Clemen-Stone S, Eigsti D, & McGuire S. (1991). *Comprehensive family community health nursing* (3rd ed.). St. Louis: Mosby.

Clements IW, & Buchanan D. (1982). *Family therapy: A nursing perspective*. New York: Wiley.

Clements IW, & Roberts FB (Eds.). (1983). *Family health: A theoretical approach to nursing care*. New York: Wiley.

Corcoran K, & Fischer J. (1987). *Measures for clinical practice: A source book*. New York: The Free Press.

Cross J. (1985). Betty Neuman. In J George (Ed.). *Nursing theories: The base for professional nursing practice* (2nd ed., pp. 258-286). Englewood Cliffs, NJ: Prentice-Hall.

Curran D. (1983). *Traits of a healthy family*. Minneapolis: Winston Press, (Harper & Row).

Curran D. (1985). *Stress and the healthy family*. Minneapolis: Winston Press (Harper & Row).

Daniel L. (1986). Family assessment. In B Logan & C Dawkins (Eds.). *Family-centered nursing in the community* (pp. 184-208). Reading, MA: Addison-Wesley.

de Chardin PT. (1955). *The phenomenon of man* (pp. 109-112). London: Collins.

Dintiman G, & Greenberg JS. (1986). *Health through discovery* (3rd ed.). New York: Random House.

Duvall E. (1977). *Family development*. Philadelphia: Lippincott.

Duvall EM, & Miller BC. (1985). *Marriage and family development*. New York: Harper & Row.

Eberst R. (1984). Defining health: A multidimensional model. *Journal of School Health 54*(3), 99-104.

Edison C. (1979). Family assessment guidelines. In D Hymovich & M Barnard (Eds.). *Family health care: General perspectives* (pp. 264-279). New York: McGraw-Hill.

Epstein N, Baldwin L, & Bishop D. (1983). The McMaster assessment device. *Journal of Marital and Family Therapy 9*, 171-180.

Epstein NE, Bishop DS, & Baldwin LM. (1982). McMaster model of family functioning: A view of the normal family. In F Walsh (Ed.). *Normal family processes* (pp. 115-141). New York: Guilford Press.

Eshleman JR. (1974). *The family: An introduction.* Boston: Allyn & Bacon.

Fawcett J. (1975). The family as a living open system: An emerging conceptual framework for nursing. *International Nursing Review 22*, 113-117.

Fawcett J. (1984). *Analysis and evaluation of conceptual models of nursing.* Philadelphia: Davis.

Fawcett J. (1989a). *Analysis and evaluation of conceptual models of nursing* (2nd ed.). Philadelphia: Davis.

Fawcett J. (1989b). Analysis and evaluation of the Neuman Systems Model. In B Neuman (Ed.). *The Neuman Systems Model* (pp. 65-92). Norwalk, CT: Appleton & Lange.

Fawcett J, & Downs F. (1986). *The relationship of theory and research.* Norwalk, CT: Appleton-Century-Crofts.

Feathers R. (1989). Orem's self-care nursing theory. In J Riehl-Sisca (Ed.). *Conceptual models for nursing practice* (pp. 369-375). Norwalk, CT: Appleton & Lange.

Feetham S. (1983). *Feetham family functioning survey.* Available from Children's Hospital National Medical Center, 7701 Glennon Drive, Bethesda, MD 20817.

Feetham SL. (1984). Family research: Issues and directions for nursing. In HH Werley & JJ Fitzpatrick (Eds.). *Annual Review of Nursing Research 2*, 3-25.

Feetham SL. (1990). Conceptual and methodological issues in research of families. In AL Whall & J Fawcett (Eds.). *Family theory development in nursing: State of the science and art.* Philadelphia: Davis.

Feetham SL, & Humenick SS. (1982). The Feetham family functioning survey. In SS Humenick (Ed.). *Analysis of current assessment strategies in the health care of young children and childbearing families* (pp. 259-268). Norwalk, CT: Appleton-Century-Crofts.

Filsinger E. (1983). Assessment. What it is and why it is important. In EE Filsinger (Ed.). *Marriage and family assessment: A sourcebook for family therapy.* Beverly Hills, CA: Sage.

Filsinger E (Ed.). (1983). *Marriage and family assessment: A sourcebook for family therapy.* Beverly Hills, CA: Sage.

Fisher L. (1982). Transactional theories about individual assessment: A frequent discrepancy in family research. *Family Process 21*, 313-320.

Fisher L, Kokes RF, Ransom DC, Phillips SL, & Rudd P. (1985). Alternative strategies for creating "relational" family data. *Family Process 24*, 213-224.

Fitzpatrick JJ, & Whall AL (Eds.). (1983). *Conceptual models of nursing: Analysis and application.* Bowie, MD: Brady–Prentice Hall.

Fitzpatrick J, Whall A, Johnston R, & Floyd J. (1982). *Nursing models and their psychiatric mental health applications.* Bowie, MD: Brady.

Foley V. (1974). *An introduction to family therapy.* New York: Grune & Stratton.

Forman BD, & Hagan BJ. (1984). Measures for evaluating total family functioning. *Family Therapy 11*(1), 1-36.

Fournier DG, Olson DH, & Bruckman JM. (1983). Assessing marital and premarital relationships: The PREPARE-ENRICH inventories. In EE Filsinger (Ed.). *Marriage and family assessment*. Beverly Hills, CA: Sage.

Fredman N, & Sherman R. (1987). *Handbook of measurements for marriage and family therapy*. New York: Brunner/Mazel.

Freeman RB, & Heinrich J. (1981). *Community health nursing practice* (2nd ed.). Philadelphia: Saunders.

Friedemann ML. (1989). The concept of family nursing. *Journal of Advanced Nursing 14,* 211-216.

Friedman MM. (1986). *Family nursing: Theory and assessment* (2nd ed.). Norwalk, CT: Appleton-Century-Crofts.

Fuhr R, Moos R, & Dishotsky N. (1981). The use of family assessment and feedback in ongoing family therapy. *American Journal of Family Therapy* 9(1), 24-36.

Gilliss C. (1989). Why family health care? In C Gilliss, B Highley, B Roberts, & I Martinson (Eds.). *Toward a science of family nursing* (pp. 3-8). Reading, MA: Addison-Wesley.

Gilliss C, Roberts B, Highley B, & Martinson I. (1989). What is family nursing? In C Gilliss, B Highley, B Roberts, & I Martinson (Eds.). *Toward a science of family nursing* (pp. 64-76). Reading, MA: Addison-Wesley.

Glass J. (1989). Levine's theory of nursing: A critique. In J Riehl-Sisca (Ed.). *Conceptual models for nursing practice* (pp. 339-348). Norwalk, CT: Appleton & Lange.

Glasser P, & Glasser L. (1970). *Families in crisis*. New York: Harper & Row.

Goldblum-Graff D, & Graff H. (1982). The Neuman model adapted to family therapy. In B Neuman. *The Neuman Systems Model: Application to nursing education and Practice* (pp. 217-222). Norwalk, CT: Appleton-Century-Crofts.

Gonot P. (1986). Family therapy as derived from King's conceptual model. In AL Whall (Ed.). *Family therapy theory for nursing: Four approaches* (pp. 33-48). Norwalk, CT: Appleton-Century-Crofts.

Good MD, Smilkstein MG, Good BJ, Shaffer T, & Arons T. (1979). The family APGAR index: A study of construct validity. *Journal of Family Practice 8,* 577-582.

Gordon M. (1982). *Manual of nursing diagnosis*. New York: McGraw-Hill.

Gordon M. (1987). *Nursing diagnosis: Process and application*. New York: McGraw-Hill.

Gray W, Rizzo ND, & Duhl FD (Eds.). (1969). *General systems theory and psychiatry*. Boston: Little, Brown.

Greenberg J. (1985). Health and wellness: A conceptual differentiation. *Journal of School Health 55*(10), 403-406.

Griffith JW. (1986). Relevance of theoretical approaches in nursing practice. In J Griffith-Kenney & P Christensen. *Nursing process: Application of theories, frameworks and models* (2nd ed., pp. 3-16). St. Louis: Mosby.

Griffith-Kenney JW, & Christensen PJ. (1986). *Nursing process: Application of theories, frameworks, and models* (2nd ed.). St. Louis: Mosby.

Grotevant HD. (1989). The role of theory in guiding family assessment. *Journal of Family Psychology 3*(2), 104-117.

Grotevant HD, & Carlson CI. (1987). Family interaction coding systems: A descriptive review. *Family Process 26,* 49-74.

Grotevant HD, & Carlson CI. (1989). *Family assessment: A guide to methods and measures*. New York: Guilford Press.

Grubb J. (1984). An interpretation of the Johnson Behavioral system model for nursing practice. In J Riehl & C Roy (Eds.). *Conceptual models for nursing practice* (2nd ed., pp. 217-254). New York: Appleton-Century-Crofts.

Gustafson MB. (1977). Let's broaden our horizons about the use of contracts. *International Nursing Review 24*(1), 18-19.

Haley J. (1976). *Problem-solving therapy*. San Francisco: Jossey-Bass.

Hall JE, & Weaver BR. (1985). *Distributive nursing practice: Systems approach to community health* (2nd ed.). Philadelphia: Lippincott.

Haller KB. (1986). Selecting measurement instruments. *Journal of Maternal Child Nursing 11*, 438.

Haney M, & Boenisch E. (1983). *Stressmap: Finding your pressure points*. San Luis Obispo, CA: Impact Publishers.

Hanson SMH. (1985). *Family health inventory: A measurement*. Paper presented at the National Council of Family Relations, Dallas, TX.

Hanson SMH. (1986). Health single parent families. *Family Relations 35*(1), 125-132.

Hanson SMH. (1987). Family nursing and chronic illness. In M Leahey & L Wright (Eds.). *Families and chronic illness* (pp. 2-32). Springhouse, PA: Springhouse.

Hanson SMH. (1988). *Family nursing curricula in accredited U.S. Schools of Nursing*. Portland: Oregon Health Sciences University. (Research report summarized for research grant from the Office of Research, Development and Utilization.)

Hanson SMH, Heims M, & Bozett FW. (In process). Family nursing curriculum in America.

Hareven TK. (1987). Historical analysis of the family. In MB Sussman & SK Steinmetz. *Handbook of marriage and the family*. New York: Plenum Press.

Hill R. (1971). *The strengths of black families*. New York: Emerson Hall.

Hill R, & Hansen D. (1960). The identification of conceptual frameworks utilized in family study. *Marriage and Family Living 22*, 299-311.

Hill R, Katz AM, Simpson RL. (1957). An inventory of research in marriage and family behavior: A statement of objectives and progress. *Marriage and Family Living 19*, 89-92.

Hill R, & Rodgers R. (1964). The developmental approach. In H Christenson (Ed.). *The handbook of marriage and the family* (pp. 171-211). Chicago: Rand McNally.

Hoffman M. (1982). From model to theory construction: An analysis of the Neuman Health-Care Systems Model. In B Neuman (Ed.). *The Neuman Systems Model: Application of nursing education and practice* (pp. 44-48). East Norwalk, CT: Appleton-Century-Crofts.

Holman AM. (1983). *Family assessment: Tools for understanding and intervention*. Beverly Hills: Sage.

Holman TB, & Burr WR. (1980). Beyond the beyond: The growth of family theories in the 1970's. *Journal of Marriage and the Family 42*, 729-741.

Holmes TH, & Rahe RH. (1967). The social readjustment rating scale. *Journal of Psychosomatic Research 11*, 213-218.

Holt S, & Robinson T. (1979). The school nurses assessment tool. *American Journal of Nursing 79*, 950-953.

Houldin A, Saltstein S, & Ganley K. (1987). *Nursing diagnosis for wellness: Supporting strengths*. New York: Lippincott.

Humenick SS. (1982). *Analysis of current assessment strategies in the health care of young children and childbearing families*. Norwalk, CT: Appleton-Century-Crofts.

Hurwitz J, Kaplan D, & Kaiser E. (1965). Designing an instrument to assess parental coping mechanisms. In H Parad (Ed.). *Crisis interventions: Selected readings* (pp. 339-348). New York: Family Service Association of America.

Hymovich D. (1983). The chronicity impact and coping instrument: Parent questionnaire. *Nursing Research 32*, 275-281.

Hymovich D, & Barnard M. (1979). Family health care: General perspectives. New York: McGraw-Hill.

Jackson DD. (1973). *Therapy, communication and change* (2nd ed.). Palo Alto, CA: Science and Behavior Books.

Jackson J. (1966). A Conceptual and measurement model for norms and roles. *Pacific Sociology Review 9*, 35-38.

Janosik EH, & Miller JR. (1980). Assessment of family function. In JR Miller & EH Janosik (Eds.). *Family-focused care* (pp. 132-146). New York: McGraw-Hill.

Johnson DE. (1980). The behavioral system model for nursing. In JP Riehl & C Roy (Eds.). *Conceptual models for nursing practice* (2nd ed., pp. 207-216). New York: Appleton-Century-Crofts.

Johnson MN, Vaughn-Wrobel B, Ziegler SM, Hough L, Bush HA, & Kurtz P. (1982). Use of the Neuman health-care systems models in the master's curriculum: Texas Women's University. In B Neuman (Ed.). *The Neuman systems model: Application to nursing education and practice* (pp. 130-152). Norwalk, CT: Appleton-Century-Crofts.

Johnson OG, & Bommarito JW. (1976). *Tests and measurements in child development: Handbook I*. San Francisco: Jossey-Bass.

Johnson SH. (1986). *Nursing assessment and strategies for the family at risk: High risk parenting* (2nd ed.). Philadelphia: Lippincott.

Johnston R. (1986). Approaching family intervention through Rogers' conceptual model. In A Whall (Ed.). *Family therapy theory for nursing: Four approaches* (pp. 11-32). Norwalk, CT: Appleton-Century-Crofts.

Jones S. (1980). *Family therapy: A comparison of approaches*. Bowie, MD: Brady.

Jones S. (1986). A reformulation of the interactional approach to family therapy. In A Whall (Ed.). *Family therapy theory for nursing: Four approaches* (pp. 95-126). Norwalk, CT: Appleton-Century-Crofts.

Jones W, & Dimond M. (1982). Family theory and family therapy models: Comparative review with implications for nursing practice. *Journal of Psychosocial Nursing and Mental Health Services 20*(10), 12-19.

Kandzari JH, & Howard JE. (1981). *The well family: A developmental approach to assessment*. Boston: Little, Brown.

Karoly P (Ed.). (1985). *Measurement strategies in health psychology*. New York: Wiley.

Kazek AE, Jarmas A, & Snitzer L. (1988). The assessment of marital satisfaction: An evaluation of the Dyadic Adjustment Scale. *Journal of Family Psychology 2*, 82-91.

King I. (1981). *A theory for nursing: Systems, concepts, process.* New York: Wiley.

King I. (1989). *King's general systems framework and theory.* In J Riehl-Sisca (Ed.). *Conceptual models for nursing practice* (pp. 149-158). Norwalk, CT: Appleton & Lange.

Knafl K. (1986). The concept of family. In B Logan & C Dawkins (Eds.). *Family-centered nursing in the community* (pp. 31-53). Reading, MA: Addison-Wesley.

Knafl K, & Grace H. (1978). *Families across the life cycle.* Boston: Little, Brown.

Lasky P, Buckwalter KE, Whall AL, Lederman R, Speer J, McLane A, King JM, & White MA. (1985). Developing an instrument for the assessment of family dynamics. *Western Journal of Nursing Research 7,* 40-52.

Leslie ER. (1976). *The family in social context.* New York: Oxford Press.

Levine M. (1971). Holistic nursing. *Nursing Clinics of North America 6*(2), 253-264.

Lewis JM. (1979). *How's your family? A guide to identifying your family's strengths and weaknesses.* New York: Brunner/Mazel.

Lewis J, Beavers W, Gossett J, & Phillips VA. (1976). *No single thread: Psychological health in family systems.* New York: Brunner/Mazel.

Lillis P, & Cora V. (1989). A case study analysis using the Neuman Nursing Process Form: An abstract. In B Neuman (Ed.). *The Neuman systems model* (pp. 51-55). Norwalk, CT: Appleton & Lange.

Lincoln YS, & Guba EG. (1985). *naturalistic inquiry.* Beverly Hills, CA: Sage.

Litman TJ. (1974). The family as a basic unit in health and medical care: A social-behavioral overview. *Social Science and Medicine 8,* 495-519.

Logan BB, & Dawkins CE. (1986). *Family centered nursing in the community.* Menlo Park, CA: Addison-Wesley.

Lowman J. (1980). Measurement of family affective structures. *Journal of Personality Assessment 44*(2), 130-141.

MacElveen PM. (1983). *Social networks.* Available from CL Attneave, 5206 Ivanhoe Place NE, Seattle, WA 98105.

Mangen DJ, Bengtson VL, & Landry PH. (Eds.). (1988). *Measurement of intergenerational relations.* Newbury Park, CA: Sage.

Margolin G, & Fernandez V. (1983). Other marriage and family questionnaires. In EE Filsinger (Ed.). *Marriage and family assessment: A sourcebook for family therapy* (pp. 317-338). Beverly Hills, CA: Sage.

McCubbin HI, Cauble AE, & Patterson JM. (1982). *Family stress, coping and social support.* Springfield, IL: Charles C Thomas.

McCubbin HI, Olson DH, & Larsen AS. (1987). F-COPES: Family Crisis Orientated Person Evaluation Scales. In HI McCubbin & AI Thompson (Eds.). *Family assessment inventories for research and practice.* Madison: University of Wisconsin-Madison (Family Stress Coping and Health Project, 1300 Linden Drive, 53706).

McCubbin HI, & Patterson JM. (1983). Stress: The family inventory of life events and changes. In EE Filsinger (Ed.). *Marriage and family assessment: A sourcebook for family therapy* (pp. 275-298). Beverly Hills, CA: Sage.

McCubbin HI, & Patterson JM. (1987). FILE: Family Inventory of Life Events and Changes. In HI McCubbin & AI Thompson (Eds.). *Family assessment inventories for research and practice* (pp. 81-98). Madison: University of Wisconsin-Madison (Family Stress Coping and Health Project, 1300 Linden Drive, 53706).

McCubbin HI, & Thompson AI. (Eds.). (1987). *Family assessment inventories for research and practice*. Madison: The University of Wisconsin-Madison (Family stress Coping and Health Project, 1300 Linden Drive, 53706).

McDowell I, & Newell C. (1987). *Measuring health: A guide to rating scales and questionnaires*. New York: Oxford University Press.

McFarland GK, & Wasli EL. (1986). *Nursing diagnoses and process in psychiatric mental health nursing*. Philadelphia: Lippincott.

McFarlane J. (1986). *Clinical handbook of family nursing*. New York: Wiley.

McGoldrick M, & Gerson R. (1985). *Genograms in family assessment*. New York: Norton.

Mead GH. (1933). *Mind, self, and society*. Chicago: University of Chicago Press.

Mederer H, & Hill R. (1983). Critical transitions over the family life span: Theory and research. *Marriage and Family Review* 6(1/2), 39-60.

Messer, A. (1970). *The individual in his family: An adaptation study*. Springfield, IL: Charles C Thomas.

Meyerstein I. (1979). The family behavioral snapshot: A tool for teaching family assessment. *American Journal of Family Therapy* 7(1), 48-56.

Miller EW, Epstein NB, Bishop DS, & Keitner GI. (1986). The McMaster Family Assessment Device: Reliability and validity. *Journal of Marriage and Family Therapy 11*, 345-356.

Miller J. (1965). Living systems: Basic concepts. *Behavioral Science 10:* 193-224.

Miller J, & Janosik E. (1980). *Family focused care*. New York: McGraw-Hill.

Miller SR, & Winstead-Fry P. (1982). *Family systems theory in nursing practice*. Reston, VA: Reston Publishing Co.

Minuchin S. (1974). *Families and family therapy*. Cambridge, MA: Harvard University Press.

Mirenda R. (1986). The Neuman systems model: Description and application. In P Winstead-Fry (Ed.). *Case studies in nursing theory* (pp. 127-159). National League of Nursing, Pub. No. 15-2152.

Mischke-Berkey K, Warner P, & Hanson S. (1989). Family health assessment and intervention. In P Bomar (Ed.). *Nurses and family health promotion: Concepts, assessment, and interventions* (pp. 115-154). Baltimore: Williams & Wilkins.

Moos RH. (1974). *Family environment scale*. Palo Alto, CA: Consulting Psychologists Press.

Moos RH. (1985). Evaluating social resources in community and health care contexts. In P Karoly (Ed.). *Measurement strategies in health psychology*. New York: Wiley.

Moos RH, & Moos BS. (1976). A typology of family social environments. *Family Process 15,* 357-371.

Moos RH, & Moos BS. (1983a). Clinical applications of the family environment scale. In E. E. Filsinger (Ed.). *Marriage and family assessment: A sourcebook for family therapy* (pp. 253-274). Beverly Hills, CA: Sage.

Moos RH, & Moos BS. (1983b). A typology of family social environments. *Family Process 15,* 357-371.

Mountain KL. (1982). FACES: A family dynamics assessment based on cohesion and adaptability. In SS Humenick (Ed.). *Analysis of current assessment strategies in the health care of young children and childbearing families* (pp. 269-277). Norwalk, CT: Appleton-Century-Crofts.

Murphy S. (1986). Family study and nursing research. *Image: Journal of Nursing Scholarship 18*(4), 170-174.

Murray R, & Zentner J. (1985). *Nursing assessment and health promotion through the life span*. Englewood Cliffs, NJ: Prentice Hall.

Neuman B. (1980). The Betty Neuman Health-Care Systems Model. In J Riehl & C Roy (Eds.). *Conceptual models for nursing practice* (2nd ed., pp. 127-131). Norwalk, CT: Appleton-Century-Crofts.

Neuman B. (1982). *The Neuman systems model: Application to nursing education and practice*. Norwalk, CT: Appleton-Century-Crofts.

Neuman B. (1983). Family intervention using the Betty Neuman Health-Care Systems Model. In I Clements & F Roberts (Eds.). *Family health: A theoretical approach to nursing care* (pp. 161-176). New York: Wiley.

Neuman B. (1989). The Neuman systems model. In B Neuman (Ed.). *The Neuman Systems Model* (2nd ed., pp. 3-50). Norwalk, CT: Appleton & Lange.

Neumann College Nursing Faculty. (1987). *Neumann College Nursing Process Tool*. Aston, PA: Neumann College, Department of Nursing.

Nye FI, & Berardo FM. (1981). *Emerging conceptual frameworks in family analysis*. New York: Praeger Scientific.

Oliveri ME, & Reiss D. (1984). Family concepts and their measurement: Things are seldom what they seem. *Family Process 23,* 33-48.

Olson DH. (1986). Circumplex model VII: Validation studies and FACES III. *Family Process 25,* 337-351.

Olson DH, Bell R, & Portner J. (1980). *Family adaptability and cohesion evaluation scales*. St. Paul: University of Minnesota Press.

Olson DH, McCubbin HI, Barnes HL, Larsen AS, Muxen MJ, & Wilson MA. (1983). *Families: What makes them work?* Beverly Hills, CA: Sage.

Olson DH, McCubbin HI, Barnes HL, Larsen AS, Muxen MJ, & Wilson MA. (1985). *Family inventories*. St. Paul: University of Minnesota Press.

Olson DH, & Portner J. (1983). Family adaptability and cohesion evaluation scales. In EE Filsinger (Ed.). *Marriage and family assessment: A sourcebook for family therapy* (pp. 299-316). Beverly Hills, CA: Sage.

Olson DH, Portner J, & Bell R. (1978). *Family adaptability and cohesion evaluation scale (FACES)*. St. Paul: University of Minnesota.

Olson DH, Portner J, & Lavee Y. (1985). *FACES III*. St. Paul: University of Minnesota.

Olson D, Russell C, & Sprenkle D. (1980). Circumplex model of marital and family systems II: Empirical studies and clinical intervention. In JP Vincent (Ed.). *Advances in family intervention, assessment, and theory* (pp. 78-87, 128-176). Greenwich, CT: JAI Press.

Olson D, Russell C, & Sprenkle D. (1983). Circumplex model of marital and family systems VI: Theoretical update. *Family Process 22,* 69-83.

Olson DH, Sprenkle DH, & Russell CS. (1979). Circumplex model of marital and family systems I: Cohesion and adaptability dimensions, family types, and clinical applications. *Family Process 18,* 3-28.

Olson DH, Sprenkle DH, & Russell CS. (1983). Circumplex model of marital and family systems VI: Theoretical update. *Family Process 22,* 60-83.

Orem D. (1979). *Nursing: Concepts of practice* (3rd ed.). New York: McGraw-Hill.

Orem DE. (1985). *Nursing: Concepts of practice* (4th ed.). New York: McGraw-Hill.

Otto HA. (1963). Criteria for assessing family strength. *Family Process 2*(2), 239-338.

Otto HA. (1973). A framework for assessing family strengths. In A Reinhardt & M Quinn (Eds.). *Family-centered community nursing: A sociocultural framework* (pp. 87-94). St. Louis: Mosby.

Paltrow K. (1980). Review of areas: Updated method of patient evaluation. *Postgraduate Medicine, 67*(1), 211-214.

Parse R. (1986). Man-living-health. In A Marriner (Ed.). *Nursing theorists and their work* (pp. 169-177). St. Louis: Mosby.

Parse R. (1989). Man-living-health: A theory of nursing. In J Riehl-Sisca (Ed.). *Conceptual models for nursing practice* (pp. 253-257). Norwalk, CT: Appleton & Lange.

Parsons T. (1951). *The social system*. Glencoe, IL: The Free Press.

Parsons T, & Bales RF. (1955). *Family socialization and interaction process*. New York: The Free Press.

Pender NJ. (1982). *Health promotion in nursing practice*. Norwalk, CT: Appleton-Century-Crofts.

Pender N. (1987). *Health promotion in nursing practice* (2nd ed.). Los Altos, CA: Appleton & Lange.

Perosa L, Hansen J, & Perosa S. (1981). Development of the structural family interaction scale. *Family Therapy 8*(2), 77-90.

Peters M. (1981). Making it black family style: Building on the strength of black families. In N Stinnett, T DeFrain, K King, D Knaab, & G Rowe (Eds.). *Family strengths 3: Roost of well-being* (pp. 73-91). Lincoln: University of Nebraska Press.

Phares EJ. *Locus of control and personality*. Morristown, NJ: General Learning Press.

Phipps L. (1980). Theoretical frameworks applicable to family care. In J Miller & E Janosik. *Family focused care* (pp. 31-58). New York: McGraw-Hill.

Pinnell NN, & de Meneses M. (1986). *The nursing process: Theory, application, and related processes* (pp. 135-140). Norwalk, CT: Appleton-Century-Crofts.

Pino CJ. (1984). The children's family environment scale (CFES). *Family Therapy 11*(1), 85-86.

Pless IB, & Satterwhite B. (1973). A measure of family functioning and its application. *Social Science and Medicine 7*, 613-621.

Polit DF, & Hungler BP. (1983). *Nursing research: Principles and methods*. Philadelphia: Lippincott.

Popkin D. (1980). Structural family intervention. In JR Miller & EH Janosik. *Family focused care* (pp. 332-345). New York: McGraw-Hill.

Pratt L. (1973). The significance of the family in mediation. *Journal of Comparative Family Studies 4*, 13-15.

Pratt L. (1976). *Family structure and effective health behavior: The energized family*. Boston: Houghton Mifflin.

Putt A. (1978). *General systems theory applied to nursing*. Boston: Little, Brown.

Reed K. (1982). The Neuman systems model: A basis for family psychosocial assessment and intervention. In B Neuman (Ed.). *The Neuman systems model: Application to nursing education and practice* (pp. 188-195). Norwalk, CT: Appleton-Century-Crofts.

Reed K. (1989). Family theory related to the Neuman systems model. In B Neuman (Ed.). *The Neuman systems model* (2nd ed., pp. 385-396). Norwalk, CT: Appleton & Lange.

Reed P. (1986). The Developmental conceptual framework: Nursing reformulations and applications for family therapy. In A Whall (Ed.). *Family therapy theory for nursing: Four approaches* (pp. 69-91). Norwalk, CT: Appleton-Century-Crofts.

Reynolds CL. (1988). The measurement of health in nursing research. *Advances in Nursing Science, 10*(4), 23-31.

Riehl-Sisca J. (1986). Symbolic interactionism. In A Marriner (Ed.). *Nursing theorists and their work* (pp. 246-255). St. Louis: Mosby.

Riehl-Sisca J. (1989). The Riehl Interaction Model: An update. In J Riehl-Sisca (Ed.). *Conceptual models for nursing practice* (pp. 383-402). Norwalk, CT: Appleton & Lange.

Roberts CS, & Feetham SL. (1982). Assessing family functioning across three areas of relationships. *Nursing Research 31*(4), 231-235.

Rodgers RH. (1964). Toward a theory of family development. *Journal of Marriage and the Family 26,* 262-270.

Rogers M. (1970). *An introduction to the theoretical basis of nursing.* Philadelphia: Davis.

Rogers M. (1989). Nursing: A science of unitary human beings. In J Riehl-Sisca (Ed.). *Conceptual models for nursing practice* (pp. 181-188). Norwalk, CT: Appleton & Lange.

Roy C. (1980). *Conceptual models for nursing practice.* New York: Appleton-Century-Crofts.

Roy C. (1983). Roy adaptation model. In I Clements & F Roberts. *Family health: A theoretical approach to nursing care* (pp. 255-278). New York: John Wiley & Sons.

Roy C. (1989). The Roy adaptation model. In J Riehl-Sisca (Ed.). *Conceptual models for nursing practice* (pp. 105-114). Norwalk, CT: Appleton & Lange.

Russell CS. (1979). Circumplex model of marital and family systems, III: Empirical evaluation with families. *Family Process 18,* 29-45.

Russell RD. (1980). Some futures of health education. *Eta Sigma Gamma* September (Supp).

Sabatelli RM. (1988). Measurement issues in marital research: A review and critique of contemporary survey instruments. *Journal of Marriage and the Family 50,* 891-915.

Satir V. (1967). Conjoint family therapy. Palo Alto, CA: Science & Behavior Books.

Satir V. (1972). *Peoplemaking.* Palo Alto, CA: Science and Behavior Books.

Satterwhite BB, Zweig SR, Iker HP, & Pless B. (1976). The family functioning index—Five year test-retest reliability and implications for use. *Journal of Comparative Family Studies 7*(1), 111-116.

Schraneveldt JD. (1973). The interactionist framework in the study of the family. In A Reinhardt & M Quinn (Eds.). *Family-centered community nursing* (pp. 119-138). St. Louis: Mosby.

Schrumm WR. (1982). Integrating theory, measurement and data analysis in family studies survey research. *Journal of Marriage and the Family 44,* 983-998.

Schrumm WR, Barnes HL, Bollman SR, Jurich AP, & Milliken GA. (1985). Approaches to the statistical analysis of family data. *Home Economics Research Journal 14*(1), 112-122.

Schuster C, & Ashburn S. (1986). *The process of human development* (2nd ed.). Boston: Little, Brown.

Scoresby L. (1979). Family systems therapy. *Journal of the Association of Mormon Counselors & Psychotherapists 5,* 2-28.

Sedgwick R. (1981). *Family mental health: Theory and practice.* St. Louis: Mosby.

Selye H. (1974). *Stress without distress.* New York: New American Library.

Selye H. (1976). *The stress of life* (rev. ed.). New York: McGraw-Hill.

Sills GM, & Hall JE. (1985). A general systems perspective for nursing. In JE Hall & BR Weaver (Eds.). *Distributive nursing practice: A systems approach to community health* (pp. 21-29). Philadelphia: Lippincott.

Sloan M, & Schommer B. (1975). The process of contracting in community nursing. In BW Spradley (Ed.). *Contemporary community nursing.* Boston: Little, Brown.

Smilkstein G. (1978). The family APGAR: A proposal for a family function test and its use by physicians. *Journal of Family Practice 6,* 1231-1239.

Smilkstein G. (1980). The cycle of family function: A conceptual model for family medicine. *Journal of Family Practice 11*(2), 223-232.

Smilkstein G, Ashworth C, & Montano D. (1982). Validity and reliability of the family APGAR as a test of family function. *Journal of Family Practice 15,* 303-311.

Snyder C, Eyres SJ, & Barnard K. (1979). New findings about mothers' antenatal expectations and their relationship to infant development. *American Journal of Maternal Child Nursing 4*(6), 354-357.

Sorochan W. (1976). Self-actualization inventory. Personal health appraisal. New York: Wiley.

Spanier GB. (1976). Measuring dyadic adjustment: New scales for assessing the quality of marriage and similar dyads. *Journal of Marriage and the Family 35,* 15-28.

Spanier GB. (1988). *Presidential address to the National Council on Family Relations.* Philadelphia.

Spanier GB, & Filsinger EE. (1983). The dyadic adjustment scale. In EE Filsinger (Ed.). *Marriage and family assessment: A sourcebook for family therapy* (pp. 155-168). Beverly Hills, CA: Sage.

Speer JJ, & Sachs B. (1985). Selecting the appropriate family assessment tool. *Pediatric Nursing 11,* 349-355.

Spradley B. (1981). *Community health nursing, concepts and practice.* Boston: Little, Brown.

Spradley B. (1986). *Readings in community health nursing* (3rd ed.). Boston: Little, Brown.

Spradley BW. (1985). *Community health nursing: Process and practice for promoting health.* St. Louis: Mosby.

Sprenkle D, & Olson D. (1978). Circumplex model of marital system IV: Empirical study of clinic and non-clinic couples. *Journal of Marriage and Family Counseling 4,* 59-74.

Stangler SR, Huber CJ, & Routh DK. (1980). *Screening growth and development of preschool children: A guide for test selection.* New York: McGraw-Hill.

Stanhope M, & Lancaster J. (1984). *Community health nursing: Process and practice for promoting health.* St. Louis: Mosby.

Stanton M, Paul C, & Reeves JS. (1985). An overview of the nursing process. In J George, (Ed.). *Nursing theories: The base for professional nursing practice* (pp. 14-33). Englewood Cliffs, NJ: Prentice-Hall.

Stinnett N. (1979). Strengthening families. *Family Perspectives 13,* 3-9.

Stinnett N, Chester B, & DeFrain J, & Knaub P (Eds.). (1979). *Family strengths: Positive models for family life.* Lincoln: University of Nebraska Press.

Stinnett N, & DeFrain J. (1985). *Secrets of strong families.* Boston: Little, Brown.

Stinnett N, DeFrain J, King K, Lindgren H, Van Zandt S, & Williams R (Eds.). (1982). *Family strengths 4.* Lincoln: University of Nebraska Press.

Stinnett N, DeFrain J, King K, Knaub P, & Rowe G. (1981). *Family strengths 3: Roots of well-being.* Lincoln: University of Nebraska Press.

Stinnett N, Sanders G, & DeFrain J. (1981). Strong families: A national study. In N Stinnett, J DeFrain, K King, P Knaoub, & G Rowe (Eds.). *Family strengths 3: Roots of well-being* (pp. 33-41). Lincoln: University of Nebraska Press.

Story E, & Roiss M. (1986). Family centered community health nursing and the Betty Neuman Systems Model. *Nursing Papers/Perspectives in Nursing 18*(2), 77-88.

Straus MA. (1964). *Family measurement techniques.* Minneapolis: University of Minnesota Press.

Straus MA, & Brown BW. (1978). Family measurement techniques: Abstracts of published instruments, 1935-1974. Minneapolis: University of Minnesota Press.

Straus MA, & Tallman I. (1971). SIMFAM: A technique for observational measurement and experimental study of families. In J Aldous, T Condon, R Hill, M Straus, & I Tallman (Eds.). *Family problem solving: A symposium on theoretical, methodological, and substantive concerns* (pp. 379-438). Hynesdale, IL: Dryden.

Sullivan J, & Fawcett J. (1990). The measurement of family phenomena. In A Whall & J Fawcett (Eds.). *Family theory development in nursing: State of the science and art.* Philadelphia: Davis.

Tapia JA. (1975). The nursing process in family health. In B Spradley (Ed.). *Contemporary community nursing.* Boston: Little, Brown.

Thomas RB. (1987). Methodological problems in family health care research. *Journal of Marriage and the Family 49,* 65-70.

Tinknam K, & Voorhies E. (1984). *Community health nursing: Evolution and process in family and community.* New York: Appleton-Century-Crofts.

Touliatos J, Perlmutter BF, & Straus MA (Eds.). (1990). *Handbook of family measurement techniques.* Newbury Park, CA: Sage.

Travelbee J, & Doona M. (1979). *Travelbee's intervention in psychiatric nursing* (2nd ed). Philadelphia: Davis.

Uphold CR, & Strickland OL. (1989). Issues related to the unit of analysis in family nursing research. *Western Journal of Nursing Research 11,* 405-417.

Venable, J. (1980). The Neuman health-care system model: An analysis. In J. Riehl & C. Roy (Eds.). *Conceptual models for nursing practice* (pp. 115-122). New York: Appleton-Century-Crofts.

von Bertalanffy L. (1968). *General systems theory.* New York: George Braziller.

Waltz CF, Strickland OL, & Lenz ER. (1984). *Measurement in nursing research.* Philadelphia: Davis.

Ward MJ, & Felter ME. (1979). *Instruments for use in nursing education research.* Boulder, CO: Western Interstate Commission for Higher Education.

Ward MJ, & Lindeman C. (1979). *Instruments for measuring nursing practice and other health care variables.* Hyattsville, MD: DHEW Publication No. HRA 78-53 (Volume 1) and HRA 78-54 (Volume 2).

Watson J. (1989). Watson's philosophy and theory of human caring in nursing. In J Riehl-Sisca (Ed.). *Conceptual models for nursing practice* (pp. 219-236). Norwalk, CT: Appleton & Lange.

Watzlawick R. (1966). A structure family interview. *Family Process 5,* 256-271.

Watzlawick P, & Weakland J (Eds.). (1977). *The interactional view: Studies at the Mental Research Institute, Palo Alto, 1965-1974.* New York: Norton.

Webster's third new international dictionary. (1986). Springfield, MA: Merriam-Webster.

Whall A. (1980). Congruence between existing theories of family functioning and nursing theories. *Advances in Nursing Science 3,* 59-67.

Whall AL. (1981). Nursing theory and the assessment of families. *Journal of Psychosocial Nursing and Mental Health Services 19*(1), 30-36.

Whall AL. (1983). Family system theory: Relationship to nursing conceptual models. In J Fitzpatrick & J Whall (Eds.). *Conceptual models of nursing: Analysis and application* (pp. 69-93). Bowie, MD: Brady.

Whall AL. (1986). *Family therapy theory for nursing: Four approaches.* Norwalk, CT: Appleton-Century-Crofts.

Whall AL, & Fawcett J (Eds.). (1990). *Family theory development in nursing: State of the science and art.* Philadelphia: Davis.

Woolridge PJ, Skipper J, & Leonard R. (1968). *Behavioral science, social practice and the nursing profession.* Cleveland: Case Western Reserve University Press.

Wright LM, & Leahey M. (1984). *Nurses and families: A guide to family assessment and intervention.* Philadelphia: Davis.

Young RK. (1982). *Community nursing workbook: Family as client.* Norwalk, CT: Appleton & Lange.

Appendix

Family Systems Stressor-Strength Inventory (FS³I)
Family Form

Family Name _____   Date _____

Family Member Completing Assessment _____

Ethnic Background _____

Referral Source _____   Interviewer _____

Family Members	Relationship in Family	Age	Marital Status	Education (highest degree)	Occupation
1.					
2.					
3.					
4.					
5.					
6.					

What is your current reason(s) for seeking health care assistance?

_____

_____

_____

Part 1: Family Systems Stressors (General)

DIRECTIONS: Each of the 45 situations listed here deal with some aspect of normal family life.[a] They have the potential for creating tension within family members, between family members, or between families and external environment. We are interested in your overall impression of how these situations affect your family life. Please circle a number (1 through 5) that best describes the amount of stress or tension they create for you. Thank you for cooperation.

	N/A	Little Stress		Medium Stress		High Stress
1. Family member(s) feeling un-appreciated	0	1	2	3	4	5
2. Guilt for not accomplishing more	0	1	2	3	4	5
3. Insufficient "me" time	0	1	2	3	4	5
4. Self-image/self-esteem/feelings of unattractiveness	0	1	2	3	4	5
5. Perfectionism	0	1	2	3	4	5
6. Dieting	0	1	2	3	4	5
7. Health/illness	0	1	2	3	4	5
8. Drugs/alcohol	0	1	2	3	4	5
9. Widowhood	0	1	2	3	4	5
10. Retirement	0	1	2	3	4	5
11. Homework/school grades	0	1	2	3	4	5
12. Communication with children	0	1	2	3	4	5
13. Housekeeping standards	0	1	2	3	4	5
14. Insufficient couple time	0	1	2	3	4	5
15. Insufficient family playtime	0	1	2	3	4	5
16. Children's behavior/discipline/sibling fighting	0	1	2	3	4	5
17. Television	0	1	2	3	4	5

18. Overscheduled family calendar	0	1	2	3	4	5
19. Lack of shared responsibility in the family	0	1	2	3	4	5
20. Moving	0	1	2	3	4	5
21. Spousal relationship (communication, friendship, sex)	0	1	2	3	4	5
22. Holidays	0	1	2	3	4	5
23. Inlaws	0	1	2	3	4	5
24. Teen behaviors (communication, music, friends, church, school)	0	1	2	3	4	5
25. New baby	0	1	2	3	4	5
26. Houseguests	0	1	2	3	4	5
27. Family vacations	0	1	2	3	4	5
28. Remarriage	0	1	2	3	4	5
29. Relationship with former spouse	0	1	2	3	4	5
30. Summer	0	1	2	3	4	5
31. Weekends	0	1	2	3	4	5
32. Religious differences	0	1	2	3	4	5
33. Predinner hour	0	1	2	3	4	5
34. Older parents	0	1	2	3	4	5
35. Economics/finances/budgets	0	1	2	3	4	5
36. Unhappiness with work situation	0	1	2	3	4	5
37. Overvolunteerism	0	1	2	3	4	5
38. Neighbors	0	1	2	3	4	5

39. Unemployment	0	1	2	3	4	5
40. Nuclear and environmental fears	0	1	2	3	4	5
41. Church-school activities	0	1	2	3	4	5
42. Unsatisfactory housing	0	1	2	3	4	5
43. Organized sports activities	0	1	2	3	4	5
44. Change in work patterns	0	1	2	3	4	5
45. Two-paycheck family	0	1	2	3	4	5

Part II: Family Systems Stressors (Specific)

DIRECTIONS: The following 10 questions are designed to provide specific information about tension producing situations, problems, or areas of concern influencing your family's health.[b] Please circle a number (1 through 5) that best describes the influence this situation has on your family's life.

What do you consider your major stressful situation, problem, or concern at this time?

_____

_____

_____

	N/A	Little or None		Medium		Very much
1. To what extent is your family bothered by this problem or stressful situation?	0	1	2	3	4	5
2. How much of an effect does this stressful situation have on your family's usual pattern of living?	0	1	2	3	4	5
3. How much has this situation affected your family's ability to work together as a family unit?	0	1	2	3	4	5

Has your family ever experienced a similar concern in the past?

YES _____ If YES, complete question 4

NO _____ If NO, proceed to question 5

	N/A	Little or None		Medium		Very much
4. How successful was your family in dealing with this situation/problem/concern in the past?	0	1	2	3	4	5
5. How strongly do you feel this current situation/problem/concern will affect your family's future?	0	1	2	3	4	5
6. To what extent are family members able to help themselves in this present situation/problem/concern?	0	1	2	3	4	5
7. To what extent do you expect others to help your family with this situation/problem/concern?	0	1	2	3	4	5

	N/A	Poor		Satisfactory		Excellent
8. Rate the overall health status of your family as a whole.	0	1	2	3	4	5

9. Rate the overall health status of each family member by name.

	N/A					
_____	0	1	2	3	4	5
_____	0	1	2	3	4	5
_____	0	1	2	3	4	5
_____	0	1	2	3	4	5
_____	0	1	2	3	4	5

Part III: Family Systems Strengths

DIRECTIONS: Each of the twenty traits/attributes listed below deals with some aspect of family life.[c] Each one contributes to the health and well-being of family members as individuals and to the family as a whole. Please circle a number (1 through 5) that best describes the extent to which family members use these traits.

My Family:	N/A	Seldom		Usually		Always
1. Communicates and listens to one another	0	1	2	3	4	5
2. Affirms and supports one another	0	1	2	3	4	5
3. Teaches respect for others	0	1	2	3	4	5
4. Develops a sense of trust in members	0	1	2	3	4	5
5. Has a sense of play and humor	0	1	2	3	4	5
6. Exhibits a sense of shared responsibility	0	1	2	3	4	5
7. Teaches a sense of right and wrong	0	1	2	3	4	5
8. Has a strong sense of family in which rituals and traditions abound	0	1	2	3	4	5

9. Has a balance of interaction among members	0	1	2	3	4	5
10. Has a shared religious core	0	1	2	3	4	5
11. Respects the privacy of one another	0	1	2	3	4	5
12. Values service to others	0	1	2	3	4	5
13. Fosters family table time and conversation	0	1	2	3	4	5
14. Shares leisure time	0	1	2	3	4	5
15. Admits to and seeks help with problems	0	1	2	3	4	5
16. Honors its elders	0	1	2	3	4	5
17. Accepts and encourages individual values	0	1	2	3	4	5
18. Values work satisfaction	0	1	2	3	4	5
19. Is financially secure	0	1	2	3	4	5
20. Is able to let go of grown children	0	1	2	3	4	5

[a]Based on Curran, D. 1985. **Stress and the healthy family.** Minneapolis: Winston Press.

[b]Based on Neuman's Systems Model. Neuman, B. 1989. **The Neuman systems model.** Norwalk, CT: Appleton-Lange.

[c]Based on Curran, D. 1983. **Traits of a healthy family.** Minneapolis: Winston Press.

Family Systems Stressor-Strength Inventory (FS³I)
Clinician Form

Family Name ——————————   Date ——————————

Part I: Family Systems Stressors (General)

Briefly discuss the 45 situations with the family member(s) and ask if
there are additional areas of concern. The purpose here is to begin
clarifying the family member(s) perceptions of stressful situations and
to zero in on their major area of concern.

——————————————————————————————

——————————————————————————————

Part II: Family Systems Stressors (Specific)

DIRECTIONS: The following 10 questions are designed to provide
specific information about the particular situation influencing the
family's health.[b] Please circle a number (1 through 5) that best
describes the influence this situation has on the family's health from
your point of view. Record the family response(s) and your
perceptions.

What do you consider to be the family's most stressful situation/
problem/or areas of concern at this time? (Identify problem area(s))

——————————————————————————————

——————————————————————————————

——————————————————————————————

	N/A	Little or none		Medium		Very Much
1. To what extent is the family bothered by this situation/ problem/concern? (Effects on psychosocial relationships communication, interactions)	0	1	2	3	4	5

Family Response

Clinician Perceptions

		Little				Very
	N/A	or none		Medium		Much

2. How much alteration in the   0   1   2   3   4   5
family's usual pattern of
living is occurring as a result
of this situation/problem/
concern? (Identify life-style
patterns and developmental
tasks)

Family Response

Clinician Perceptions

		Little				Very
	N/A	or none		Medium		Much

3. How much has this situation   0   1   2   3   4   5
affected the family's ability
to work together as a family
unit? (Identify roles and
tasks and how these are being altered.)

Family Response

Clinician Perceptions

		Little				Very
	N/A	or none		Medium		Much

4. Has the family ever experi- 0   1   2   3   4   5
   enced similar situations in
   the past? If so describe what
   the family did. How successful were they in resolving the situation/problem/
   concern? (Identify past
   coping patterns, adaptive
   strategies, and what success
   means to family.)

Family Response

Clinician Perceptions

		Little				Very
	N/A	or none		Medium		Much

5. How strongly do you think   0   1   2   3   4   5
   the present situation/
   problem/concern will affect
   the family and family members in the future? What effects do you expect? What
   are the anticipated consequences? (Identify current
   and potential coping patterns.)

Family Response

Clinician Perceptions

	N/A	Little or none		Medium		Very Much
6. To what extent are family members able to help themselves in the present situation/problem/concern? Identify self-assistive behaviors, family expectations, and spiritual influence.	0	1	2	3	4	5

Family Response

Clinician Perceptions

	N/A	Little or none		Medium		Very Much
7. To what extent does the family expect others to assist them with their present situation? What roles do family members expect others to play? (Describe roles and availability of extrafamily resources.)	0	1	2	3	4	5

Family Response

Clinician Perceptions

	N/A	Poor		Satisfactory		Excellent

8. Describe the overall health   0   1   2   3   4   5
   status of the family system.
   Consider four major categories: physical status, psychosocial characteristics,
   developmental characteristics, and spiritual influence

Family Response

Clinician Perceptions

9. Rate the overall health status of each family
   member using 5 variables as reference
   points: physiological, psychological,
   developmental, sociocultural, and spiritual
   influence.

	N/A	Poor		Satisfactory		Excellent
a. _____	0	1	2	3	4	5
b. _____	0	1	2	3	4	5
c. _____	0	1	2	3	4	5
d. _____	0	1	2	3	4	5
e. _____	0	1	2	3	4	5

Family Response

Clinician Perceptions

Part III: Family Systems Strengths

DIRECTIONS: Each of the 20 trait and/or attributes listed here deal with some aspect of family life.[c] Each one contributes to the health and well-being of family members as individuals and to family as a whole. Briefly describe your perception of how these strengths are operationalized in this family and circle the number (1 through 5) that best describes the extent to which they are used.

This Family:	N/A	Seldom or not at all		Usually		Always
1. Communicates and listens to one another	0	1	2	3	4	5

Clinician Perceptions

2. Affirms and supports one another	0	1	2	3	4	5

Clinician Perceptions

3. Teaches respect for others	0	1	2	3	4	5

Clinician Perceptions

4. Develops a sense of trust in members	0	1	2	3	4	5

Clinician Perceptions

5. Has a sense of play and humor	0	1	2	3	4	5

Clinician Perceptions

6. Exhibits a sense of shared responsibility	0	1	2	3	4	5

Clinician Perceptions

7. Teaches a sense of right   0   1   2   3   4   5
   and wrong

Clinician Perceptions

8. Has a strong sense of   0   1   2   3   4   5
   family in which rituals
   and traditions abound

Clinician Perceptions

9. Has a balance of interac-   0   1   2   3   4   5
   tion among members

Clinician Perceptions

10. Has a shared religious   0   1   2   3   4   5
    core

Clinician Perceptions

11. Respects the privacy of   0   1   2   3   4   5
    one another

Clinician Perceptions

12. Values service to others   0   1   2   3   4   5

Clinician Perceptions

13. Fosters family table time 0   1   2   3   4   5
    and conversation

Clinician Perceptions

14. Shares leisure time	0	1	2	3	4	5

Clinician Perceptions

15. Admits to and seeks help with problems	0	1	2	3	4	5

Clinician Perceptions

16. Honors its elders	0	1	2	3	4	5

Clinician Perceptions

17. Accepts and encourages individual values	0	1	2	3	4	5

Clinician Perceptions

18. Values work satisfaction	0	1	2	3	4	5

Clinician Perceptions

19. Is financially secure	0	1	2	3	4	5

Clinician Perceptions

20. Is able to let go of grown children	0	1	2	3	4	5

Clinician Perceptions

[a]Based on Curran, D. 1985. **Stress and the healthy family.** Minneapolis: Winston Press.
[b]Based on Neuman's Systems Model. Neuman, B. 1989. **The Neuman systems model.** Norwalk, CT: Appleton–Lange.
[c]Based on Curran, D. 1983. **Traits of a healthy family.** Minneapolis: Winston Press.

Family Systems Stressor-Strength Inventory (FS³I)
Summary Form

Family Name _____   Date _____

Family Member(s) Completing Assessment _____

Ethnic Background(s) _____

Religious Background(s) _____

Referral Source _____   Interviewer _____

Family Members	Relationship in Family	Age	Marital Status	Education (highest degree)	Occupation
1.					
2.					
3.					
4.					
5.					
6.					

Family's current reason for seeking health care assistance?

_____

_____

_____

_____

_____

_____

_____

Scoring Key

Family Member Perceptions
Section 1: Family Form

Part I Family Systems Stressors (General)

Add scores from questions 1 to 45 and calculate an overall score for Family Systems Stressors (General). Ratings are from 1 (most positive) to 5 (most negative). Subscale scores range from 45 to 225.

Family Systems Stressors (General) Score

$$\frac{(\quad)}{45} \times 1 = \underline{\hspace{2cm}}$$

Graph subscale score on Quantitative Summary Form: Family Systems Stressors: General, Family Member Perceptions.

A. Intrafamily Systems Subscale Score:

Add scores from questions 1-11 and calculate a subscale score. Ratings are from 1 (most positive) to 5 (most negative). Subscale scores range from 11 to 55.

Intrafamily Systems Stressors Score

$$\frac{(\quad)}{11} \times 1 = \underline{\hspace{2cm}}$$

Graph score on Quantitative Summary Form: Family Systems Stressors (Intrafamily), Family Member Perceptions.

Family Member Perceptions
Section 1: Family Form

B. Interfamily Systems Subscale Score:

Add scores from questions 12-34 only and calculate a subscale score. Ratings are from 1 (most positive) to 5 (most negative). Scores range from 23 to 115.
Interfamily Systems Stressors Score

$$\frac{(\quad)}{23} \times 1 = \underline{\hspace{2cm}}$$

Graph subscale score on Quantitative Summary Form, Family Systems Stressors (Interfamily), Family Member Perceptions.

C. Extrafamily Systems Subscale Score:

Add scores from questions 35-45 and calculate a subscale score. Ratings are from 1 (most positive) to 5 (most negative). Scores range from 11 to 55.
Extrafamily Systems Stressors Score

$$\frac{(\quad)}{11} \times 1 = \underline{\hspace{2cm}}$$

Graph subscale score on Quantitative Summary Form: Family Systems Stressors (Extrafamily), Family Member Perceptions.

Part II Family Systems Stressors (Specific)

Add scores from questions 1 to 8 only and calculate a score for Family Systems Stressors (Specific). Ratings are from 1 (most positive) to 5 (most negative). Questions 4, 6, 7, and 8 are reverse scored.* Scores range from 8 to 40.

Family Systems Stressors (Specific) Score

$$\frac{(\ \ )}{8} \times 1 = \underline{\hspace{2cm}}$$

Graph score on Quantitative Summary Form: Family Systems Stressors (Specific) Family Member Perceptions. Scores for question 9 are recorded on Qualitative Summary Form 2D: Family Systems Stressors (Specific).

Part III Family Systems Strengths

Add scores from questions 1 to 20 and calculate a score for Family Systems Strengths. Ratings are from 1 (seldom used) to 5 (always used). Scores range from 20 to 100.

Family Systems Strengths Score

$$\frac{(\ \ )}{20} \times 1 = \underline{\hspace{2cm}}$$

Graph score on Quantitative Summary Form: Family Systems Strengths.

*Reverse Scoring:

Question answered as **one** is scored as 5 points

Question answered as **two** is scored as 4 points

Question answered as **three** is scored as 3 points

Question answered as **four** is scored as 2 points

Question answered as **five** is scored as 1 point

Clinician Perceptions
Section 2: Clinician Form

Part I Family Systems Stressors (General)

Identify predominant tension producing situations from list of 45 situations/problems/concerns and prioritize them in order of importance to family. Record on Qualitative Summary Form: Family Systems Stressors (General).

Additional Comments:
General Stressors:

Intrafamily:

Interfamily

Extrafamily:

Part II Family Systems Stressors (Specific)

Calculate quantitative scores for questions 1 to 8 in same manner as for Section 1, Part II. Family Member Perceptions. Graph on Quantitative Summary Form for Family Systems Stressors (Specific), Clinician Perceptions.

Identify specific tension producing situation/problem/concern that is influencing family health and record on Qualitative Summary Form 2A: Family Systems Stressors (Specific).

Part III Family Systems Strengths

Calculate quantitative scores for questions 1 to 20 in same manner as for Section 1, Part III. Family Member Perceptions. Graph on Quantitative Summary Form for Family Systems Strengths, Clinician Perceptions.

Identify Family Systems Strengths that contribute to family stability, health and can serve as a basis for prevention/intervention activities. Record on Qualitative Summary Form Part III: Family Systems Strengths.

Quantitative Summary

DIRECTIONS: Graph the scores from each family member inventory by placing an "X" at the appropriate location and connect with a line. (Use first name initial for each line.)

Scores for Wellness and Stability	Family Systems Stressors Family Member Perceptions					Family Systems Stressors Specific	
	General	Intra-Family	Inter-Family	Extra-Family		Fam. Mem. Perceptions	Clinician Perceptions
5.0					5.0		
4.8					4.8		
4.6					4.6		
4.4					4.4		
4.2					4.2		
4.0					4.0		
3.8					3.8		
3.6					3.6		
3.4					3.4		
3.2					3.2		
3.0					3.0		
2.8					2.8		
2.6					2.6		
2.4					2.4		
2.2					2.2		
2.0					2.0		
1.8					1.8		
1.6					1.6		
1.4					1.4		
1.2					1.2		
1.0					1.0		

Sum of strengths available for prevention/ intervention mode	Family Systems Strengths	
	Family Member Perceptions	Clinician Perceptions
5.0		
4.8		
4.6		
4.4		
4.2		
4.0		
3.8		
3.6		
3.4		
3.2		
3.0		
2.8		
2.6		
2.4		
2.2		
2.0		
1.8		
1.6		
1.4		
1.2		
1.0		

*PRIMARY Prevention/Intervention Mode: Flexible Line   ) 1.0-2.3
*SECONDARY Prevention/Intervention Mode: Normal Line) 2.4-3.6
*TERTIARY Prevention/Intervention Mode: Resistance Lines) 3.7-5.0
*Breakdown of numerical scores for stressor penetration are suggested values

Qualitative Summary*
(Family and Clinician Perceptions)

Part I: Family Systems Stressors: General

Identify predominant tension producing situation(s) in family and list them in order of importance to the family.

Situation/Problem/Concern	Priority for Family
1. _____	_____
2. _____	_____
3. _____	_____
4. _____	_____
5. _____	_____

Comments:

*Combines information from Family Form and Clinician Form.

Part II: Family Systems Stressors: Specific

Identify specific tension producing situation/problem/concern
influencing family health.

_____

_____

_____

_____

_____

_____

Comments:

Part II: Family Systems Stressors: Specific
B. Summarize perceptions of the specific family situation/problem/
concern and identify discrepancies between family and clinician
perceptions.

Stressor (Situation)	Famiy Perception
1. Extent family bothered by situation/problem/concern: effects on psychosocial relationships, communications, and interactions	
2. Alterations in usual life-style patterns and family developmental tasks	
3. Effects on family's ability to work together: alteration in roles and tasks	
4. Similar situations, problems, concerns: family's past coping patterns; what "success" means to family	
5. Effects of present situation on family health in future: anticipated consequences; current and potential coping patterns	
6. Family's ability to help themselves in situation; self-assistive behaviors; family expectations and spiritual influence	
7. Family expectations of others and their role in helping family; extrafamily resources and their role	

Clinician Perception	Discrepancies

C. Summarize significant health status data for each family member using five variables.

	Family Member 1	Family Member 2	Family Member 3
Physiological			
Psychological			
Developmental			
Sociocultural			
Spiritual			

Family Member 4	Family Member 5	Family Member 6

D. Using the four major categories of the family system, combine significant health status data from family member variables.

Major Category	Family System
Psychological Relationship	
Physical Status	
Spiritual Influence	
Developmental Characteristics	

Part III: Family Systems Strengths
Identify family systems strengths that contribute to family stability and
support actual and potential prevention/intervention activities.

Family Systems Strengths
1.
2.
3.
4.
5.
6.
7.

Part IV: Family Care Plan*
List the three most significant clinician diagnoses (prioritize).

Diagnosis General and Specific Family Systems Stressors	Family Systems Strengths Supporting Family Care Plan	Goals Family and Clinician

Prevention/Intervention Mode		Outcomes
Primary, Secondary, or Tertiary	Prevention/Intervention Activities	Evaluation and Replanning

Index

A

Ability to learn, 32
Adaptation, 29-30
Adaptation Model, 4
Adequate family, 48
Aging parents, 93
Allergy, 88
American Nurses' Association
    (ANA), 18
  Social Policy Statement of, 18, 51
  Standards of Nursing Practice of,
    18
ANA: *see* American Nurses'
    Association
Appropriateness of assessment/
    measurement instrument, 248
Areas of concern, 72
Assessment, 2, 20-37, 52, 54, 148,
    226-227, 231-242
Assessment/Intervention Tool, 12

B

Baccalaureate nursing students, 231
Basic structure, 25
Beavers-Timberlawn Family
    Evaluation Scale (BT),
    248-249
Behavioral Systems Model for
    Nursing, 9
Blended childbearing family, health
    promotion and, 85-88
Boundary, 6, 30-31
  semipermeable, 6
Boundary lines, 25
Bowen's Multigenerational approach,
    15, 16
BT; *see* Beavers-Timberlawn Family
    Evaluation Scale

C

Calgary Family Assessment Model
    (CFAM), 9, 12, 47-48, 230,
    242, 249
Cancer, ovarian, 93
Case studies, 84-97
CFAM; *see* Calgary Family
    Assessment Model
Childbearing family
  blended, 85-88
  nuclear, 88-93
Chronicity Impact and Coping
    Instrument: Parent
    Questionnaire (CI-CI:PQ),
    245, 249-250
CI-CI:PQ; *see* Chronicity Impact and
    Coping Instrument: Parent
    Questionnaire
Client, 23
Client/client system, 25
Clinical nursing theory, 2
Clinical relevance of assessment/
    measurement instruments, 248
Coaching, 17
Cognition, 32
Communication level, 13
Communication system, 4
Content, 25
Contract, nursing, 60
Control, stress and, 38-39
Couples, stress and, 40-41

D

DAS; *see* Dyadic Adjustment Scale
Defensiveness, 72
Degree of reaction, 26
Development, 35-36
Developmental theory, 10-12
Developmental variance, 17, 33

Diagnosis, nursing, 2, 52, 53, 54,
    55-58, 82, 96
Dyadic Adjustment Sclae (DAS),
    246, 250-251

E

Emotional health, 32
Emotional level, 13
Emotional systems, 4, 15-16
Employment, 37
Energized family, 48
ENRICH; see Enriching and
        Nurturing Relationships
        Issues, Communication and
        Happiness
Enriching and Nurturing
        Relationships Issues,
        Communication and Happiness
        (ENRICH), 246, 251
Entropy, 26
Environment, interaction with, 23, 26
Environmental stressors, 24
Exploratory laparotomy, 93
Extrafamily system stressors, 30,
    45-46, 72, 73, 77, 80, 86
Evaluation, 52, 54

F

FACES; see Family Adaptability and
        Cohesion Evaluation Scale
Faculty-developed instruments, 242
FAD: see Family Assessment Device
Family, 23
    adequate, 48
    basic structure of, 64-65
    development of, 33
    energized, 48
    goals of, 82
    healthy, strengths found in, 48, 49
    nuclear childbearing, 88-93
    nursing process and, 51-71
    as social system, 8
    stability of, 34, 62, 67-68
    strengths of, 46-50, 74, 75, 80,
        82, 86-87, 91-92, 95-96
    theoretical approaches used to
        study, 3-4
    as unit of care, 1, 2-3
Family Adaptability and Cohesion
        Evaluation Scale (FACES),
        245, 251-252

Family Adaptability Partnership,
        Growth, Affection, and
        Resolve Tests (Family
        APGAR), 242, 245, 252-253
Family APGAR; see Family
        Adaptability, Partnership,
        Growth, Affection, and
        Resolve Tests
Family Assessment Device (FAD),
        245, 253-254
Family Assessment Guide, 254
Family Assessment Tool (FAT), 254
Family assessment/measurement
        instruments, 232-241
Family concerns, concepts, and
        interaction patterns, 35-36
Family Coping Index, 254-255
Family Crisis Orientated Personal
        Evaluation Scales (F-COPES),
        255
Family Dynamics Measure, 245
Family energy resources, 64-65
Family Environment Scale (FES),
        245, 255-256
Family Form, 76-79
Family Functioning Index (FFI), 245,
        256-257
Family Health Assessment Form,
        231, 257
Family Health Assessment Guide,
        257
Family Health Inventory, 230, 246,
        257-258
Family instrumentation, 227-230
Family Inventory of Life Events
        (FILE), 258
Family member assessment variables,
        30-34
Family Nursing Assessment/
        Measurement Instrumentation,
        226-262
Family nursing curriculum, 231-242
Family nursing instrumentation,
        230-231
Family Strengths Assessment, 242
Family Strengths Scale, 258-259
Family systems, 17, 34-37; see also
        Family
    nursing assessment applied to,
        20-37

Family systems—cont'd
    stressor factors in, 38-46, 85-86,
        90-91, 94-95
    theoretical orientations used to
        understand, 1-19
Family Systems Stressor Strength
    Inventory (FS³I), 71, 72-83,
    247
Family systems therapy, 15-17
Family theory models, 3-4, 8-12, 17,
    18
Family therapy models, 3-4, 12-17,
    18
FAT; see Family Assessment Tool
F-COPES; see Family Crisis
    Orientated Personal Evaluation
    Scales
Feedback, 7, 26
Feeling response, subjective, 16
Feetham Family Functioning Scale,
    242
Feetham Family Functioning Survey
    (FFFS), 245, 259
FES; see Family Environment Scale
FFFS; see Feetham Family
    Functioning Survey
FFI; see Family Functioning Index
Field theory, 22
FILE; see Family Inventory of Life
    Events
Flexible line of defense, 26, 64, 67,
    86, 94
Friedman Family Assessment Model,
    257
FS³I; see Family Systems Stressor
    Strengths Inventory

G

General Systems Framework and
    Theory, 4
General systems theory, 4-8, 15, 22,
    249
Genograms, 242
Gestalt, 22-23
Goal, 26, 82
    family, 82
    nursing, 53, 59-60, 82
Graduate nursing students, 231
Guidelines for Family Assessment, 9,
    12

H

Harmful stress, 39
Health, 26, 59
Health families, strengths found in,
    48, 49
HHN; see Home health nurse
HOME; see Home Observation for
    Measurement of the
    Environment
Home health nurse (HHN), 93
Home Observation for Measurement
    of the Environment (HOME),
    259-260
Human-to-Human Relationship
    Model, 10

I

IFF; see Inventory of Family Feelings
Implementation, 52, 54
Individual strategies, 245
Input/output, 26
Instability, family, 34, 67-68
Instrumentation
    faculty-developed, 242
    family, 227-230
    family nursing, 230-231
Interaction Model, 15
Interactional therapy, 14-15, 17
Interfamily system stressors, 30, 45,
    72, 73, 77, 80, 85-86
Intervention, 2
Intrafamily system stressors, 30, 44,
    72, 73, 77, 80, 85
Intrapersonal stressors, 44
Inventory of Family Feelings (IFF),
    260

K

Knowing, 32

L

Laparotomy, exploratory, 93
Learning, 32
Life, totality of, 23
Likert numerical rating scale, 77, 78,
    79, 82, 251, 258
Line
    of defense, 27, 59, 64, 77, 79, 80,
        88
        flexible, 26, 64, 67, 86, 94

Line—cont'd
  of defense—cont'd
    normal, 23, 27, 29, 64, 68, 94
  of resistance, 24, 27, 29, 59, 64,
      68, 77, 79, 80, 88
  internal, 27

M

McMaster Family Assessment
    Device, 245, 253-254
McMaster Model of Family
    Functioning, 253
Measurement, 226-227, 231-242, 248
  instruments for, 232-241
  strategies for, 244-247
Mental health, 32
Mental processes, 31-32

N

NANDA approved Nursing
    Diagnostic Categories, 55-58
NCAST; *see* Nursing Child
    Assessment Satellite Series
Negentropy, 27
Neuman College Nursing Process
    Tool, 81
Neuman's Systems Model, 4, 12, 22,
    50, 51-71, 72, 78, 81, 84
  applied to family systems, 22-23
  basic assumptions in, 23-24
  case study in, 17
  definition of terms in, 24-29
  family stressors and, 42-44
  operationalized, 29-37, 62-65
Ninth National Conference on
    Classification of Nursing
    Diagnoses, 55
Nitroglycerin, 89
Normal line of defense, 23, 27, 29,
    64, 68, 94
Nuclear childbearing family, 88-93
Nuclear middlescent family, 93-97
Nurse form, 79-80
Nursing, 27
Nursing assessment applied to family
    systems, 20-37
Nursing Child Assessment Satellite
    Series (NCAST), 260-261
Nursing contract, 60
Nursing diagnosis, 53, 55-58, 82, 96

Nursing goals, 53, 59-60, 82
Nursing instruments, psychometric
    evaluation of, 242-244
Nursing outcomes, 53, 60, 83
Nursing processes, 51-71

O

Objective thinking response, 16
Observational instrument, 230
Open system, 27
Otitis media, 84, 85-88
Outcomes, nursing, 53, 60, 83
Ovarian cancer, 93

P

Parent-Interaction Model, 10
Parents, aging, 93
Permeability of boundaries, 4, 30-31
Physical status, 35
Physiological variable, 31
Planning, 2, 52, 54
Positive stress, 39
Practice model approach, 13
Premarital Personal and Relationships
    Evaluation (PREPARE), 246,
    251
PREPARE; *see* Premarital Personal
    and Relationships Evaluation
Prevention, levels of, 23, 24
Prevention/intervention, 27, 61,
    65-71, 82-83
  primary, 24, 60, 61, 65–67
  secondary, 24, 60, 61, 67-69
  tertiary, 24, 60, 61, 69, 70-71
Primary prevention/intervention
    mode, 24, 60, 61, 65-67
Problem situation, 72
Process/function, 28
Propositions, 23
Psychometric evaluation of nursing
    instruments, 242-244
Psychosocial relationship
    characteristics, 35
Psychological variable, 31-32

R

Reconstitution, 28, 29-30
Relational strategies, 245-246
Relationship systems, 15, 31-32
Reliability, 76, 242-243, 248

Research, 227
Riehl Interaction Model, 10
Role relationship model, 12-13

S

Science of Unitary Human Beings, 4
Secondary prevention/intervention
mode, 24, 60, 61, 67-69
Selected Family Assessment/
Measurement Instruments,
248-261
Self-Care Nursing Theory, 15
Self-report instruments, 230
Semipermeable boundaries, 4
Sensitization, 243-244
SFIS: see Structural Family
Interaction Scale
SIMFAM; see Simulated Family
Activity Measure
Simulated Family Activity Measure
(SIMFAM), 246
Social Policy Statement of American
Nurses' Association, 18, 51
Social system, family as, 8
Sociocultural variable, 32-33
Spiritual variable, 33-37
Stability, family, 7, 28, 34, 59, 62,
67-68
Standards of Nursing Practice of
American Nurses'
Association, 18
Strengths, family, 46-50, 74, 75, 80,
82, 86-87, 91-92, 95-96, 242,
258-259
Stress, 7, 23, 38-50
control and, 38-39
couples and, 40-41
family life and, 40-41
harmful, 39
positive, 39
Stressors, 28, 29, 38-50, 69-70, 72,
86
environmental, 24
extrafamily, 45-46

Stressors—cont'd
family, 43
interfamily, 45
intrafamily, 44
intrapersonal, 44
Structural Family Interaction Scale
(SFIS), 261
Structural system, 4, 17
Structural therapy, 13-14
Structural-functional therapy, 8-9
Structure-function, 17
Structured Family Interview, 246
Subjective feeling response, 16
Symbolic interaction theory, 9-10, 17
System balance and feedback, 7
System control, 6
System structure, 6
Systems models, 13

T

Teacher, 17
Tertiary prevention/intervention
mode, 24, 60, 61, 69, 70-71
Theoretical orientations used to
understand family systems,
1-19
Theory
of Goal Attainment Model, 10
of Nursing, 15
Thinking response, objective, 16
Totality of life, 23
Total-Person Approach, 24
Traits found in healthy families, 49

V

Validity, 76, 242-243, 248
Value, 7
von Bertalanffy, 4, 15

W

Wellness/illness, 28, 30, 34, 59
Wellness/stability state, 23-24
Wellness variance, 96
Wholistic, 29